Effective Literacy Instruction

for Students with Moderate
or Severe Disabilities

Effective Literacy Instruction

for Students with Moderate or Severe Disabilities

by

Susan R. Copeland, Ph.D.

and

Elizabeth B. Keefe, Ph.D.

University of New Mexico
Albuquerque

with invited contributors

Baltimore • London • Sydney

Paul H. Brookes Publishing Co.
Post Office Box 10624
Baltimore, Maryland 21285-0624

www.brookespublishing.com

Typeset by Integrated Publishing Solutions, Grand Rapids, Michigan.
Manufactured in the United States of America by
George H. Buchanan Printing, Bridgeport, New Jersey.

The case studies in the book represent real situations, but the names and identifying details
of the children and family members have been changed to protect their privacy. Activities
involving individuals with disabilities and teachers or therapists are used by permission.

Second printing, February 2009

Library of Congress Cataloging-in-Publication Data

Copeland, Susan R.
   Effective literacy instruction for students with moderate or severe disabilities by Susan R.
   Copeland and Elizabeth B. Keefe with invited contributors.
     p.   cm.
   Includes bibliographical references and index.
   ISBN-13: 978-1-55766-837-0 (alk. paper)
   1. Students with disabilities—Education—United States. 2. Language arts—Remedial
   teaching—United States.   I. Keefe, Elizabeth B.   II. Title
LC4028.C66 2007
371.9'0446—dc22
                                                      2006101715

British Library Cataloguing in Publication data are available from the British Library.

Contents

About the Authors

Susan R. Copeland, Ph.D., Assistant Professor, Department of Educational Specialties, Special Education Concentration in Mental Retardation and Severe Disabilities: Studies in Educational Equity for Diverse Exceptional Learners, University of New Mexico, Albuquerque, New Mexico 87131

Dr. Copeland's primary research interest is in developing strategies that allow individuals with disabilities to provide their own supports, direct their own lives, and enhance their active participation in their families, schools, and communities. Her research has focused on use of self-management strategies within inclusive settings, peer supports, and preparation of educators to be effective reading and literacy teachers. Her research on these topics has appeared in a variety of journals in the field, including the *American Journal on Mental Retardation*, *Remedial and Special Education*, and the *Journal of the Association for Persons with Severe Disabilities*. She teaches courses in reading/literacy instruction, advocacy and empowerment of individuals with disabilities, applied behavior analysis, and the history of and current understanding about intellectual disability. She earned a bachelor's degree in music therapy from Southern Methodist University, a master's degree in special education from the University of Arkansas at Little Rock, and her doctorate in education and human development from Vanderbilt University.

Elizabeth B. Keefe, Ph.D., Associate Professor, Department of Educational Specialties, Special Education Concentration in Mental Retardation and Severe Disabilities: Studies in Educational Equity for Diverse Exceptional Learners, University of New Mexico, Albuquerque, New Mexico 87131

Dr. Keefe received her bachelor's degree in sociology from the University of Newcastle-upon-Tyne in the United Kingdom, her master's degree in anthropology from the University of Nebraska, and her master of arts and doctoral degrees in special education from the University of New Mexico. She is Coordinator of the Special Education Program at the University of New Mexico. She has taught in inclusive settings at the elementary school level and is actively involved throughout New Mexico in various educational reform issues. Her research interests have focused on inclusive practices, co-teaching, and how systems change occurs and is sustained at elementary, middle, and high schools. She has written articles on these topics for numerous publications and has collaborated with students, families, and practitioners to ensure that their voices are heard in the professional literature.

About the Contributors

Jonathan D. Brinkerhoff, Ph.D., Assistant Professor, Department of Teacher Education, University of New Mexico, Albuquerque, New Mexico 87131

Dr. Brinkerhoff teaches graduate and undergraduate courses in educational technology and educational psychology. Prior to joining the faculty of the University of New Mexico, Dr. Brinkerhoff spent 17 years as an elementary classroom teacher. During that time, he worked as a consultant to the California State Department's Tri-Tec Program, as a mentor teacher of practicing teachers, and as a master teacher of preservice teachers. In each of these capacities, Dr. Brinkerhoff worked to enhance teachers' effective use of research-based teaching techniques.

J. Anne Calhoon, Ph.D. (Cherokee), Assistant Professor, Department of Language, Literacy, and Sociocultural Studies, University of New Mexico, Albuquerque, New Mexico 87131

Professor Calhoon earned her doctorate in educational psychology from Marquette University. She teaches graduate courses in reading process, assessment, and American Indian children's literature. Her research has focused on aspects of literacy and American Indian identity, and her research on early literacy development has appeared in publications such as the *Journal of Autism and Developmental Disorders* and the *Journal of Literacy Research*. She is principal author of a chapter titled "Gender Equity for American Indian Students" in the *Handbook on Gender Equity Through Education* (Lawrence Erlbaum Associates) to be published in the spring of 2007.

Beth E. Foley, Ph.D., CCC-SLP, Associate Professor and Head of the Department of Communicative Disorders and Deaf Education, Utah State University, Logan, Utah 84322

For more than two decades, Dr. Foley's career has focused on using assistive technology to improve educational, social, and vocational outcomes for individuals with significant disabilities. Dr. Foley's primary research interests are language and literacy development in children with complex communication needs and inclusion of students who use augmentative and alternative communication (AAC) in general education settings. Her numerous publications, conference presentations, and workshops on these topics speak to the critical need for integrating best practices in assistive technology and AAC language and literacy intervention in educational programming for students with significant disabilities.

Julia Scherba de Valenzuela, Ph.D., Associate Professor, Special Education Concentration in Mental Retardation and Severe Disabilities: Studies in Educational Equity for Diverse Exceptional Learners, University of New Mexico, Albuquerque, New Mexico 87131

Professor Scherba de Valenzuela coordinates the interdisciplinary doctoral program in educational linguistics and teaches in the bilingual education/TESOL program, in addition to her faculty appointment in special education. She is a nationally certified speech-language pathologist, and her research interests include bilingual special education, language socialization and communication development among culturally and linguistically diverse populations, and alternative assessment/evaluation. She has contributed to assessment development efforts at the state and national levels. Her recent publications include contributions to *The Handbook of Special Education* (Sage, 2007) and *The Bilingual Special Education Interface* (Prentice Hall, 2004) and to the journal *Exceptional Children*.

Amy Staples, Ph.D., Assistant Professor, Department of Special Education, University of Northern Iowa, Cedar Falls, Iowa 50614

Dr. Staples teaches methods courses, with a focus on literacy and inclusion. Her research in literacy learning, spanning 20 years, led to an interest in the need for more equitable education for all children, especially those labeled as having a disability. Her research examines the role technology can play in supporting both the literacy development and active participation of children with disabilities in inclusive educational settings.

M. Marilyn Tracey, M.A., Doctoral Student, Special Education Concentration in Mental Retardation and Severe Disabilities, University of New Mexico, Albuquerque, New Mexico 87131

Ms. Tracey is a member of the Diné Nation of northeastern Arizona. She is a certified bilingual teacher, counselor, and diagnostician. Her research interests include bilingual special education, language retention and revitalization, communication development among culturally and linguistically diverse populations, and alternative assessment/evaluation. She has contributed to assessment development efforts at the state levels.

Foreword

According to Kliewer, Fitzgerald, and Meyer-Mork (2004), literacy can be defined as "making meaning" of messages in your environment. Similarly, Teale and Sulzby (1986) indicated that literacy encompasses the use of listening, speaking, reading, and writing in an individual's everyday life. Put another way, literacy comprises the manner in which an individual interacts with people and participates in activities across contexts. When addressing instruction on the four components of literacy, therefore, we must consider how they are interrelated, how they develop both simultaneously and interactively, and how instruction must blend all four components in genuine opportunities to listen, speak, read, and write (Koppenhaver, Pierce, Steelman, & Yoder, 1995; Notari-Syverson, O'Connor, & Vadasy, 1996; Ryndak, Morrison, & Sommerstein, 1999).

Most students with moderate or severe disabilities have been denied effective instruction to become fully participating members of our literate society (Kliewer & Biklen, 2001; Ryndak et al., 1999). For example, for several years I have been involved with school districts attempting to make systemic change that incorporates the development and implementation of effective services for students with moderate or severe disabilities in inclusive general education contexts, including services that reflect literacy instruction. One of the middle schools was serving students in a traditional self-contained special education class in which only students labeled as having multiple disabilities (i.e., severe/profound cognitive impairments along with severe physical impairments) had been placed. In fact, since being identified as having multiple disabilities as young children, these students annually had received their special education and related services in self-contained special education settings. Throughout the educational careers of these students, their education teams had consistently determined that they required intensive instruction on either developmental skills (e.g., colors, numbers, motor skills) or functional life skills (e.g., self-care) rather than on the general education content that their peers without disabilities were learning and the use of that content across meaningful contexts. This general education content includes the development of literacy, extended to its proficient use in a literate world. When considered as a pattern over years, it is clear that students with moderate or severe disabilities had been denied access to effective instruction that would have allowed them to become literate.

In addition, the placement of students with moderate or severe disabilities in self-contained classes reflected a determination that they required consistent one-to-one support that could only be provided in "specialized" settings by adults, rather in diverse meaningful settings by a variety of people, including classmates and other students without disabilities, in conjunction with adults. In essence, this self-contained placement denied the students access to a combination of settings and supports that would have addressed their instructional needs and learning characteristics (Koppenhaven, 2000; Ryndak & Alper, 2003) by embedding instruction in meaningful activities with individuals who are important to the learners across a variety of real-life contexts for students of their chronological age. Such instructional contexts would have provided genuine opportunities to need, learn, and use literacy as well as genuine age-matched literacy role models.

On entering the self-contained class, I met Ken and Victor. Throughout the day, both boys had one-to-one support from an adult (e.g., special education teacher, related services provider, paraprofessional) and were receiving instruction on responding to rudimentary yes/no questions (e.g., "Do you want [an item]?") either with vocalizations or by touching differentiated switches. As such, their augmentative and alternative communication (AAC) systems comprised two options, powered either by voice or by two switches requiring one touch each. Instruction on the use of their AAC systems was provided by an adult during multiple sessions of massed training trials; that is, each student had multiple trials to answer yes/no questions during three 10- to 15-minute periods across the day. Little variation occurred in the contexts or activities during which this instruction took place; activities were loosely defined, rather than defined as the initiation, completion, and termination of a task that had an outcome that was meaningful to the student.

Through the process of school system change, this self-contained placement ended for Ken and Victor because the principal and teachers at the middle school, with support from the district director of special education, decided to provide these students with opportunities to interact with their schoolmates without disabilities. Initially this was discussed as "social inclusion." To accomplish this, the students were placed in general education classes with support provided by special education personnel and by peers from the next grade level through a formal peer-support program that resulted in academic credit. Within a couple of months, it became clear to the general education teachers and peer supporters that Ken and Victor were able to do much more academically than they previously had been asked to do. Not only were they answering rudimentary yes/no questions correctly with their cursory AAC systems, they also were correctly answering yes/no questions about grade-level academic content and correctly making choices from multiple options of content answers. It was clear that their current communication systems were inadequate and did not reflect their literacy abilities—abilities that Ken and Victor had developed *in spite of* the limited nature of the literacy skills on which they had been receiving inadequate instruction for years. In fact, the middle school general education teachers and peer supporters had to convince the special education personnel that Ken and Victor were demonstrating an understanding of grade-level academic content and required more complex AAC systems. Within months of Ken and Victor joining general education classes with accommodations/modifications and supports, their education teams had identified and acquired more sophisticated AAC systems for the boys. It was determined that Ken and Victor already had literacy and mobility skills that allowed them to choose from an eight-item array, as well as to select from five levels of arrays. Each AAC system was sophisticated enough to be expanded as Ken and Victor required more communication options, as well as mobile enough to be used across contexts both in and out of school. For the first time in their educational careers, Ken and Victor were provided with a method to communicate their needs, desires, and knowledge of academic content in a meaningful way, and they had AAC systems that allowed them to communicate across activities, contexts, and communication partners when *they* needed or wanted to communicate. The boys finally were able to participate in real middle school experiences simply by being provided with 1) opportunities to interact with other middle school students; 2) access to literacy instruction, situations in which literacy was required, and literacy models; and 3) appropriate AAC systems to demonstrate literacy skills they had developed *in spite of* years of ineffective instruction in self-contained settings.

The issues epitomized by this experience are twofold. First, as a field we must be concerned with, if not outraged by, the lack of access to the general education curriculum, in particular literacy instruction for students like Ken and Victor. As I have spoken with colleagues nationally and internationally, it has become increasingly evident that my experience with Ken and Victor is not unique; rather, several colleagues have described similar experiences in multiple schools. If, as a society that calls for accountability for *all*, we expect students with moderate or severe disabilities to become competent consumers and participants in the literate world along with their same-age classmates and schoolmates without disabilities, then students with moderate or severe disabilities *must* have access to the same curriculum content (McSheehan, Sonnenmeier, Jorgensen, & Turner, 2006; Sturm et al., 2006). In addition, students with moderate or severe disabilities *must* have access to individualized accommodations and modifications (Gillette, 2006) that enable them to participate in literacy instruction. Although students with disabilities may not be able to demonstrate literacy in a manner traditionally recognized (Sturm et al., 2006), increasingly, general education teachers and education administrators are recognizing that students like Ken and Victor *can* understand general education curriculum content, they *can* understand content presented to them either verbally or in writing (Van der Bijl, Alant, & Lloyd, 2006), and they *can* demonstrate their understanding using verbal or written expression (Basil, 2003). There is a growing recognition that just because a student's verbal or written expression may incorporate assistive technology devices (e.g., switches, voice output devices, and/or computers), the students' expression of *knowledge* through the use of literacy is in no way diminished.

Second, given the research base that demonstrates the effectiveness of instructional strategies for students with moderate or severe disabilities in inclusive contexts (Ryndak & Fisher, 2003) and the effectiveness of inclusive education practices (McGregor & Vogelsberg, 1998), as a field we must be concerned by the lack of attention to the settings in which instruction for students like Ken and Victor is occurring. If, as a society that values high achievement leading to personal independence and community contribution, we *expect* outcomes for students with moderate or severe disabilities that include their participation in a literate world along with their same-age schoolmates without disabilities, then students with moderate or severe disabilities *must* have access to the same instructional activities for general education content, the same highly qualified teachers of that content, and the same quality of effective and evidence-based instructional strategies. In addition, students with moderate or severe disabilities *must* have access to individualized accommodations and modifications that focus on the development and use of literacy across activities and contexts in which literacy naturally is embedded (McSheehan, Sonnenmeier, Jorgensen, & Turner, 2006; Sturm et al., 2006). These would include accommodation and modifications to instructional strategies, the distribution of instructional opportunities across meaningful activities and contexts, natural supports from people who are important to them, and accountability processes. While some students with moderate or severe disabilities may not be able to participate in instructional activities in the same manner as their schoolmates without disabilities, general education teachers and education administrators increasingly are recognizing how differentiated instruction and demonstration of knowledge can and should be embedded in their educational efforts. Furthermore, as they embed differentiated instruction and knowledge demonstration, they are grasping more fully the extent to which their educational efforts lead to student learning and better outcomes for *all* students.

If general education teachers and education administrators are recognizing the abilities of students like Ken and Victor with moderate or severe disabilities, surely it is time for special education teachers, as well as teacher educators, to reflect on their own assumptions about students with moderate or severe disabilities and their own practices. In this book, Susan Copeland and Liz Keefe tackle these issues. They present the rationale, research base, and effective instructional strategies required for reconceptualizing how the field looks at literacy in the education and lives of students with moderate or severe disabilities. Their insights and strategies bring new hope to the field—hope for more effective instruction that leads to students with moderate or severe disabilities being more literate and using literacy in everyday life. This increased literacy can only lead to students with moderate or severe disabilities having more meaningful participation in, and making a greater contribution to, our literate society.

Diane Lea Ryndak, Ph.D.
Associate Professor
Department of Special Education
University of Florida

REFERENCES

Basil, C. (2003). Acquisition of literacy skills by children with severe disability. *Child Language Teaching & Therapy, 19*(1), 27.

Gillette, Y. (2006). Assistive technology and literacy partnerships. *Topics in Language Disorders, 26*(1), 70–84.

Kliewer, C., & Biklen, D. (2001). "School's not really a place for readings": A research synthesis of the literate lives of students with severe disabilities. *Journal of the Association for Persons with Severe Handicaps, 26*(1), 1–12.

Kliewer, C., Fitzgerald, L.M., & Meyer-Mork, J. (2004). Citizenship for all in the literate community: An ethnography of young children with significant disabilities in inclusive early childhood settings. *Harvard Educational Review, 74*(4), 373–403.

Koppenhaver, D.A. (2000). Literacy in AAC: What should be written on the envelope we push? *Augmentative & Alternative Communication, 16*(4), 270–279.

Koppenhaver, D.A., Pierce, P.L., Steelman, J.D., & Yoder, D.E. (1995). Contexts of early literacy intervention for children with developmental disabilities. In M. Fey, J. Windsor, & S. Warren (Vol. Eds.), *Communication and language intervention series: Vol. 5. Language intervention: Preschool through the elementary years*. Baltimore: Paul H. Brookes Publishing Co.

McGregor, G., & Vogelsberg, T. (1998). *Inclusive schooling practices: Pedagogical and research foundations. A synthesis of the literature that informs best practices about inclusive schooling*. Baltimore: Paul H. Brookes Publishing Co.

McLane, J.B., & McNamee, G.D. (1990). *Early literacy*. Cambridge, MA: Harvard University Press.

McSheehan, M., Sonnenmeier, R.M., Jorgensen, C.M., & Turner, K. (2006). Beyond communication access: Promoting learning of the general education curriculum by students with significant disabilities. *Topics in Language Disorders, 26*(3), 266–291.

Notari-Syverson, A., O'Connor, R., & Vadasy, P. (1996). *Facilitating language and literacy development in preschool children: To each according to their needs.* Paper presented at the annual American Educational Research Association meeting, New York. (ERIC Document Reproduction Service No. ED395692)

Ryndak, D.L., & Alper, S. (2003). *Curriculum and instruction for students with significant disabilities in inclusive settings* (2nd ed.). Boston: Allyn & Bacon.

Ryndak, D.L., & Fisher, D. (Eds.). (2003). *The foundations of inclusive education: A compendium of articles on effective strategies to achieve inclusive education* (2nd ed.). Baltimore: TASH.

Ryndak, D.L., Morrison, A.P., & Sommerstein, L. (1999). Literacy prior to and after inclusion in general education settings. *Journal of the Association for Persons with Severe Handicaps, 24*(1), 5–22.

Sturm, J.M., Spadorcia, S.A., Cunningham, J.W., Cali, K.S., Staples, A., Erickson, K., et al. (2006). What happens to reading between first and third grade? Implications for students who use AAC. *Augmentative & Alternative Communication, 22*(1), 21–36.

Teale, W.H., & Sulzby, E. (1986). Emergent literacy as a perspective for examining how young children become writers and readers. In W.H. Teale & E. Sulzby (Eds.), *Emergent literacy: Writing and reading* (pp. vii–xxv). Norwood, NJ: Ablex Publishing.

Van der Bijl, C., Alant, E., & Lloyd, L. (2006). A comparison of two strategies of sight word instruction in children with mental disability. *Research in Developmental Disabilities, 27*(1), 43–55.

Acknowledgments

We couldn't have put this book together without the teachers and students who graciously shared their instructional activities and literacy creations with us. Our grateful thanks go to Jeanne Desjardins, Gail Baxter, Michelle Trujillo, Sandra Crowell, Melanie Brawley, MaryAnna Palmer, Debra Huggins, James Panky, Kay Osborn, Frances Duff, Kaia Tollefson, Veronica Moore, Rob Spooner, Mary Clark, Frances Farrah, and Jesus Castillo.

Karen Potter, Kathy Roberson, Seon Sook Park, Peggy Hulick, Clare Stott, Peggy MacLean, and Baylor del Rosario all provided valuable assistance during the researching and writing of this book. We especially want to acknowledge the staff and students at John Adams Middle School who so generously shared their ideas and literacy products with us.

Special thanks go to Leslie, Jeff, Karen, and Danny Lederer for their vision of what is possible for students with disabilities. Thanks also to Kent Logan for being ever willing to collaborate and share his expertise about providing access to general education for all students.

We would also like to thank our colleagues Julia Scherba de Valenzuela and Ruth Luckasson for taking time to share their ideas with us and give us invaluable feedback and encouragement as we worked on the book. Finally, thanks go to Mike, Andrew, and Meg Keefe and to Jim, Heather, and Christopher Copeland for their love and support during the research and writing of the book.

To my mother, Maxine Spooner, and my brother, Rob Spooner,
who showed me the incredible power literacy can have
in all of our lives (SC)

With love and appreciation to George Barker
and Margaret Keefe (LK)

Effective Literacy Instruction

for Students with Moderate
or Severe Disabilities

Chapter 1

The Power of Literacy

Susan R. Copeland

The *American Heritage Dictionary* (2000) defines *empower* as "equip[ing] or supply[ing] with an ability." A critical purpose of education is to equip students with the knowledge and skills that will lead to increased opportunities, choices, and autonomy. One of the skills valued by and, in fact, required in our society is literacy. Being a *reader* is a highly valued social role. Acquiring even basic literacy skills can create opportunities to participate more fully in one's community, to be less dependent on others, and to make individual choices about what one wants to do or learn. For instance, having literacy skills increases opportunities for employment; expands opportunities for communication of one's ideas, thoughts, and intentions; enhances safety, health, and well-being; increases opportunities to gain new knowledge and explore new areas of learning; and facilitates participation in leisure and social activities. As our society becomes more and more focused on technological skills that require reading and writing skills, it becomes even more important that all citizens be given the opportunity to gain these essential skills.

It is particularly important that schools provide literacy instruction for individuals with moderate or severe disabilities that will enable them to have access to the important benefits associated with literacy. Too often the educational system has either denied literacy instruction to students with significant disabilities, viewing them as incapable of learning, or offered instruction that is inadequate or ineffective (McGill-Franzen & Allington, 1991). Such lowered expectations have resulted in less than positive outcomes for many persons with disabilities. For example, students with significant disabilities have higher rates of post-school unemployment or are employed in low-wage jobs, resulting in lower status and greater social isolation than their typically developing peers (Wagner, Newman, Cameto, Garza, & Levine, 2005).

The potential consequences of not providing literacy instruction to individuals with moderate or severe disabilities are too serious to ignore. Michael Bach's statement on the importance of literacy, as cited by Ewing (2000), illustrates the critical need for appropriate instruction and support:

> "No longer viewed as a set of particular skills, literacy refers to a status that accords people the opportunities and supports to communicate, given the skills and capacities they have and can develop. To be literate is to have status, respect, and accommodation from others; to have skills in communication (verbal, written, sign, gestural, or other language); and to have access to the information and technologies that make possible self-determined participation in the communication processes of one's communities and broader society."

1

Our field can no longer deny individuals the opportunity to acquire such valuable skills based simply on a disability label. Instead, we must act on the least dangerous assumption: that all individuals can acquire valued skills if given appropriate instruction and supports. To do otherwise is to deny the rights of these individuals to full participation in their communities. Yoder, Erickson, and Koppenhaver (1997) expressed the critical importance of these rights in the Literacy Bill of Rights found in Figure 1.1.

The current national focus on improving reading instruction for all our nation's children (e.g., Reading First) must include students with severe disabilities, as well as their typically developing peers. Indeed, this renewed interest in improving literacy instruction offers a unique opportunity to reexamine literacy instruction for students with significant disabilities and put into place more effective programs that *will* result in individuals who are "equipped with knowledge and skills that lead to increased opportunities, choices, and autonomy." (*American Heritage Dictionary*, 4th ed., 2000)

All persons, regardless of the extent or severity of their disabilities, have the basic right to use print. Beyond this general right are certain literacy rights that should be assured for all persons. These basic rights are

1. The right to an *opportunity to learn* to read and write. Opportunity involves engagement in active participation in tasks performed with high success.

2. The right to have *accessible,* clear, meaningful, culturally and linguistically appropriate texts at all time. *Texts,* broadly defined, range from picture books to newspapers, novels, cereal boxes, and electronic documents.

3. The right to *interact with others* while reading, writing, or listening to text. *Interaction* involves questions, comments, discussions, and other communications about or related to text.

4. The right to *life choices* made available through reading and writing competencies. *Life choices* include but are not limited to employment and employment changes, independence, community participation, and self-advocacy.

5. The right to *lifelong educational opportunities* incorporating literacy instruction and use. Literacy *educational opportunities,* regardless of when they are provided, have the potential to provide power that cannot be taken away.

6. The right to have teachers and *other service providers who are knowledgeable* about literacy instruction methods and principles. *Methods* include but are not limited to instruction, assessment, and the technologies required to make literacy accessible to individuals with disabilities. *Principles* include but are not limited to the belief that literacy is learned across places and time and that no person is too disabled to benefit from literacy learning opportunities.

7. The right to live and learn in *environments* that provide varied models of print use. Models are demonstrations of purposeful print use such as reading a recipe, paying bills, sharing a joke, or writing a letter.

8. The right to live and learn in environments that maintain the *expectations and attitudes* that all *individuals are literacy learners.*

Figure 1.1.   A literacy bill of rights. (From Yoder, D.E. [2001]. Having my say. *Augmentative and Alternative Communication, 17*[1], pp. 1–10.)

LITERACY INSTRUCTION FOR STUDENTS
WITH MODERATE OR SEVERE DISABILITIES

The purpose of this book is to provide educators and other practitioners and parents with information on effective literacy instruction for students with moderate or severe disabilities. These students include those who have been labeled as having intellectual or multiple disabilities or autism spectrum disorders. Literacy instruction for these students, even more than for students with other mild disabilities, has often been neglected. In fact, historically, society has not seen individuals with moderate or severe disabilities as "readers." They have not been viewed as capable of what Kliewer and colleagues called "literate citizenship" (Kliewer et al., 2004, p. 373), so the opportunity to acquire literacy skills has not always been offered to them or provided in ways that meet their unique learning needs.

Overview of Previous Models of Literacy Instruction for Students with Moderate or Severe Disabilities

For many years, educational programs for children with moderate or severe intellectual disabilities utilized a readiness model. This model required students to first master subskills considered to be prerequisites for more advanced literacy skills before being allowed to continue literacy instruction (Mirenda, 2003). So, for example, a child might be expected to learn and name all the letters of the alphabet in the correct order before being taught to read his or her name. Unfortunately, many of these subskills were taught in a decontextualized, disconnected manner, which made it very difficult for learners with moderate or severe disabilities to master them. The end result was that they often got stuck on lower-level skills and were never provided with additional literacy instruction because they weren't considered ready for it. Furthermore, this model frequently resulted in age-inappropriate instruction that had little useful value for students. In classrooms using this model, for instance, it was not uncommon to see 17-year-olds still singing the alphabet song or being drilled on color words.

Beginning in the mid-to-late 1970s, the curriculum focus for students with moderate or severe disabilities changed to functional skills (Browder et al., 2004). In terms of literacy instruction, this meant that educators taught students sight words considered necessary for survival in the school and community (Connors, 1992; Katims, 2000). For example, students might spend time learning words like *exit* and *poison* or learning to write the words needed to complete job applications. In many ways, this instructional approach was an improvement over the readiness model. Students learned to read words that they could use immediately in their schools, job settings, and communities, and accordingly their dependence on others was decreased.

Potential Limitations of a Functional Literacy Approach

Although functional literacy instruction has many benefits, it also limits the range of literacy skills a student can acquire and therefore their opportunities for full participation in their communities. This approach does not teach students literacy skills that might allow a broader and richer range of literacy experiences such as reading for pleasure or acquiring the writing skills needed to e-mail a friend. More recent research on literacy and children with moderate or severe disabilities has shown how important it is to not underestimate these children or inadvertently limit their development of literacy skills (Connors, 1992; Katims, 2000). While not all children will become conventional readers or writers, educators can no longer come to that conclusion merely by looking at the assigned disability labels. Instead, practitioners must give these students the opportunity to develop a broad range of literacy skills. They must view these individuals as readers and writers, have high expectations for what they can learn, and provide appropriate literacy instruction in meaningful ways that will allow the students to develop their skills to the fullest extent possible.

NATIONAL DISCUSSION ON LITERACY

Since release of the National Reading Panel (NRP) Report in 2000, there has been a renewed focus on reading instruction in public schools. Researchers, policy makers, and practitioners are once again engaging in lively debate about what are the essential components of beginning reading instruction. Related legislation (e.g., No Child Left Behind [NCLB]) has emphasized that schools must implement effective instruction that will allow *all* children to learn to read. This debate leaves parents, teachers, and other related service providers of children with moderate or severe disabilities wondering if *all* includes children with more significant disabilities. Did researchers and policy makers who crafted the current national policies on beginning reading instruction take these children into consideration in making their instructional and policy recommendations? Should practitioners use the results of the NRP report to guide literacy instruction for these learners?

Renewed Focus on Literacy Instruction
for Students with Moderate or Severe Disabilities

Questions such as these have led to increased interest in the literacy development of children with moderate or severe disabilities. We suggest that although the NRP report (2000) did not include research on children with tested IQ scores below 70 (i.e., children considered to have an intellectual disability) or children who use alternative means of communication, this is still a highly opportune time to examine the state of literacy instruction for children with moderate or severe disabilities. The national focus on literacy for all children presents an ideal opening to provide practitioners with resources on what is known about effective, evidence-based literacy instruction for this group of individuals.

Supporting Research

Although more and more researchers are examining effective literacy practices for children with moderate or severe disabilities, the number of studies in this area is still relatively small. The available research supports use of the instructional components identified in the NRP report with some noteworthy qualifications. First, even more effort to teach literacy skills in context must be made with this group of learners than with their typically developing peers. Practitioners must be sure that they are focusing instruction on the purpose of literacy to create or gain meaning and not just on teaching isolated word recognition (pattern recognition) skills. This means teaching literacy within meaningful situations (Connors, 1992; Katims, 2000) and assisting students to make the connection between the skills they are learning and their own lives. Second, we must recognize the unique strengths and needs of each student and adapt literacy instruction to meet those needs (Yoder, 2001). Our field has a vast knowledge base for effective use of adaptations and technology to provide access to learning for individuals with a variety of disabilities. We must now apply this knowledge to teaching literacy effectively.

OVERVIEW OF THE BOOK

In this book, the authors of each chapter describe effective, evidence-based literacy practices for individuals with moderate or severe disabilities. The book is not intended as a text on how to teach reading in general; there are numerous excellent books already available for that purpose. Instead, the authors provide practitioners with up-to-date information on how to incorporate components of effective instruction into their daily literacy lessons for individuals with moderate or severe disabilities. The book is not geared only toward young children who typically are in the beginning stages of literacy acquisition. In fact, the instructional strategies presented are deliberately focused on learners of any age who are developing literacy skills. This decision was made because the authors recognized that individuals with severe disabilities have not had an opportunity to receive systematic, effective literacy instruction. Thus, older students at the beginning levels of literacy will benefit from the instructional strategies presented in each chapter.

The book is organized around the critical components of instruction for beginning readers (see Figure 1.2). It is important to point out that the literacy practices described in each chapter are applicable to students with a range of learning needs. This includes students with and without identified disabilities. However, for the purposes of this book, the authors highlight their use for students who have moderate or severe disabilities.

Each chapter focuses on a key component of instruction and describes evidence-based teaching strategies found to be effective for this group of learners. The focus of the book is not on merely providing access to instruction in each of these components, although that is a vital consideration when working with students with diverse abilities. Rather, the authors of each chapter provide information on why these instructional components are significant in designing an effective literacy program and on how to implement each component into comprehensive literacy instruction.

Each chapter also emphasizes providing literacy instruction for students within inclusive settings. It is not enough to place students with moderate or severe disabilities in general education classroom settings for social interaction purposes only. As important as social interaction is, practitioners have a responsibility to assist all students in acquiring the critical academic skills that will lead to their full participation in their communities. The authors make the assumption that general education classrooms or other postschool inclusive settings are the optimal locations for the literacy instruction of students with moderate or severe disabilities. Indeed, literacy instruction is most effective for individuals with mod-

The following are the components of effective reading instruction identified by the NRP (2000) with the addition of oral language.

Oral Language: Language forms the basis for literacy. Understanding the sound system of a language (its phonology), the rules for how words can be combined to create different meanings (its grammar and syntax), how to use language in social contexts (pragmatics), and word meanings (semantics) all influence development of literacy skills.

Phonological Awareness: Phonological awareness is the ability to recognize and manipulate the units that make up spoken language. It involves recognition that sentences are made up of words, words of syllables, and syllables of individual sounds or phonemes. *Phonemic awareness* is particularly important for developing reading skills. It entails detecting and manipulating the individual sounds in spoken words.

Phonics: Phonics is knowledge of the relationship between letters (graphemes) and their associated sounds (phonemes). Phonics knowledge allows children to map spoken language (speech) onto letters. This knowledge can be applied to decode unknown words or used to spell words when creating text (encoding).

Fluency: This is the ability to read text accurately and at a reasonably rapid, smooth pace. To be a fluent reader, a child must recognize words automatically without having to slow down to decode each word in a text. Fluent reading allows the child to concentrate on the meaning of what is being read instead of concentrating on each letter sound. Fluent readers can comprehend what they are reading more easily than readers who read slowly or in a choppy manner.

Vocabulary: A child's vocabulary is comprised of the words a child understands and uses in listening, speaking, reading, and writing. *Listening* vocabulary consists of words a child understands when she or he hears them spoken; it includes words that the child understands but may not use in his or her everyday conversation. *Speaking* vocabulary consists of words students understand and routinely use when speaking. *Reading* vocabulary consists of the words a child can read and understand. *Writing* vocabulary consists of words a child understands and can use when composing text. Having a well-developed vocabulary is important for beginning readers because to read a word in print requires having that word in your vocabulary. For example, decoding a word that you have never heard won't be very useful to you because you have no point of reference to understand its meaning.

Text Comprehension: Text comprehension is understanding the meaning of printed text, or, in other words, making sense out of what you read. It is the point of reading! Text comprehension can range from understanding the meaning of a single word ("Stop!") to understanding the nuances of meaning found in a Shakespeare sonnet. Effective comprehension requires several skills including efficient word recognition, a well-developed vocabulary, fluent reading, and adequate background knowledge ("knowledge of the world").

Figure 1.2.   Components of effective reading instruction. (From Armbruster, B.B., Lehr, F., & Osborn, J. [2001]. *Put reading first: The research building blocks for teaching children to read: Kindergarten through grade 3*. Washington, DC: The Partnership for Reading.)

erate or severe disabilities when it takes place within an inclusive setting (Erickson, Koppenhaver, & Yoder, 1994). This is supported by research findings suggesting that literacy instruction for this group of students must be done within meaningful, context-based situations. A classroom full of students of diverse abilities and with diverse interests provides powerful models for observational learning. Moreover, inclusive settings offer opportunities for richer, more diverse and more sophisticated literacy experiences than are likely to be offered within segregated, self-contained classrooms. (See, for example, Chapter 2, Brinkerhoff and Keefe's discussion of the use of brain-based learning strategies to create a rich literacy-learning environment.) The instructional practices provided in each chapter are easily implemented within settings that include learners with and without disabilities, and the practices described will benefit both groups.

Creating Rich Literacy Learning Environments for All Students

Jonathan D. Brinkerhoff and Elizabeth B. Keefe

A major focus and challenge for teachers of students with moderate or severe disabilities has been providing access to the general education classroom while still individualizing instruction (Brown, Wilcox, Sontag, Vincent, Dodd, & Gruenewald, 2004; Jackson, Ryndak, & Billingsley, 2000; Villa & Thousand, 2005). A perusal of recent publications in special education reveal an increasingly sophisticated educational knowledge and instructional practices aimed at providing meaningful access to the general education curriculum through such strategies as the Infused Skills Grid (e.g. Castegnera Fisher, Rodifer, & Sax, 1998), Program at a Glance (e.g., Snell & Janney, 2000), and Ecological/Discrepancy Analysis (Downing, 2002, 2005; Ryndak & Alper, 2003; Snell & Brown, 2006).

Research clearly indicates that students with moderate or severe disabilities benefit from placement in general education classes (Villa & Thousand, 2000). Research has shown gains in many areas including increased learning (Fisher & Meyer, 2002; Ryndak, Morrison, & Sommerstein, 1999), increased engaged time (Katz, Mirenda, & Auerbach, 2002; Logan, Bakeman, & Keefe, 1997), improved social and play skills (Fisher & Meyer, 2002; Keefe & Van Etten, 1994), and higher quality IEPs (Hunt, Farron-Davis, Beckstead, Curtis, & Goetz, 1994). At the same time, research indicates that students without disabilities do as well or better from education in inclusive classrooms (Cole, Waldron, & Majd, 2004; Sharpe, York, & Knight, 1994; Staub & Peck, 1994). No research base exists to show that students with disabilities gain any educational benefits from segregated educational placements (Downing, 2005).

What is happening in these inclusive classrooms that leads to positive educational outcomes for all students? We believe that by improving access for students with disabilities, teachers are implementing instructional strategies that create richer learning environments for all students whether or not they have disabilities. In this chapter we examine the latest research and literature on creating rich learning environments for students. Brain-based learning is a new and exciting area of research in education focused on an examination of the chemical and structural aspects of how brains learn. We propose that this brain-based research provides a solid foundation to justify the use of such educational innovations as differentiated instruction, multiple modalities, and cooperative learning with all students, including those with severe disabilities. This chapter will provide an overview of the most recent research on brain-based learning, describe some examples of instructional strategies that are consistent with this research, and look at how individual individualized education program (IEP) objectives can be taken into account.

BRAIN-BASED LEARNING

Advances in imaging technologies such as magnetic resonance imaging (MRI), functional magnetic resonance imaging (fMRI), and positron emission tomography (PET) have allowed researchers to examine the functioning of the brain in unprecedented detail. In contrast to classic studies in educational psychology that focused on external observation of human behavior as the basis for intuiting how brains functioned, these imaging technologies provide a window into the real time neuronal activity associated with the perception of environmental stimuli, how that sensory input is processed, and how information is stored in memory—in other words, how brains learn. Results from classic educational psychology research in combination with studies using the newest brain imaging technologies have produced a new level of understanding concerning the learning process—information that can guide educators interested in maximizing the impact of instruction for their students.

How Do Brains Work?

To better understand the educational implications of brain research, we must first understand what brains are made of and how they receive, process, and store information. The brain is part of the nervous system. The basic building blocks of the nervous system are specialized cells called neurons that differ from other cells in that they are designed to communicate with one another using a combination of chemical and electrical signals.

While neurons come in a variety of shapes, the typical neuron is shaped like a tree. The tree's canopy is composed of the main cell body. In place of leaves, the neuron's cell body is covered with multiple projections called dendrites that lie in contact with adjacent neurons. The function of a cell's dendrites is to receive information in the form of chemical signals from surrounding neurons. If the received signals are sufficiently strong, the neuron is activated, meaning it transmits the signal down the length of its trunk, or axon, and on to the roots. The roots are filaments that lie adjacent to the dendrites of other neurons. The filaments of one neuron don't actually touch the dendrites of adjacent cells; they're separated by a tiny gap. This gap is called the synapse. Neurons transmit signals across these synapses by releasing chemicals called neurotransmitters. Examples of neurotransmitters include glycine, epinephrine, dopamine, serotonin, cortisol, and endorphins.

The brain is made of billions of these interconnected neurons, which are arranged into various structures, the most obvious of which are the two halves, or hemispheres, of the brain, which are connected by thick chords of neurons called the corpus callosum. Other brain structures generally come in pairs, with one in the left hemisphere, and one in the right. Some of these structures control bodily functions automatically, without active thought. For example, the brain stem controls breathing and the beating of the heart, the cerebellum controls balance and muscle coordination, and the amygdala moderates emotion. While these structures can influence learning, of greater interest to teachers are brain structures that play a role in conscious thought and memory, as it is here that the most active aspects of learning take place.

Conscious thought occurs in a part of the brain called the cerebral cortex. The cerebral cortex is made up of lobes, each with primary responsibility for specific aspects of brain function. For example, the occipital lobes are primarily responsible for vision; the temporal lobes for hearing; and the parietal lobes for both body awareness, such as sensations of heat, cold, pain, or pressure, and for control of which of these sensations to pay attention to at any given time. Last are the frontal lobes, which are the seat of consciousness. The frontal lobes control conscious thought or cognition and the body's voluntary movement. For example, when engaged in a conversation, it is the frontal lobes that allow you to understand the conversation, decide that you have something to say, and direct the muscles in your throat and mouth so you can speak.

This structural description of the brain's various parts and associated functions, however, is tremendously simplified. In truth, the functioning of the brain is both highly complex and integrated across all of its parts in both hemispheres. Attempting to isolate a single part of the brain and *teach* it leads to educational fads such as the right brain–left brain hoopla in vogue some years ago where lessons were designed to accommodate specifically either left-brained individuals who were said to be more verbal and analytical or right-brained individuals who were supposed to be more artistic and emotional. In truth, both halves of the brain are actively engaged at all times during all activities, either analytic or creative. Yet, while efforts to consider left–right-brained teaching strategies may have been misguided, the intention of making instruction more effective based on a more sophisticated understanding of how brains learn is a valid enterprise. Achieving that goal may be more fruitfully achieved by looking at the brain functionally rather than structurally.

The Information Processing Model

The information processing model (Gagne & Driscol, 1988; see Figure 2.1) describes the functions of the brain responsible for learning while ignoring the specific biological structures underlying those functions. The model begins with the environment generating a variety of stimuli that activate the body's sensory receptors. So, light enters the eye and triggers neurons on the retina, sound enters the ears and triggers neurons in the inner ear, particles enter the nose or mouth and trigger neurons associated with smell or taste, and stimulation of the skin triggers neurons associated with pressure, temperature, or pain.

Neurons transmit these stimuli to the brain where they enter the sensory register, which is responsible for perceiving the prominent features of the stimuli through a process of pattern recognition. For example, the visual stimulus generated by looking at the letter X would be recognized as two crossed lines. This process takes the merest fraction of a second before the information is transferred to the short-term or conscious memory. Here the information is coded into a meaningful concept (i.e., the crossed line pattern is associated with a stored memory of the letter X retrieved from long-term memory). The con-

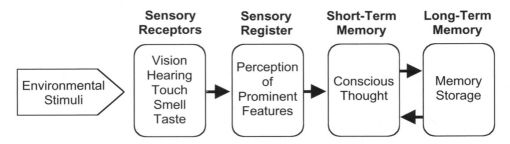

Figure 2.1. Example of the information processing model. (From Gagne, R.M., & Driscol, M.P. [1988]. *Essentials of learning for instruction* [2nd ed., p. 13]. Englewood Cliffs, NJ: Prentice Hall.)

sciousness is now aware that the letter X has been seen. This information will reside in short-term or conscious memory for at most a few seconds unless it is actively dealt with. Conscious memory might actively consider some aspect of the X or its meaning as part of a word within a sentence, which would result in its retention for a longer period. If information in conscious memory is to be remembered, it is sent to the long-term memory where it is stored for later retrieval. You may be wondering how this functional description of the brain relates to improving student literacy. Good question, and to answer it we need to examine both conscious or short-term and long-term memory more deeply.

Short-Term Memory

Short-term memory is constantly bombarded with incoming stimuli, far more than can be consciously dealt with. For example, right now neurons are sending messages to your brain about the feel of your clothes against your skin, of the pressure of your body against the chair you're sitting on, and of the ambient sounds around you, yet until you read this sentence, you weren't consciously aware of any of those things. Instead, you've focused your attention on reading this book. While people can consciously focus their attention for a period of time, choosing what to pay attention to is most often an unconscious process. As Patricia Wolfe, author and consultant on brain-based teaching, suggests, children may be criticized for not paying attention, but in truth, everyone is always paying attention to something; it's just that what students pay attention to may not represent what teachers would like (Wolfe, 2001). Most teachers would probably agree that students might learn more if they paid more attention to instructional tasks. Research offers clues as to what factors influence short-term memory in deciding where attention will be focused.

Novelty   People pay greater attention to what is new or different. Something as simple as putting up a new bulletin board or rearranging classroom desks will foster greater attention in a classroom. So will varying instructional styles such as whole class versus small group, or instructional delivery methods such as overheads, lectures, videos, PowerPoint, or manipulatives. Fisher and Frey (2003) discussed the importance of getting students' attention in order to teach literacy skills more effectively. They suggested that this can be done through demonstrations, discrepant events, visual displays, and/or thought-provoking questions. Similarly, many lesson plan formats include an anticipatory set as a critical element to gain student attention and interest before instruction.

Intensity   Students typically pay greater attention to stimuli that are more intense. Therefore, stimuli that are louder, faster, or more colorful than other competing stimuli are more likely to attract attention. Teachers make use of this fact when they use their *teacher voice*, or incorporate colorful illustrations into instructional materials. Movement is another factor affecting where short-term memory focuses its attention. Teachers who act out the action of a story or use props while reading aloud will command greater attention than those who sit passively in a chair.

Meaning   Meaning also influences attention. For example, if we are in a group that spontaneously begins speaking Spanish, and we speak only English, the meaning of the conversation vanishes and our attention begins to wander. It's no different for a child when instruction is unclear, disorganized, presented in steps that are too large, or riddled with unfamiliar words. Under such circumstances, students' attention will invariably wander.

Emotions   Robert Sylwester, emeritus professor of education at the University of Oregon, is well known for his assertion that "emotion drives attention, and attention drives learning" (Sylwester, 1995). A study conducted by Larry Cahill and James McGaugh at the University of California at Irvine demonstrates the point. Study participants were split into two groups, with each group viewing a slide show and listening to an accompanying story. Both stories used the same images of what appeared to be an accident scene. One story indicated that the accident scene was a disaster drill with a slide showing a young victim's badly mangled legs attributed to make-up used to make the drill realistic. The other story indicated that the images showed a real accident scene where the young victim's legs were severed from his body and surgeons later struggled to reattach them. Two weeks later, the participants were tested to see how well they remembered specific story details. Results showed that those who were told that the accident scene was real remembered significantly more than those told it was staged (Cahill & McGaugh, 1995). What this and similar studies demonstrate is that people are more likely to remember things that engage them on an emotional level.

As teachers, there are many ways we can increase our students' emotional engagement in learning. One way is to allow the students to pick their own topics of interest to study. For example, rather than being assigned a poem to analyze, or an animal to write about, the students can suggest questions they'd like to answer through science experiments. Another strategy for increasing students' emotional engagement is to present a conundrum or puzzle that piques the students' curiosity as the lead-in to a lesson. Allowing students to work in groups can raise their emotional engagement, as can tying instruction to real world questions and issues facing society; for example, they could investigate the plight of an endangered animal or they could write a state legislator and present an argument or proposal concerning a local issue. Letting students know that certain information will be covered on a test will also increase emotional engagement, although too much negative emotion in the form of anxiety or stress can be detrimental.

The design of the children's television show *Sesame Street* is research based; in thinking about it, the elements influencing attention are obvious. Consider Big Bird. A giant, talking bird is certainly novel, his coloration is intense, he moves as he walks and talks, he interacts with children on a level that is meaningful, and, if you've ever seen children with a *Sesame Street* fixation, they are definitely emotionally engaged!

The "Miller Seven"   There are other characteristics of short-term memory that are important for teachers to consider. Short-term memory has a limited capacity. Research by George Miller, psychology professor emeritus at Princeton University, demonstrated that at most an adult's short-term memory can hold seven elements, plus or minus two, at any given time. For children, the limits are lower. At 7, the limit is two; at 9, the limit is four; at 11, the limit is five; and at 13, the limit is six (Miller, 1956). It is important to remember that students with moderate or severe disabilities may have even lower limits.

Teachers see evidence of these limits every day. Consider a student reading aloud. She comes to an unfamiliar word and stops, and then she starts sounding out the word letter by letter. After several seconds, she manages to piece together the word, but now has forgotten what the sentence was about, so she jumps back to the beginning of the sentence and starts over again. Reading is a complex task requiring the decoding of letters and a given word while maintaining a memory of the of the previous words and the overall meaning of the sentence. Stumbling over an unfamiliar word and having to stop and sound it out letter by letter consumes the entire capacity of short-term memory with the result that the meaning of the overall sentence is lost.

Ways to Improve Short-Term Memory   What practical steps can teachers take to help students overcome the limited capacity of short-term memory? There are many.

Segment and Sequence Instruction   First and foremost, instructional materials should segment and sequence what is to be learned into manageable, logical steps. When each learning step is small and ordered in a logical sequence, students are able to follow the instruction without overwhelming short-term memory limitations in attempts to make sense of the instruction. Task analysis is an example of an instructional strategy using segmentation and sequencing that is particularly effective with students who have moderate or severe disabilities. Teachers should also check for understanding during instruction to ensure that students aren't lost. Such checking should be based on specific questions that require students to demonstrate their understanding through an ability to answer the questions rather than simply asking if students understand or have questions of their own. Students who are nonverbal can show through gestures, sign, or demonstration that they understand the instruction.

Provide Clear and Explicit Instructions   Another strategy for limiting cognitive load is to provide clear, explicit instructions as well as examples. If students are confused about what it is they should be doing to complete an assignment, figuring out what to do becomes the focus of attention and usurps short-term memory capacity that would be better used to focus on learning from the activity. Providing examples in the form of a completed sample item on a test or worksheet can help clarify what is to be done, thereby allowing students to focus mental resources on the activity at hand.

Provide Scaffolds   Scaffolds are supports that teachers use to help students by reducing the amount of information they need in their short-term memory while completing tasks. In the area of literacy instruction, some examples of scaffolds are ABC charts, name models, word walls, graphic organizers, and prompt questions for comprehension. These supports could be individualized or available to the whole class through a bulletin board, a chalkboard, handouts, manipulatives, or classroom wall space. Scaffolds are not meant as long-term supports; they are there to support students thinking while they learn new information or processes. By removing some of the burden of what kids are trying to mentally juggle while completing a task, teachers can help ensure that students' short-term memory limitations aren't exceeded. Some students with moderate or severe disabilities may continue to need individual scaffolds to independently complete tasks.

Use Images and Graphics   Another strategy for lessening the demands on limited short-term memory resources during instruction is the use of images and graphics. We've all heard the saying "A picture is worth 1,000 words." Insights into why this is so were revealed through a series of studies conducted by Ray Kulhavey in association with various graduate students at Arizona State University, which suggested that an entire image is processed as a single entity in short-term memory, so all the spatial and other information in the image can be conveyed as just one of the seven plus or minus two elements available during mental processing (Kulhavey, Stock, Verdi, Rittschof, & Savanye, 1993). Embodying all of this information as a single entity reduces the impact on short-term memory limits. Therefore, using any form of graphic such as pictures, diagrams, flow charts, time lines, or graphs in support of instruction will help prevent overburdening short-term memory capacity.

Many of the strategies useful for reducing demands on short-term memory are also effective for supporting students' ability to use long-term memory for storing and retrieving information. And it is through an understanding of how brains store and organize information in long-term memory that teachers can find the greatest insight into specific strategies for supporting student learning.

Long-Term Memory

Long-term memory is tasked with both storing everything a person learns and making it available for future recall on demand. How is this possible, given the vast quantity of information a person acquires over a lifetime and the limited number of neurons available for storage? It used to be thought that the brain organized information like a filing cabinet full of file folders, with the file folders made up of neurons. This theory supposed that a given localized group of neurons was responsible for the storage of a given piece of information such as the concept of an apple.

But brain imaging technologies show that when a person thinks of an apple, areas all over the brain are activated including parts of the occipital lobes responsible for vision, parts of the temporal lobes for hearing, and many other areas. Thinking of an apple activates all of those parts of the brain responsible for processing the incoming stimuli associated with experiencing an apple: seeing the shape and red color of the apple, smelling the apple's scent, hearing the crunch when the apple is bitten, feeling the texture of the apple when it's held in the hand, and the feel and taste of the apple in the mouth. Researchers realized the concept of the apple wasn't stored by a dedicated set of neurons in a single location, but instead was stored as a spider web-like pattern of neuronal activation throughout the brain. If a person is asked to think of a banana, a different pattern of neuronal activation in each of the processing areas of the brain will result. It is these differing spider-web patterns of activation that represent stored learning and memory, and it is highly efficient because any given neuron can play a part in many different memories.

These complex spider-web patterns are called *schemes*. You have a scheme for apple, and another for banana, and yet another for a Ford Mustang. But the scheme doesn't stop at the physical properties of each of these things. The scheme also includes any other related pieces of information. In the case of the apple, the scheme links to the concept of stories having to do with apples, and from there it links to specifics of the stories of Adam and Eve and Snow White. The scheme also links to the different types of apples—their colors and tastes—as well as to the varied dishes that can be made from apples including candied apples, applesauce, and apple pie. The scheme might include links to historical information about the spread of apple trees and Johnny Appleseed, as well as links to information about the cultivation of apples in orchards, or how apples are propagated and harvested or crushed for their juice. The links within the scheme keep expanding, tying together more and more information. Recalling any given piece of information requires accessing that part of the scheme where the specific information lies, and that can be accomplished by following any series of links within the scheme that lead to it.

Ways to Improve Long-Term Memory   Once you understand that a scheme is a complex pattern of informational nodes connected by links, and that recalling something you've learned is a process of following those links back to the appropriate information node, you have a powerful insight into how to make instruction more effective. Suppose you want your students to learn something such as how the letter "c" can make the sound /k/ or /s/. You know that this phonics fact represents a node that will be linked to other information as part of a scheme. You also know that recalling that fact later will require following links back to the original information node. How can you increase the probability that a student will be able to do that?

One way is to create as many links as possible to the newly learned fact. Poorly defined schemes with few links make accessing an information node more difficult, while more robust, better developed schemes with more links to a given piece of information make accessing any given information node easier. This is true because with a greater number of well developed links, if the student isn't successful recalling the information following one set of links, there are other options that could be used to access the information. In contrast, when using a scheme with only a few tenuous links, the student has few options for re-call. If the first attempt doesn't work, there may be no other options to try with the result that the information can't be accessed.

Create Links Through Multiple Senses   How can teachers support students in creating multiple links to a given concept or fact? Recall that brain scans of people thinking of an apple showed activity in all of those areas of the brain associated with the sensory experience of an apple. So, when teaching "c" makes the sound /k/ or /s/, if you can associate that learning with multiple senses, each sense will contribute its own links to the scheme and the result will be more links to use leading back to the learning. Many reading programs use multisensory approaches with students (e.g., Wilson Reading Program, Animated Literacy, Patterns for Success). Accordingly, you could have students use ma-nipulatives to show different representations of the letter "c" in the beginning, middle, and end of words; this would use sight and touch. You could recite words and rhymes using the letter "c" that involve speaking and hearing. Students could make the letter "c" with their body or draw it in shaving cream, thereby using sight, touch, and kinesthetics. Many creative teachers have known for years that engaging multiple senses in instruction results in better learning. But there are other factors contributing to the creation of more robust schemes with increased numbers of links that involve linking new learning to what's already known.

Connect to Prior Learning   Research done in the 1880s graphically demonstrated how difficult it can be to learn information with few if any links to previous learning. German researcher Hermann Ebbinghaus investigated learn-ing in the absence of the previous knowledge, learning, and experiences that are normally available to people by memorizing random lists of nonsense syllables such as *doj* or *geb* to the point that he could confidently repeat the lists when given the first syllable. By using nonsense syllables, he ensured that there was no connection between the syllables and any prior knowledge he might have. He dis-covered that after 24 hours, he could recall fewer than 50% of the syllables, and after 48 hours, only 35% (Ebbinghaus, 1913). This clearly suggests that rote mem-orization, the learning of isolated facts not tied to an existing scheme, is far from a successful learning strategy.

There is much we can do as teachers to support students in linking new learning to existing schemes. When designing instruction, we can begin lessons by connecting the topic of the day's lesson to prior lessons or learning. Thus, a lesson on the stepped pyramids of the Incas might begin by asking students to think about what they know about Egyptian pyramids. Connecting to prior learn-ing represents the first step in most systematic lesson design models—for ex-ample, the seven step model created by Madeline Hunter taught in preservice teaching programs (Hunter, 1994).

Teachers can help students forge links by relating new content to prior learning during lessons. One way of doing this is through use of metaphors, sim-iles, and analogies, each of which compares something new with something known. For example, in this chapter, the shape of a neuron was compared with a tree. Knowledge of a tree's shape helped support learning how a neuron is shaped. During a lesson on Incan pyramids, the thousands of workers cooperat-ing to construct the pyramids could be linked through metaphor, simile, or analogy to bees working to construct a hive to help students understand the organization and cooperation of the workers.

Engage Students at Higher Levels of Bloom's Taxonomy   Another way to forge more links within a scheme is to engage students on a deeper mental level during learning. Benjamin Bloom (1956) created a taxonomy describing different levels of thinking in which the lowest levels are *knowledge* and *comprehension*. Knowledge and comprehension represent the type of thinking required to memorize and regurgitate facts—for example, recognizing the symbol M and knowing the sound it stands for. Above these two levels is *application*, a level of thought where knowledge is used to solve real-world problems. This would be reflected in having a knowledge of letter sounds in order to read. Above the application level are the levels *analysis*, *synthesis*, and *evaluation*, with each representing a deeper level of thought and engagement. Analysis, an assessment of meaning, would be reflected in finding the theme of a poem or the pattern in a set of data; synthesis, the creation of something new, might involve rewriting *Goldilocks and the Three Bears* from the perspective of the bears; and evaluation, the judging of something by a set of criteria, would be reflected in the critique of a novel or painting.

Instruction that engages students in deeper levels of thinking as represented by the higher levels of Bloom's taxonomy results in the development of a more complex scheme with increased numbers and complexity of information nodes and their associated links. Such instruction is the exact opposite of the rote memorization investigated by Ebbinghaus. In contrast to the rapid loss of recall for nonsense syllables, research demonstrates that instruction engaging students at higher levels of Bloom's taxonomy results in greater recall in both the short and long-term.

Bring Recall to the Level of Automaticity   So far, all of the strategies for supporting long-term memory have focused on increasing the number and complexity of links within a scheme as a way to increase the likelihood of accessing and understanding a given fact or memory. Another means for supporting the recall of information from long-term memory is to make those links leading to the information as strong as possible. This is analogous to following a path through a forest: It's easier to follow a well-worn path than one used less often. In the same way, it's easier to follow a well-worn path of links in the brain.

How does this translate to teaching in a classroom? There are certain types of learning that we as teachers want students to know to the point where they can access and use the learning automatically. This is called bringing learning to a point of automaticity, and examples of skills teachers would want students to master at this level include sound–symbol relationships, sight words, and writing conventions (e.g., capitalization, punctuation). Skills such as these are so basic we want students to access and utilize them without conscious thought, and the way to achieve that is through practice. Each time a student decodes "c" as /k/ or /s/, the link to that fact is reinforced. With sufficient repetition, the neuronal links within the scheme become so engrained that accessing that information becomes fast and automatic. With no conscious thought required to recall the information, no imposition on short-term memory limits are made, allowing conscious memory to engage in more meaningful pursuits.

In the example of decoding print, with basic sound–symbol relationships at a level of automaticity, short-term or conscious memory can focus fully on the process of comprehension. In the example of basic writing conventions including capitalization and punctuation, requiring students to use these conventions for all curricular areas and assignments will result in their use becoming automatic over time. Therefore, beyond expecting students to use complete sentences in writing assignments, spelling words can be embedded into complete sentences, with students responsible for writing the entire sentence on their papers. Similarly, short-answer questions on a science test can be written in complete sentences. Through repetition, use of correct writing conventions will be raised to a level of automaticity, freeing short-term memory resources to focus on the content of what is being written. The rest of the chapter will describe and discuss specific instructional strategies that lead to the creation of rich literacy learning environments.

INSTRUCTION SUPPORTING BRAIN-FRIENDLY CLASSROOMS FOR ALL STUDENTS

Information from research on how brains learn is applicable to all students in all settings, so teachers who keep brain function in mind when designing and implementing instruction are likely to be more successful at reaching their instructional goals. Let's review what such teaching is like overall and then consider specific instructional strategies that teachers can use to create brain-friendly classrooms.

Brain-based teaching recognizes that short-term memory is constantly bombarded with stimuli and that gaining student attention can be facilitated through instruction that incorporates novelty, intensity, or movement. Instruction should engage students emotionally by making learning personally meaningful. To avoid overloading short-term memory resources, instruction should be presented in small, logically sequenced steps that include use of images and graphics as well as appropriate scaffolds such as process steps written on a blackboard. Further relieving short-term memory demands are use of clear directions and worked examples of problems.

To help students integrate new learning into existing long-term memory schemes, instruction should support students in forming links between new and previously learned information by making clear how the present lesson builds on previous lessons and by using similes, metaphors, and analogies that focus student attention on how the new learning relates to known information. Use of similes, metaphors, analogies, pictures, graphics, and models have the added benefit of reducing demands on short-term memory by allowing students to apply known information to the understanding of new learning. To support formation of more robust schemes, instruction should make use of multiple senses and require thinking at higher levels of Bloom's taxonomy. To facilitate automaticity for basic skills, instruction should include multiple instances and types of practice to burn in appropriate long-term memory links. In turn, bringing basic skills to a level of automaticity reduces demands on short-term memory, as students can focus on problem solving and comprehension rather than decoding phonics facts, or on expressing their thoughts rather than on capitalization and punctuation.

The following section describes some examples of instructional strategies that can be used by teachers to plan effective instruction for all learners. Specific examples of how these strategies apply to students with moderate or severe disabilities are given. These strategies are effective because they are consistent with the most recent research on how the brain works.

Differentiated Instruction

A differentiated classroom is based on the assumption that students are varied in their abilities, interests, and learning preferences (Tomlinson, 2001). Instruction in a differentiated classroom is designed for a diverse group of learners right from the start rather than assuming that all students learn in the same way and at the same rate. This is in contrast to many general education classrooms where curriculum is delivered in the same way to all students in the class, requiring teachers to retrofit curriculum for students with disabilities (Udvari-Solner, Villa, & Thousand, 2002). In the undifferentiated classroom, instruction might be adjusted after students have failed to make progress due to a mismatch between instruction and student needs. At worst, students who fail to make expected progress might be viewed as problem students who do not belong in the general education classroom.

In a differentiated classroom, multiple approaches are offered to enable the students to master content, process information, and demonstrate their learning through varied products. Assessment is dynamic and ongoing to ensure that the classroom instructional approaches meet the needs of students. Instruction is differentiated according to students' readiness, interest, and learning profiles (Tomlinson, 2001). A differentiated classroom will be better able to adapt to the needs of students with moderate or severe disabilities because the teacher is already assuming that the student population is diverse. Students with moderate or severe disabilities will typically be below their grade-level peers in readiness. A differentiated classroom already has varied content based on readiness, and therefore the student with moderate or severe disabilities is not the only student doing something different, as would be the case in the undifferentiated classroom. Students with moderate or severe disabilities have varied interests and learning styles in the same ways as students without disabilities, and will benefit from differentiation based on these factors.

An Example of Differentiated Instruction   A third-grade class is completing a research project on animals. The competencies for the unit include reading, writing, and oral-language skills; research and critical thinking skills; and scientific knowledge of animals. One of the students in the class, Jonah, has Down syndrome. Jonah's individual goals include identifying basic sight words, writing his name, following directions, working appropriately with peers, and making choices. Through differentiation, all students in this class can have their needs met. Content is differentiated by readiness level through offering reading materials at varied levels, from picture books to encyclopedias. Content is differentiated by interest through allowing students to pick the animals they would like to research. Content is differentiated by learning profile through offering a variety of materials for research including books, videos, audiotapes, and web sites. Process is differentiated by allowing students to work in small groups, pairs, or individually. Product is differentiated by allowing students to choose from a menu of assignments that include making up a poem or song about the animal, creating a diorama or poster about the animal, creating a play about the animal, and creating a brochure about the animal. The use of grading rubrics clearly communicates expectations for the assignments. The differentiation of content, process, and product gives the student with moderate or severe disabilities access to the curriculum by providing materials at his ability level, allowing Jonah to work with his peers, and designing assignment choices that allow him to meet his individual learning goals.

Multiple Modalities

Schema theory indicates that instruction incorporating multiple modalities will result in more robust schemes that enable students to more easily recall learned information. This occurs as each different modality used during the learning process contributes its own links within the scheme, and each link can serve as a potential means for recalling the information. Teaching by using multiple modalities helps all students learn but can be particularly important for those with special needs. Howard Gardner (1983) has popularized teaching using multiple modalities through the theory of multiple intelligences. The theory of multiple intelligences (MI) questions the narrow definition of intelligence embodied in traditional intelligence and achievement tests used by educators. Gardner proposed that there are at least seven intelligences: logical–mathematical, linguistic, spatial, musical, kinesthetic, interpersonal, and intrapersonal. Gardner was concerned that many students in schools are not viewed as intelligent because they cannot perform well on tests designed to measure solely logical–mathematical and linguistic abilities. Armstrong (2000) took Gardner theory and proposed many ways in which it could be used to design classroom instruction that would enable a diverse group of learners to be successful. MI theory does not suggest that there are seven *types* of people, rather that all people possess and can develop each intelligence. In addition, the intelligences are not mutually exclusive and often work together. The importance of the MI theory is that students are acknowledged for their intelligences and allowed to use all intelligences to increase their learning.

An Example of Multiple Intelligences   In a 10th-grade world history class the students are studying World War I. Competencies to be addressed include the ability to describe and discuss the causes of the war and the impact of the war on the economic, political, and social development of different countries. In addition, students also will be demonstrating reading, writing, and oral-language skills and their ability to use varied sources to research a topic. Karen is a 16-year-old girl in this class who has multiple disabilities including intellectual and physical disabilities. Karen's individual goals include using an augmentative communication device for communication and improving her receptive language and sight word reading skills, maintaining her range of motion in limbs, and improving her fine motor skills through grasping objects. Instructional strategies and activities for the unit include

- Lectures (linguistic)
- Advance organizers, overheads, and videos (spatial)
- Discussion and working in groups (interpersonal)

- Journals and letter writing (interpersonal)
- Music from the 1914–1918 era (musical)
- Reenactment of life in the trenches (kinesthetic)
- Debate on the causes of the war and factors leading to victory (logical)
- Graphs of the casualties and population change in participating nations (logical)
- Museum exhibit for the school library exploring various aspects of the war and its aftermath (linguistic, logical, spatial, and interpersonal)

These instructional strategies and activities enable Karen to participate meaningfully by listening and answering questions, using her communication device to join the discussion, learning sight words connected to the unit, using the computer to research information, and using gross and fine motor skills to help make the museum display, all of which contribute to the creation of increased links within her scheme and an increased chance that she will successfully recall the information when desired.

Cooperative Learning

Research has demonstrated that cooperative learning benefits students with and without disabilities (Johnson & Johnson, 1989; Putnam, 1998; Sapon-Shevin, Ayres, & Duncan, 2002). Cooperative learning is structured group work designed to incorporate five major elements (Johnson, Johnson, & Holubec, 1993):

1. *Positive interdependence*, which requires that there be a reason for students to work together. Students with moderate or severe disabilities can have meaningful roles in the group.
2. *Individual accountability,* which requires that students be held accountable for their learning within the group. Goals can be adapted to the individual needs of students with moderate or severe disabilities.
3. *Cooperative skills*, which must be taught to the students as part of cooperative learning. Teachers cannot assume that students will know how to work together effectively. Cooperative learning groups provide an opportunity for students with moderate or severe disabilities to learn and practice social skills.
4. *Face-to-face interaction,* which is important to ensure interaction among group members.
5. *Group processing*, which is important in evaluating the effectiveness of the group. Students will often have better ideas than adults about how to modify the cooperative group structures for students with moderate or severe disabilities.

When students with moderate or severe disabilities are included in general education classrooms, cooperative learning is an effective way to facilitate meaningful participation and interaction with peers.

Examples of Cooperative Learning   Barbara is a student with moderate or severe disabilities in a second-grade classroom. The class is working in cooperative groups to recreate a model of their small rural town. Each group has chosen one building to recreate for the project. Students work in groups of four to build their structures (face-to-face interaction). Group members must share materials (positive interdependence and cooperative skills). Each student must tell the class about which part of the building he or she created (individual accountability). Students talk to the teacher about how well their group was able to share and work together (group processing). Barbara needs no special modifications for this activity because it does not involve reading and writing. The activity gives Barbara a natural opportunity to work on her social interaction and communication skills.

Michael is a nonverbal student with moderate or severe disabilities and extremely limited movement. During a cooperative group activity in a sixth-grade science class where students are measuring the pH of various foods, Michael is the materials manager providing a place for the materials to be used on his wheelchair tray (positive interdependence). When the students pick up their material, they interact verbally with Michael and note whether he makes eye contact and smiles at them (individual accountability, cooperative skills, and face-to-face interaction). After the group activity, the students are asked to evaluate their interactions and to suggest ways in which Michael could better participate in the future (group processing).

Celeste is a student with autism. Her ninth-grade classroom is doing a cooperative math activity that involves developing a budget for a simulated career and living situation. Celeste plays the role of fact checker and uses her calculator to make sure that her group's checkbook calculations are correct (positive interdependence and individual accountability). She is working on physically staying with her group (face-to-face interaction and cooperative skills). Celeste and the other students in the group complete a self-evaluation about how well they contributed to their group (group processing).

SUMMARY

This chapter has discussed the importance of research into how the brain works to design literacy instruction for students with moderate or severe disabilities. Our assumption is that the brains of students with disabilities are more similar to than different from the brains of students without disabilities. Our least dangerous assumption is that providing a rich learning environment for all students by using instructional strategies consistent with what we know about how the brain works is a best practice for students with moderate or severe disabilities. The next chapter will look at conceptual models for organizing literacy instruction for all students right from the start.

Chapter 3

The Role of Language and Communication as the Basis for Literacy

Julia Scherba de Valenzuela and M. Marilyn Tracey

T he purpose of this chapter is to define and discuss concepts fundamental to understanding the development of communication. This is necessary in a book about literacy for all students, as literacy is an important and highly socially valued form of communication and one that often has been perceived as beyond the reach of many students with intensive communication needs. As one of several potential forms of communication, literacy development must be understood within the individual's overall communication skills. The multiple forms of communication that may be present within an individual's repertoire might include: oral language, signed language, written language, graphic or tactile representation of objects or concepts (i.e., picture cards or miniature objects), conventional and unconventional gestures, eye gaze, facial expressions, vocalizations, and body movements and habitual behaviors that others interpret as meaningful.

It is important to recognize that all individuals use multiple forms of communication with those around them, even those with the most significant needs for supports. According to the National Joint Committee for the Communicative Needs of Persons with Severe Disabilities (NJC), communication is "both a basic need and a basic right of all human beings" (NJC, 1992, p. 3). Johnson, Baumgart, Helmstetter, and Curry (1996) reminded us that "each individual communicates in some fashion" (p. 5) and that it is the responsibility of professionals to provide the context and supports necessary to learn new and maintain existing communication skills. Johnson and colleagues cautioned against excluding any individual from participating in a communication system, even if the individual responds inconsistently, is believed to be incapable of using the system independently, or is at a pre-intentional level of communication ability. This argues strongly for immersing all individuals in a print-rich environment and engaging in literacy activities, even if professional evaluation does not predict that they will become proficient and/or independent readers or writers.

This chapter was deliberately written from a multicultural and multilingual perspective. The first author, Julia Scherba de Valenzuela, is a Spanish–English bilingual special educator and bilingual speech–language pathologist. She is a native English speaker who was born and raised in a multicultural part of Southern California. She was exposed to several different languages from an early age, beginning with Hebrew as part of her Jewish education during early childhood. She has lived in several Latin American countries and uses both Spanish and English on a daily basis in both professional and personal contexts. The second author, Marilyn Tracey, is a Navajo–English bilingual educational diagnostician and educator. She is a member of the Diné people, as Navajos refer to themselves. She has spoken Navajo since birth and was raised within the boundaries of the Navajo Nation. Ms. Tracey has lived and worked in several different Native American communities in Arizona, New Mexico, and Montana. She has deep and continuing ties with her traditional community and uses her language skills in Navajo and English in personal and professional settings daily. We disclose this personal information as a way of contextualizing the text that follows. In this chapter we will include examples from our experiences as practitioners, teacher–educators, and members of multicultural and multilingual communities as a way of making the information presented more understandable and realistic. It is therefore important that readers understand where we come from, geographically, culturally, and linguistically, in order to understand the context of our examples and perspectives. It is also important that readers understand that the suggestions of characteristics/behaviors of Navajo and other Native Americans are not definitive and will not apply to all Navajo people and Native Americans as a whole. These may be some characteristics of most or some traditional individuals but will vary depending on circumstances such age, acculturation, and geographic region in which they live (i.e., on or off the reservation, their community within the reservation). The same holds true for any description of common behaviors, beliefs, and characteristics of any group of people, including those with disabilities.

DEFINING FUNDAMENTAL CONCEPTS

It is critical to have a clear understanding of commonly used terms within a particular discipline. Agreement about the meaning of terms enhances the effectiveness of communication between professionals and the families of individuals requiring their support. This is especially important because a number of terms used by education professionals and academics have meanings that are different when used in a professional context from the common usage. This can be especially problematic when it is not clear that two people are using and understanding a particular term in two different ways. For example, an educator might ask a parent whether his or her child can talk. The professional might really be asking whether the child uses language, a very specific term that is defined below. However, the parent might interpret the question to mean "Does your child use oral language?" and respond no because the child uses sign not spoken language. Or, the parent might understand the educator's use of *talk* to mean any kind of oral production and say "Yes, my child talks" because the child communicates using a combination of gestures and vocalizations.

Sometimes terms are used in a very generic sense—so generic that they may become quite meaningless. For example, *nonverbal* is a term that is incorrectly applied to many students who are able to produce meaningful and understandable, although limited, speech. In addition, this term sometimes is applied to students who are deaf, but who also are fluent sign language users. Although it is true that many individual who use sign language do not speak, they certainly are not limited in their language production. They simply use a non-oral mode of language. Therefore, the term *nonverbal* loses any useful meaning in accurately describing communication abilities when applied to such a wide and varied group of individuals.

When terms are not used accurately or specifically, it is not possible to get a clear picture of an individual's actual communication abilities. There is an extremely wide range of communication abilities that individuals who are described as nonverbal and having severe disabilities might possess. Without clearly understanding and being able to accurately describe an individual's actual present level of performance, it is difficult to determine what type of supports would best meet his or her needs. For example, students may be provided with an augmentative and alternative communication (AAC) system that is either well below or well above their current communication abilities. We have seen students with functional, although limited, oral speech given a picture card system that restricts them to communicating one-word object requests at a level below their current expressive abilities. Sometimes this happens because the student comes from a home where the primary language is not English. The student's multi-word oral speech may be interpreted as gibberish simply because his or her language abilities have not been assessed bilingually and there was no clear communication among the professionals, the student's family members, and any translators (if present). This can result in a waste of time, resources, and a great deal of frustration for the individual who has not been provided with access to an appropriate and functional communication system.

Communication

The following definition of communication is well accepted within the community of professionals who work with individuals who have intensive communication needs.

> Communication is any act by which one person gives to or receives from another person information about that person's needs, desires, perceptions, knowledge, or affective states. Communication may be intentional or unintentional, may involve conventional or unconventional signals, may take linguistic or nonlinguistic forms, and may occur through spoken or other modes. (NJC, 1992, p. 3)

This definition emphasizes the multiple forms that a communicative act may take. Human beings can communicate in a variety of ways besides words. The above definition also recognizes that communication can take place even when individuals are not aware of their own ability to communicate (communicative intent), do not use commonly recognized forms of communication (conventional signals), and have not yet developed language.

The NJC (1992) also produced a Communication Bill of Rights, which we strongly recommend all individuals obtain, including and especially family members of individuals with intensive communication needs. In addition to setting forth the 12 basic communication rights, this Bill of Rights states that "all persons, regardless of the extent or severity of their disabilities, have a basic right to affect, through communication, the conditions of their own existence" (p. 3). This places responsibility on the partners of individuals who do not have intentional or conventional ways to express themselves to find ways to communicate that are within the means of that individual. Communication partners must recognize, respond to, and value the expressive communication that the individual already produces.

Communication is an important and integral part of living in a community. People communicate with others in multiple contexts: in homes, in workplaces, in the groups they belong to, and in the community. No matter how well individuals think they understand each other, communication is hard. Joe and Miller (1987) stated that culture is often the root of communication challenges. Because all communication is cultural and draws on culturally embedded assumptions about appropriate ways of communicating, culture influences how people engage in communicative interactions with others. An example of this is the way Navajos in the American Southwest initiate interactions by stating their clan or role in relation to the other, "my son, my daughter, my brother." In addition, most Native Americans rarely greet others with a physical touch, especially in public. However, many individuals from Latin American countries will greet friends and even teachers with a hug and a kiss on the cheek. Differences in cultural patterns of communication can pose problems for individuals with cognitive disabilities when they interact with others from a different cultural group, unless there is an understanding that these differences in communication are natural, to be expected, and do not indicate incompetence on the part of either person.

Intentional Communication

Although it is common in Western societies to assume that even very young infants have an intent to communicate when they cry, scream, or babble, in actuality this important cognitive skill develops over time. The transition from preintentional to intentional communication is thought to emerge in typically developing infants by nine months of age (Wetherby, Warren, & Reichle, 1998).When discussing intentional communication, professionals typically refer to whether an individual has developed the capacity for intentional communication, not whether a particular instance of communication was intended or not. Sometimes people say, "But I didn't mean to say that!" or "That's not what I meant," in reference to a specific communicative act. However, assessment of intentional communication refers to whether an individual has developed the awareness that communication can achieve some effect on a listener and whether they do communicate purposefully in pursuit of a predetermined goal. It is not in reference to any one specific act of communication.

It can be difficult to determine whether an individual with intensive communication needs has developed intentional communication or not. Wetherby and Prizant (1989) suggested that the following behaviors can provide evidence of communicative intent:

> 1) alternating eye gaze between goal and listener, 2) persistent signaling until a goal is accomplished or failure is indicated, 3) changing the signal quality until the goal has been met, 4) ritualizing or conventionalizing communicative forms, 5) awaiting a response from the listener, 6) terminating the signal when the goal is met, and 7) displaying satisfaction when the goal is attained and dissatisfaction when it is not. (p. 78)

They also suggested that the development of intentional communication is not a clearly demarcated stage, where one could state equivocally that previously an individual did not have communicative intent but now he or she does. Like most cognitive or behavioral phenomena, the development of communicative intent is gradual. Wetherby and Prizant (1989) argued that intentionality emerges along a continuum, from "no awareness of a goal" (p. 79) to the conscious awareness and ability to reflect upon the means of achieving the communicative goal, with the more advanced aspect of intentionality emerging through 18 months of age in typically developing children.

Sometimes there may be disagreements between families and professionals as to whether an individual with severe disabilities has developed intentional communication. However, as recognized in the NJC definition of communication cited above, communication does not have to be intentional for it to occur. The important point is that there needs to be a recipient who is willing to attempt to figure out the possible meaning of a behavior. Development of intentionality is fostered by consistent responses to an individual's non-intentional communication. Therefore, when in doubt 1) assume that an individual does have something meaningful to communicate, 2) attempt to understand what the meaning of a particular behavior might be, and 3) respond as though communication is intentional.

Conventional Communication   Communicative acts are recognized when two or more people agree upon their meaning. For example, a wink, nod, or other gesture might have a special meaning between two siblings, friends, or family members. When a communicative act is *conventional*, it is recognized outside of a limited social context and is widely understood within a larger community or cultural group. Sometimes people assume that conventional communication is universal. However, if you have ever traveled to other countries or lived within different cultural groups, you know that even common gestures, such as raising two fingers in the peace sign or making a circle with the thumb and index finger while raising the other fingers to indicate *good* are not understood or used in the same way in every country. Among the Diné it is common to indicate agreement or answer yes by raising the eyebrows, usually in combination with nodding the head. Some Latinos in the Southwest say "hi" with a quick upwards head nod. These communicative conventions have developed, been adopted, used, and learned within particular historical, social, and cultural contexts. Conventional communicative behaviors are not universal or innate.

As such, individuals with the most significant needs for supports may not have learned or used conventional means to communicate. If they have had sensitive and responsive partners their unique forms of communication have been recognized as meaningful, and consistent attempts have been made to discover the meaning of the communication. It is therefore very important not to dismiss the interpretations of family members or caregivers as unrealistic. Just as physicians and other medical personnel have learned to detect and interpret the physical responses of individuals in a coma as communicating meaningful and relevant information about their health and state, caretakers of individuals with intensive communication needs also may have learned to identify which behaviors consistently occur during which contexts and indicate certain states, needs, or wants. For example, a mother may have learned that her daughter relaxes and vocalizes in a certain way when her favorite soft sweater is put on her. Through trial and error, over time, responsive caregivers learn to accurately identify unconventional communicative acts. Another example was shared by a teacher who noticed that a student of hers indicated that he was hungry by walking over to the classroom microwave and opening and slamming the door. The teacher knew that she was correct in her interpretation because when she gave him something to eat, he took the food and ate it, but when she did not give him food, his behavior escalated. Because the communication of individuals with severe disabilities may be different from that typically expected, it is vital that caregivers and educators of individuals with unconventional communication maintain and share a communication dictionary, so that new people can learn to understand and respond to communication appropriately and effectively.

Definition of Language

The following definition of language has been adopted by the American Speech-Language-Hearing Association (ASHA, 1982):

> Language is a complex and dynamic system of conventional symbols that is used in various modes for thought and communication.
> Contemporary views of human language hold that
>
> * Language evolves within specific historical, social, and cultural contexts
> * Language, as rule-governed behavior, is described by at least five parameters: phonologic, morphologic, syntactic, semantic, and pragmatic
> * Language learning and use are determined by the interaction of biological, cognitive, psychosocial, and environmental factors
> * Effective use of language for communication requires a broad understanding of human interaction including such associated factors as nonverbal cues, motivation, and sociocultural roles. (p. 499)

This definition helps distinguish communication, which can be accomplished via multiple means, from language, which is a special and unique form of communication.

Language can be spoken, signed, or written. Regardless of the modality, language can be differentiated from other, nonlinguistic forms of communication by the use and combination of abstract, conventional symbols, in a *generative* and *rule-governed* manner. Linguists and many child-language specialists use the term *symbol* in a precise sense, as in the definition above, to indicate a particular and important type of relationship between something (i.e., an object, an action, or a concept) and how it is represented. A symbol has an arbitrary, abstract relationship to its referent. In contrast, an icon is a direct or obvious representation. The key to whether a particular representation is a symbol or an icon is not in the representation itself, but in the relationship to what it represents (its *referent*). For example, a picture of an apple could be either an icon or a symbol, depending on what it is designed to represent. If the apple picture is used to represent an actual apple, it would be an icon, because the relationship between the representation and its referent is direct and obvious. Most people who see an apple and a picture of an apple should be able to link the two, regardless of their cultural background or knowledge about apples. However, if the apple picture is supposed to stand for New York, then it is a symbol, because this relationship is abstract and arbitrary. Unless you knew that New York was referred to as "the Big Apple," you would have no way of knowing that the apple picture referred to that particular city.

The reason we dwell on the difference between symbol and icon here is that symbol is often used by educators in a more generic sense for any representation, whether arbitrary or direct. This is often true in the AAC literature. For example, Beukelman and Mirenda (2005) referred to all representations as symbols but distinguished them along a continuum of abstractness, ranging from *opaque symbols* (true, abstract symbols) to *transparent symbols* (icons). Yet, in the definition of language presented above, the term *symbol* is used in its technical linguistic sense as an abstract, arbitrary representation. This can be seen in the following quote from Fromkin, Rodman, and Hyams: "The relationship between the sounds and meanings of spoken languages and between the gestures and meanings of sign languages are for the most part arbitrary" (2003, p. 27).

This implies that a prerequisite for the development of language is the comprehension and use of abstract symbols. This may be very challenging for some individuals with cognitive disabilities. Like the transition to intentional communication, the transition to symbolic communication is a critical step toward more complex communication development. Gestures and early words develop symbolic qualities as they begin to be used in creative ways and are no longer tied to the contexts in which they were first learned (Iverson & Thal, 1998; Wetherby, Reichle, & Pierce, 1998). According to Wetherby, Reichle, and Pierce "a word is considered a symbol when it has been decontextualized or dissociated from the occurrence of a particular event" (p. 200). Wilcox and Shannon (1998) argued that decontextualization "requires a child to form associations between words and more generalized concepts. Decontextualization is facilitated by exposure to words in different contexts representing varying communicative functions" (p. 388). This is an important point as it suggests that it is vital that individuals who are developing symbolic communication do so in language-rich environments with multiple opportunities to engage in communication about a variety of topics and in a variety of contexts. Repetitive communication in a restrictive range of contexts will not foster a transition to symbolic, and eventually, linguistic communication.

Language is also a unique form of communication because it is a generative, rule-governed system. Generative refers to the fact that "speakers of all language are capable of producing and comprehending an infinite set of sentences" (Fromkin et al., 2003, p. 27). The reason this is possible is that there are rules that all speakers of a language follow, even if they are not conscious of doing so. These rules govern how sounds and words are combined in regular and expected patterns by competent speakers of each language. In fact, speakers can apply these rules to new words, regardless of whether they understand their meaning or not. For example, if you heard the new verb "trif," you would know how to say that someone did it yesterday ("triffed"), was doing it now ("is triffing"), or does it as a habitual action ("trifs"). An important part of developing a language is learning these unconscious rules, especially for the correct formation of words (morphology) and sentence (syntax). Words and parts of words cannot be combined willy-nilly—there are conventions in each language variety that govern what is acceptable and what is not. For example, in English, it would not be correct to say "it left running the dog." However, that same word order ("Salió corriendo el perro") would be just fine in Spanish. These examples illustrate the fact that grammatical conventions are also arbitrary—they have developed over time within particular language communities. There is nothing inherently better or worse about the different ways grammar in languages is constructed. For example, double negatives are not used in Standard American English; speakers of this dialect would say things like "we don't have any." However, speakers of other dialects of English, as well as other languages such as Spanish, do use double negatives. Speakers of those language varieties say things like "I don't have none" or "No tengo nada," following the language patterns, or rules, of their particular language or dialect.

As part of culture, human language has many functions. Chief among them is communication. People also identify themselves as part of a social group by which language variety they speak. Language is developed through participation in social interactions and community systems (Ochs, 1986). Another important part of learning a language, therefore, is learning how to use it appropriately in different social settings—what is referred to as the "discourse norms" (Corson, 1993) of a particular community. Different language communities have different rules for indicating politeness, respect, and interest in and importance of a topic, taking turns in a conversation, using eye gaze, maintaining a topic, and selecting speakers, among many others. For example, wait time—the amount of time speakers are given to speak and respond—is substantially longer in Native American cultures than in the dominant American culture.

Corson (1993) suggested that different discourse norms "usually reflect quite different cultural values" (p. 36). Therefore, through learning to use a language appropriately in different social and cultural contexts, individuals also learn about the values, attitudes, customs, beliefs, and structure of their culture and community. Because people learn how to become members of a community as they learn the language of that community, it is critical to recognize the importance of the home language of students with disabilities. If one of the goals of educating students with severe disabilities is to provide tools for greater community participation, then support of the home language should be a primary goal for instruction, as this will be one of the principal means for providing community access.

Many people have the idea that some languages are better for expressing certain things than others. For example, we have heard that French is more useful for expressing romantic ideas than German, and that describing different types of snow is possible in certain Native Alaskan or Native American languages but not in English. Neither of these popular conceptions is true. According to Fromkin et al. (2003): "There are no 'primitive' languages—all languages are equally complex and equally capable of expressing any idea in the universe. The vocabulary of any language can be expanded to include new words for new concepts" (p. 27). This means that all languages are adequate for expressing and developing complex concepts such as academic knowledge. Indeed, use of the home language can be an important educational support for students who are in the process of beginning to learn English. However, it should also be recognized that some Native American communities, in response to historic patterns of invasion and oppression, have chosen to restrict the use and teaching of their languages to community members (Sims, 2006). Therefore, it is always important to ask what family preferences are when choosing the language(s) of instruction, while recognizing that many families may not know about the importance or availability of bilingual instruction, especially for students with more significant needs for supports.

Literacy

In this book, written language has been defined as conventional reading and writing; however, literacy can be defined in a broader sense. Indeed, unless educators and other professionals take a more expanded perspective on literacy, individuals who have not yet developed language, as defined above, would be excluded from participating in literacy activities in meaningful ways.

Recently, the definition of literacy has evolved from an exclusive focus on reading and writing to encompass a more inclusive and expansive perspective. We present some of these definitions to illustrate the different perspectives. Some of this work has come from researchers involved in exploring literacy among diverse populations and across cultural, political, and socioeconomic boundaries. For example, Dubin and Kuhlman (1992) stated that

> The past decade has been marked by significant new directions in literacy research brought about by questions which seek to discover how literacy functions in families . . . in communities . . . and in workplaces. . . . What does it mean to be 'literate' as a member of a particular culture? What are the patterns of literacy use within fields of work, within professions, within age-groups? (p. vii)

Hiebert (1991) applied an explicitly constructivist perspective to the definition of literacy:

> For some time now, a new perspective on literacy, and the learning processes through which literacy is acquired, has been emerging. This new perspective does not consist of old ideas with a new name, but rather it represents a profound shift from a text-driven definition of literacy to a view of literacy as active transformation of texts. In the old view, meaning was assumed to reside primarily within text, whereas, in the new view, meaning is created through an interaction of reader and text. (p. 1)

Langer (1991) took this notion of interaction of reader with text a step further, contrasting "literacy as the act of reading and writing and literacy as *ways* of thinking" (p. 13). Langer suggested that the definition of literacy depends on the context within which one functions: "Literacy can be viewed in a broader and educationally more productive way, as the ability to think and reason like a literate person, *within a particular society*" (p. 11). Langer further argued that

> It is the culturally appropriate way of thinking, not the act of reading or writing, that is most important in the development of literacy. Literacy thinking manifests itself in different ways in oral and written language in different societies, and educators need to understand these ways of thinking if they are to build bridges and facilitate transitions among ways of thinking. (p. 13)

Although the above definitions emphasize a more interactive, inclusive perspective by considering literacy as culturally situated and defined, they may be problematic when considering what literacy means for individuals with intensive communication needs and/or significant cognitive impairments. Some authors have considered the complexity of applying definitions of literacy to individuals with severe disabilities. Although most authors in this area have recognized literacy as "interactive, constructive, strategic, and meaning-based" (Steelman, Pierce, & Koppenhaver, 1994, p. 201), they also typically maintain the notion that comprehension and use of *written* text is central to literacy. Steelman and colleagues' definition is a good example: "To be literate is to be able to gather and to construct meaning using written language" (p. 201). Foley (1994) emphasized the importance of oral language development to written language by highlighting both in her definition of literacy: "Used broadly to refer to the mastery of language, in both its spoken (or augmented) and written forms, which enables an individual to use language fluently for a variety of purposes" (p. 184). Yet Foley also cautioned that although "there is general agreement today that spoken language abilities are closely related to the development of literacy skills in the normal population" (p. 185), "linguistic ability, as opposed to speech production ability, appears to be the more critical factor" (p. 186). Returning to the definition of language presented earlier in this chapter, readers should remember that language requires the use of abstract arbitrary symbols. As Foley emphasizes, this would be a requirement for the development of conventional reading and writing.

An important question to consider, however, is whether students who have not developed or who are not likely to develop any form of symbolic communication could be considered *literate*. An alternative perspective was suggested by the committee developing Alternate Assessments for reading and writing in New Mexico. The definitions of reading and writing used during the development of expanded performance standards in these content areas were the following:

- The end result of writing instruction is the ability to produce a permanent product that can be understood by others. This implies the use of a tool.

- The end result of reading instruction is the ability to comprehend others' graphic symbols[1] used to communicate.

This expanded perspective on literacy is critical, as Beukelman, Mirenda, and Sturm (1998) reminded us:

> Because of these individuals' cognitive limitations, educators may not consider literacy learning as an educational goal. As a result, individuals with cognitive impairments are at risk of being held to reduced expectations and lacking exposure to literacy materials, both at home and at school. If educators believe that reading does not begin until individuals possess certain prerequisite skills, and if educators think of literacy as an "all or none" ability, they will not consider the potential for varying degrees of literacy learning by individuals with cognitive impairments. In truth, individuals with cognitive impairments can and should engage in the same emergent literacy activities as their peers without disabilities (e.g., listening repeatedly to stories, having access to writing tools). We cannot overemphasize the importance of intensive exposure to literacy materials in the early years (p. 361).

---

[1]The term *symbol* was used here in the generic sense, including both concrete, direct, iconic representations, as well as more abstract symbolic representations.

INSTRUCTIONAL IMPLICATIONS

There are a number of important instructional implications deriving from the information presented above. These implications can be grouped into three main areas: understanding students' level of communication, recognizing students' home language and culture, and using best practices for facilitating students' communication and language development. All three of these areas are vital to providing effective and appropriate instruction to students with intensive communication needs.

Levels of Communication

When providing literacy instruction for students with intensive communication needs, it is critical to understand their level of communication development. Whether the student demonstrates communicative intent, uses conventional or unconventional communication, communicates symbolically or non-symbolically, and has developed language or not should be determined. If a student has some form of conventional communication, it is probably safe to assume that he or she has communicative intent. However, this is much harder to determine when students use unconventional means of communication such as rocking or vocalizations. It is necessary to determine the student's level of communication in order to assure that a communication system is available that will be functional and effective for him or her.

Although it is necessary to provide students with access to information within their current levels of ability, it is also important to expose them to materials that they do not yet understand and forms of communication that they cannot yet use independently. It is through engaging in communicative interactions with the support of more competent others that students will develop advanced forms of communication. Therefore, even though a particular student may not yet have developed symbolic communication, print should be widely available in the environment and the student should have opportunities to engage with text with the support of others. Hopefully, through repeated exposure to written language, the student will develop an interest and eventually abilities in conventional reading. For example, it might be appropriate to provide the written word for pictures in a student's communication book with the goal of later fading the use of pictures if and when the student learns to read conventional print. However, it is important to reiterate that students should always be provided with ways to communicate that are within their current communication levels. Providing text without any pictorial support for students who have not yet developed any form of symbolic communication would probably be a frustrating and ineffective instructional strategy with which to begin literacy instruction.

The Importance of Students' Home Language and Culture

Instruction should begin with a good understanding of the student's home language and culture, regardless of the individual's level of communication development. We have heard teachers and other educational personnel say that the home language does not need to figure into instructional planning for students with cognitive disabilities who have not yet acquired language. This argument is not logical when we consider all that typically developing children must learn before they utter their first word.

Professionals need to be aware of the impact of second language acquisition and cultural and sociological differences on academic achievement and assessment. Typical patterns of second language development are often confused with learning and/or language disabilities. Because English language learners (ELLs) are sometimes overrepresented in special education (de Valenzuela, Copeland, Qi, & Park, 2006), it is vital that students are appropriately assessed and identified. Educators need to be aware that language minority students, especially those who are not yet proficient in English, need special attention, appropriate assessment, support for continued development of their home language, and a challenging curriculum. Even if students have been identified with moderate or severe cognitive disabilities, their native language abilities must be assessed by a competent bilingual evaluator with knowledge of both first and second language development and the needs of students with more significant disabilities.

Professionals also must be sensitive to the ways in which students engage in classroom settings. Expectations for appropriate participation can be varied in different cultures, and students who come from different countries or from non-dominant-culture backgrounds may have a difficult time adjusting to the dominant American culture and educational system. For example, the expected participation structure for conversation is not the same for Native American students as for dominant-culture students. The Diné culture tends to take a reflective approach rather than an analytical one. They observe and listen more than they demand to know why. As discussed earlier, Native Americans tend to have longer wait times than those used by speakers of Standard American English. Winterton (1976) found that with Pueblo Indian children, extended wait time was significantly related to the length of students' responses and the amount of student-to-student interaction. These differences, if not recognized and valued, can cause difficulties for children from non–dominant-culture backgrounds. For example, students may react by withdrawing from classroom activities and interactions.

In addition, professionals need to be aware of the complex belief systems and values affecting the perception of disability for families from culturally diverse backgrounds, including the influence of traditional and spiritual beliefs; beliefs about health and healing, religion, folk medicine and folk healers; and expectations of a child's social roles. For example, for the Diné, the human world is not the only place where forms of life communicate with one another. Through animals, events, spirits, and visions, the Diné people experience signals and signs as evidence of the connectedness or communication of all of creation through dreams and déjà vu types of experiences. There is an understanding that people are equal to animals; we are all equal because we are all part of Great Spirit and equal participants in the world and universe. These communicative experiences are interpreted as a type of divine guidance. It is essential that professionals respect family beliefs and values, even when they differ from those of the dominant culture. Professionals must also be aware of the ways in which their own beliefs and value systems influence how they evaluate the words, actions, and decisions of culturally and linguistically diverse families.

Along with respect for different beliefs and values, professionals also must respect community preferences for communication modes. For example, in some Native American communities it is considered impolite to directly point to another person or things with the index finger. Therefore, some Navajo people tend to point with their lips instead of with their fingers. In addition, in some traditional Navajo communities, using sign language in public may not be acceptable. Teaching students who have intensive communication needs to use a picture communication system might be preferable and more functional than teaching the use of gestures and sign language. Or, it might be more functional to teach students to use both gestures and a pictorial system and to work with the students to learn when and where to use each system. This is another example of why it is important to gain an understanding of families' perspectives and preferences when developing and implementing a communication system.

Strategies for Facilitating Communication and Language Development

In this section we will suggest general approaches to facilitate the development of communication and language with individuals who have intensive communication needs. There are a number of excellent resources that provide in-depth information about specific instructional strategies for students at a variety of levels of communication development and from a number of different perspectives. These include books and chapters referencing students with severe disabilities (Downing, 1999), students who use non-symbolic communication (Siegel & Wetherby, 2006), students for whom a functional communication approach would be appropriate (Kaiser & Grim, 2006), and students who use AAC (Beukelman & Mirenda, 2005; Light & Binger, 1998; Reichle, Beukelman, & Light, 2002). Readers are encouraged to explore the above resources for further information. The following are general recommendations:

1. The communication partners of individuals with significant communication needs should be provided with instruction and support for engaging in effective communication interactions. For example, in a school environment, teachers should not assume that other students will know how to interact with their peers with disabilities. Students will need ongoing support to learn to wait until the individual with communication needs has had time to respond, to scaffold responses rather than provide answers for the individual, and to engage the individual in their activities and conversations. Depending on the age and maturity of the potential communication partners, they can be provided with strategies for facilitating communication development, such those that follow.

2. Individuals with severe disabilities may use unconventional means of communication. It is the responsibility of the individual's communication partners to respond to attempts to communicate and develop a shared system of communication. Rather than imposing a conventional system on the individual with disabilities, it may be more effective to begin by understanding the means through which the individual currently communicates and expanding on that system. In a classroom, that means that peers can learn sign language or become familiar with the AAC system the student with a disability uses.

3. As mentioned earlier, it is the responsibility of families of and professionals who work with individuals using unconventional communication to ensure

that others are aware how those individuals express themselves. A communication dictionary should be developed, kept current, and shared with everyone who comes into routine contact with the individual.

4.   Parents, siblings, and service providers must be responsive to an individual's current and varied forms of communication. Sometimes educators emphasize one particular form of communication that a student is learning (e.g., a system of graphic symbols). This is important but should not be done to the extent of discouraging other effective forms of communication that are part of the student's functional repertoire. For example, most people naturally use gestures as part of their communication. Although the use of more complex forms of communication such as oral or sign language or picture communication systems should be encouraged, the individual's use of natural gestures and facial expressions should not be discouraged or prohibited.

5.   Communication partners must notice, encourage, and provide opportunities for expressive communication. This means focusing on *meaningful* communication. All too often, individuals are limited to indicating needs and wants. However, the social needs for communication also are extremely compelling and motivating. Having pictures of or information about favorite events, people, pets, and activities that individuals can share with others can be an important opportunity for engaging in communication with others. Just as many typically developing individuals want to share pictures of their family members or a special trip, so, too, might individuals with significant disabilities.

6.   When fostering communication development, it is more effective to follow an individual's focus of attention and to interact around topics of interest to that person than to attempt to get him or her to engage with an introduced topic or attentional focus. That means that communication partners need to ensure that the environment includes things that people would want to communicate about. As suggested above, this could mean making sure that the individual has pictures of people, places, or events that he or she would want to share. Or, it could simply mean waiting until the individual looks at or expresses an interest in something and using that as a starting place for interaction, rather than trying to attract the individual's attention to the object or activity.

7.   If replacing one form of communication with another is an instructional goal, it is vital that the new form be as or more effective and efficient than the form being replaced. This means that communication partners must be aware of and responsive to the individual's attempts to use the new form. For example, if the goal is to replace shouting out in class with hand raising, the teachers and other adults must ensure that the hand raising works better than shouting out in getting attention for the student. If it doesn't, the student will soon revert to the more effective form of communication—shouting.

8.   Professionals need to consider a student's home language and culture when developing and implementing educational interventions. The individual's home language, culture, and community are resources and strengths to be built on, not barriers that must be removed. The question for students with disabilities who have a home language other than English is not whether they can become bilingual—they must, unless they will never be exposed to En-

glish—the question is how to do that in a way that supports the continued development of their home language. It is important to remember that, most likely, if a student has a home language other than English, that other language is a useful means of communication with people who are important to them. They should be provided with access to that other language, for example, by having both English and their home language represented in any AAC system or materials. That may seem an undue burden for teachers and other educators, but it is far easier for professionals to learn a few words or phrases of a new language than for the student to learn English. When students with disabilities speak a non-English language that is used in school or district bilingual education programs, the students and teachers of those programs would be ideal communication partners. Efforts at inclusion should be directed toward making sure that these programs and individuals are accessible to students with disabilities who come from a minority language background.

CHALLENGES

There are numerous challenges faced by individuals with intensive communication needs, their families, and teachers. Three challenges that we will focus on in this section are 1) fostering communication development in segregated educational settings, 2) developing cultural and linguistic sensitivity, and 3) overcoming assumptions of limitations.

Developing Communication in Segregated Settings

A question we sometimes face when working with educators in the field is how to best facilitate communication development of students with intensive communication needs who are isolated from their typically developing peers in segregated classrooms. The most honest answer we can provide is that most segregated classrooms, especially those where all the students have significant communication challenges, are not appropriate settings in which to implement an effective language development program. People develop competence using language and other forms of communication by communicating about things that interest them with engaged and responsive communication partners. When all the students in a classroom have very limited expressive and/or receptive language skills, they will not be able to provide models of more advanced communication nor strategically modify their output to the needs of the other students in the classroom. Although teachers and educational assistants certainly can be responsive communication partners and provide models of appropriate adult language use, typically developing age-peers are more appropriate (and most likely more motivating) conversational partners.

In addition, teachers of segregated classrooms often do not have opportunities to engage in multipartner dialogue because they are responsible for attending to the needs of all students in the classroom. Students not only need to participate in communicative interactions, they also need to observe effective interchanges between others. In inclusive classrooms, students with disabilities can observe their peers engaging in conversation. However, in segregated classrooms, most of the communicative interactions a student is likely to observe are either between 1) two adults, which would most likely not be at an appropriate level or deal with typical topics of student interest, or 2) between an adult and another student who has similarly limited expressive communication abilities. In the latter case, the student is not likely to observe the kind of expanded output necessary for increasing his or her own communication abilities.

We believe the limited and limiting communication environment of segregated classrooms is perhaps one of the most compelling reasons for including students with severe disabilities in the general education classroom. Increasing students' communicative abilities is a critical educational goal. Communication is the one of the primary means through which people affect the world around them and establish and build social relationships. It is absolutely imperative that educators of students with intensive communication needs find consistent and sustained opportunities for their students to engage in ongoing meaningful communication with their age-peers. Just as they need to learn the norms of communication in their home community and the wider society, students also need to learn the norms of communicating with other children, youth, and adults within their age group. Educators must provide opportunities for students with disabilities to communicate with their peers about topics in which they are interested and in supportive contexts where they can learn and practice their developing communication skills.

Developing Cultural and Linguistic Sensitivity

When a teacher and students from different cultural backgrounds attempt to communicate, confusion and misunderstanding can arise as their communicative styles interact. Corson (1993) cautioned that "teachers can easily misinterpret different discourse norms . . . especially when the signs used by students are similar to familiar signs but carry different meanings" (p. 36). For example, Guilmet (1979) compared Navajo and dominant-culture mothers who viewed videotaped episodes of Navajo and dominant-culture children participating in a classroom. In one particular episode, a boy who was of the dominant culture engaged in high levels of verbal and physical activity. The differences in the mothers' interpretations were striking. The Navajo mothers believed the boy's high level of verbal and physical activity was negative. In contrast, the dominant-culture mothers evaluated these same behaviors positively. Differing communication norms are particularly challenging when the communication partners have little or no prior experience with each other's cultural group.

Cultural sensitivity also includes understanding the impact education materials and conversational topics have on students. For example, non–dominant-culture students may not be motivated to participate in instructional interactions at school if they are not interested in the materials they are presented. Often these materials are based on the experiences of the dominant culture and may not seem relevant to the lives of minority students. However, it may be a challenge to find culturally relevant, age-appropriate materials that are at the level of students with more significant disabilities. One possibility is for the peers of students with intensive communication to produce stories and texts to use as reading materials. This is the kind of reciprocal and mutually beneficial activity in which students with and without disabilities can engage. Learning how to produce texts, for example, by story boarding and draft writing, especially when involving the use of multimedia (i.e., digital cameras, PowerPoint, narration, animation, and sound) can be a worthwhile educational project for students who are not identified with disabilities. In turn, their peers who have disabilities would benefit from age-appropriate texts produced specifically for them. When the texts involve topics from the students' home community and culture, they can be motivating and engaging.

It also can be a challenge for teachers to gain experience with and knowledge about the culture and language norms of their students. However, schools with higher percentages of culturally and linguistically diverse students are often located in diverse communities. Teachers can learn much about typical communication patterns by attending and participating in community events, patronizing local businesses, and becoming involved in the local community. School districts often have information and resources for learning about the diverse cultures and languages represented in the student body. Parents and local community members can provide information about customs, beliefs, and typical ways of interacting, especially when asked about this in a respectful and interested manner. We have found that many people enjoy talking and sharing information about their culture and language, especially when they are approached in an interested and uncritical manner. When educators and other professionals recognize the importance of becoming informed about their students' cultures, languages, and communities, are open and interested in learning about this in nonjudgmental ways, and actively seek opportunities to learn more, these challenges can be overcome.

Overcoming Assumptions of Limitations

How disability is defined—how it is socially constructed—determines what opportunities are available for people identified with a disability. Although it is true that the cognitive abilities of some individuals will limit the extent to which they develop conventional forms of communication, including conventional literacy, it also is true that people will not learn to read and write if they are not provided with access to literacy materials. Segregated classrooms often have a dearth of literacy materials. Books and other print media are removed or locked away. And the classrooms of students with severe disabilities often are visually uninteresting—the walls are not decorated with posters, with the work of other students, or with seasonal bulletin boards, as they are in most general education classrooms. The message this provides is that literacy is not important in the lives of students with severe disabilities because they cannot and will not be able to read or write. In this way, individuals with disabilities are constructed as nonliterate beings, which reinforces to others who visit these classrooms, their peer tutors, educational assistants, administrators, and family members that literacy instruction would be a waste of time.

We strongly believe that individuals with disabilities should not be assumed incapable of learning to use effectively a wide variety of communication strategies. The only way to guarantee that an individual will not learn to communicate is to fail to provide opportunities to participate in meaningful and responsive communication exchanges. All too often, the possibility of individuals with intensive communication needs developing literacy skills is limited because others believe they will not be able to do so and, therefore, the individuals are not provided with opportunities to engage meaningfully with age-appropriate texts. The denial of opportunity, even more so than the individual's cognitive, sensory, or physical limitations, will assure failure to develop communication and literacy. In the end, this demonstrates a limitation of imagination on the part of individuals without disabilities who cannot envision alternative ways of communicating, alternative ways of being and becoming literate, and alternative ways of participating meaningfully in communities.

Chapter 4

Word Recognition Instruction

Susan R. Copeland and J. Anne Calhoon

In the past, as mentioned in Chapter 1, educators have not always believed that students with significant disabilities could acquire conventional literacy skills. Even when students were given literacy instruction, such instruction usually consisted only of learning functional sight words. Most practitioners did not think these students could learn phonics or other word analysis strategies, so the students were rarely taught to read using phonics-based approaches. However, relying solely on the sight word approach to identify words restricts students' opportunities to participate in literacy experiences. Students who are taught only sight words have to memorize words based on their appearance. When trying to read a new word, they don't have many strategies to apply. This means that their reading vocabulary will be limited to the number of words they can memorize.

In this chapter we present information on several word recognition approaches. We examine those based on both word analysis (phonics) and on automatic word recognition (sight words). Teachers of students with moderate or severe disabilities must be knowledgeable about multiple word recognition strategies and also be able to teach them effectively to their students.

PHONOLOGICAL AWARENESS

Researchers and educators have realized that many students with moderate or severe disabilities can learn word identification strategies beyond sight word recognition. Many individuals can acquire and apply phonics knowledge to read text. In doing so, they are able to greatly increase their repertoire of literacy skills, which may lead to more meaningful literacy experiences. In fact, working memory (the ability to keep words and sounds in memory when segmenting a word) seems more predictive of children's ability to learn to read by applying phonics knowledge than does general intelligence (Connors, Atwell, Rosenquist, & Sligh, 2001; Olson, Forsberg, & Wise, 1994). Although not all students with moderate or severe disabilities will master all phonics generalizations, educators should know how to provide appropriate phonics instruction so that students are at least given an opportunity to learn these important skills. Acquiring basic sound–letter knowledge, such as knowledge of initial consonant sounds, for example, can be helpful by equipping students with more strategies to apply when encountering an unfamiliar word (Kay-Raining Bird, Cleave, & McConnell, 2000).

In this section of the chapter, we review crucial components needed for developing phonics skills, beginning with phonological awareness. We also give examples of effective phonological awareness and phonics instruction for students with moderate or severe disabilities. Please note that there is a fine distinction between phonological awareness instruction and phonics instruction (O'Connor & Bell, 2004, p. 486). For example, research supports linking phonological awareness instruction with teaching visual letters to form sound–symbol knowledge (e.g., the sound for the letter *t* is /t/) (Ehri et al., 2001), something typically thought of as phonics. Theoretically, there is a point at which each beginning reader gathers sufficient sound–symbol knowledge for generalization to take place and *decoding* to begin, but this point is highly individual (Ehri, 2005; Ehri & Robbins, 1992). For ease of organization, phonological awareness and phonics are described here as two separate issues, but a quality reading instruction program will include both components in daily lessons.

Role of Phonological Awareness in Learning to Read

Phonological awareness is a term literacy practitioners are hearing more and more often. Lane, Pullen, Eisele, and Jordan (2002) defined this term as "conscious sensitivity of the sound structure of language" (p. 101). Put another way, it is the ability to perceive that sentences are made up of words, words of syllables, and syllables of individual sounds or phonemes. Phonological awareness is an *oral* and *aural* language skill that characteristically begins developing as young children acquire language and continues to develop throughout the elementary school years (Troia, 2004). It is influenced both by heredity (i.e., the neurological basis for phonological processing) and by language and literacy experiences (Torgesen & Mathes, 2000). Many of the traditional activities in which young children engage actually build phonological awareness. Think for a moment of all the games and activities young children enjoy that involve word play such as reciting nursery rhymes or playing singing games like Miss Mary Mack. Activities such as these are all opportunities for children to develop an awareness of the sound units that make up speech, that is, phonological awareness.

Although researchers debate the exact role of phonological awareness in learning to read, they do agree that developing these abilities is important in becoming a competent reader (Armbruster et al., 2001; Torgesen, 2000; Troia, 2004). In fact, there is a reciprocal relationship between phonological awareness and learning to read (Perfetti, Beck, Bell, & Hughes, 1987; Stanovich, 1986, 1998; Yopp, 1992). Instruction in phonological awareness can affect positively a child's reading skills and instruction in reading can improve a child's phonological awareness skills (Cupples & Iacono, 2000).

How does phonological awareness help children learn to read? Being aware of the sound structure of language helps children understand the alphabetic principle (Torgesen & Mathes, 2000). Children who have grasped this principle realize that speech sounds can be represented by symbols (letters), and, thus, written down and read by themselves and others. English, for example, is made of approximately 48 different sounds. Each sound can be written down (spelled) using a letter or letter combination. What makes learning to read and spell in English so difficult is that there are often multiple ways to represent the same sound, especially for vowels! For example, the /ā/ sound in the word *baby* is represented with the letter *a*, but the /ā/ sound in the word *play* is represented by two letters, *ay*, while /ā/ sound in the word *rain* is written as *ai*. Strong phonological awareness helps beginning readers with the difficulties encountered in learning to read and spell. If they understand that written words are made up of letters that represent individual speech sounds and that as the sounds in words change, the letters used to represent them also change, they are well on their way to becoming competent readers and writers. By paying attention to the letters in words, students can gain the important knowledge needed to decipher new words or to spell words and create their own texts.

Generally, children develop phonological awareness skills in sequence. First, they become aware that speech is made up of words. Then, they understand that words are made up of smaller units (syllables; Liberman, Shankweiler, Fischer, & Carter, 1974; Treiman, 1983). Next, they perceive that onsets (the part of a syllable that includes the consonant sound[s] that come before the vowel sound) and rimes (the portion of a syllable that includes the vowel sound and any consonant sounds that come after it) are present in words (Goswami, 2001; Treiman, 1985). Finally, children are able to detect that words are made up of individual sounds (phonemes). Children who have developed phonological awareness can detect these units of speech and can also manipulate them within sentences or words.

Phonemic Awareness   The last type of phonological awareness described above, phonemic awareness, is especially important if one is to become a skilled reader (Armbruster et al., 2001). A phoneme is the smallest unit of sound in a language. A child who has developed phonemic awareness can, for example, detect that two spoken words differ by only one sound (e.g., *mat* and *bat* are the same except for their initial sounds) and can manipulate individual sounds within words (Yopp, 1992). Students with well-developed phonemic awareness can

- Isolate individual sounds in words, phoneme identification (e.g., "What is the last sound in *pat?*" [/t/])

- Identify common sounds within words, oddity tasks (e.g., the common sound in *cat* and *cup* [/k/])

- Segment sounds in words, phoneme segmentation (e.g., "How many sounds are in the word *fish?*" [3])

- Categorize sounds by recognizing which in a series of words does not have the same sound, phoneme categorization (e.g., *cat, cot, tree [tree]*)

- Delete sounds within words, phoneme deletion (e.g., "What word do you make when you remove the /d/ sound from *Dan?*" [an])

- Blend separately spoken sounds into words, phoneme blending (e.g., "What word do these sounds make: /l/ /o/ /g/?" [*log*])

- Substitute sounds within words, phoneme manipulation (e.g., "If I take the /sh/ out of *ship* and replace it with /l/, what word do I make?" [*lip*])

Phonological Awareness and Children Whose First Language Is Not English

Children develop phonological awareness of the sounds in the language they first acquire. When learning a new language, they may have difficulty hearing the phonemes in the language that are different from phonemes in their native language or that are not present in their native language (Iverson et al., 2003). Native Japanese or Chinese speakers may, for example, struggle to hear, produce, and manipulate the phoneme /r/ in English because it does not exist in their languages. Consequently, children with disabilities whose native language is not English may have a doubly difficult time mastering phonological awareness skills and, later, reading skills in a nonnative language. They may be struggling with the language issues faced by all nonnative speakers of a language and with any language difficulties related to their disabilities.

Historically, researchers and educators have paid little attention to the language and literacy learning of bilingual children with moderate or severe disabilities. Many believed that these children's language abilities were so impaired as a result of their disabilities that it made little difference to consider how the disparities between their native language and their new language (usually English) might affect their learning. Thankfully this is changing, but there remains a large gap in what is known about effective second language and literacy instruction for this group of students. What practitioners can do is to be aware of the difficulties these students may encounter with phonological awareness and literacy tasks in their new language and to support students in developing language and literacy in their native language (see Chapter 3).

Phonological Awareness and Students with Moderate or Severe Disabilities

Do students with moderate or severe disabilities develop phonological awareness and is it also related to their becoming more successful readers? Although much research remains to be done in this area, the answer seems to be yes. Just as with typically developing children, better developed phonological awareness is associated with higher levels of reading skill in children with intellectual and/or other severe disabilities (e.g., Cupples & Iacono, 2000; Kennedy & Flynn, 2003).

Phonological Awareness Research

A large body of research exists indicating that phonological awareness is predictive of later reading ability (Allor, 2002; Torgesen, 2000). Most research studies of phonological awareness, however, have not included children with moderate or severe disabilities. More recent studies, particularly of children with Down syndrome, suggest that children with intellectual disabilities do develop phonological awareness and that there is a positive association between their phonological awareness abilities and later reading skills (e.g., Connors et al., 2001; Kay-Raining Bird et al., 2000).

Several studies have found that children with Down syndrome typically have great difficulty detecting rhymes, even when they posses phonemic awareness (e.g., Cardoso-Martins, Michalick, & Pollo, 2002; Snowling, Hulme, & Mercer, 2002). This is not the pattern of phonological awareness acquisition seen in typically developing children (rhyme detection characteristically develops before phonemic awareness), causing researchers to speculate that phonological awareness develops in a qualitatively different manner in children with an intellectual disability (at least for children with Down syndrome). However, these children do develop phonological awareness and it does contribute to acquisition of reading skills, so it should be included in literacy instruction.

Research also supports explicit instruction in application of phonological awareness skills to literacy tasks. Snowling et al. (2002) found that even when children with Down syndrome acquired phonological awareness skills and letter–sound knowledge, they didn't necessarily use this knowledge to identify unfamiliar words. In fact, they relied more on their sight word vocabulary than on their knowledge of letter–sound associations. These finding suggest that phonological awareness instruction for these students is most effective when it includes systematic teaching of how to apply this knowledge to text.

These research findings illustrate an important point to remember: students with moderate or severe disabilities need explicit instruction in how to use their phonological awareness skills. Merely teaching phonological awareness is not enough. These students also need consistent and clear instruction on how to use that knowledge to help identify written words or to spell words. As with other areas of learning, the students are not likely to generalize or transfer their knowledge without being explicitly taught to do so (Harris & Pressley, 1991; Torgesen et al., 1999).

Another point to keep in mind is that children with moderate or severe disabilities may not be developmentally ready to work on acquisition of phonological awareness at the same time as their typical age-peers. In other words, these students may not be ready for phonological awareness instruction that is often provided in kindergarten or first grade until they are older. Unfortunately, this may mean that they may miss this important instruction, because teachers will have moved on to instructing other skills by the time many of these students are ready to work on phonological skills.

Phonological Awareness Assessment and Instruction

Assessment information is helpful for practitioners in providing information about a student's current level of performance for instructional planning and as a means of determining the effectiveness of an instructional program. Phonological awareness is developmental, and tasks that measure phonemic and phonological awareness evolve with both language experiences in the home and reading instruction at school (Yopp, 1988). Yopp's (1988, 1992) work has formed the basis from which teachers can be successful in creating their own informal or classroom assessments of phonological awareness.

Assessment   Phonological awareness can be assessed in several ways, both formally and informally. Formal assessments of phonological awareness include standardized tests that measure skills such as identification of rhymes, isolation, and manipulation of individual sounds within words, or phonological memory. (See Resources at the end of the book for a list of commonly used formal [published] assessments of phonological awareness, the skills assessed in each test, and publisher information.)

Informal assessment is also useful in determining a student's level of phonological awareness skills and providing a practical way to monitor his or her progress in acquiring new skills. When assessing students with moderate or severe disabilities, it is important to think carefully about the type of assessment tasks selected. Be certain that you are evaluating the skill you are interested in (in this case, phonological awareness) and not inadvertently measuring a different skill such as the child's expressive speech ability or vocabulary knowledge. Using a task that is difficult for or unfamiliar to students gives an inaccurate picture of their phonological awareness abilities. Assessment tasks that put a large demand on cognitive or memory skills or that use unfamiliar vocabulary may be so difficult that students don't really understand what is being asked of them. Then their responses to these difficult tasks may not actually reflect their knowledge of phonological awareness and so will not reveal much about their skill levels.

It is also critical to present testing materials in a format students can access. Just as with the issues discussed above, we want to ensure that students' phonological skills are being assessed, and to do so, we must eliminate any barriers that interfere with that process. Paying attention to things such as the child's seating position, where assessment materials are placed, size of print, type of font, and so forth, is critical to successful assessment. The print access checklist (see Chapter 5, Figure 5.1) is an excellent tool to use to evaluate access issues that might interfere with assessment.

Fortunately, researchers and practitioners have developed phonological awareness measurement tasks that take into account some of the assessment problems that practitioners may encounter with students who have intellectual or severe disabilities (e.g., Boudreau, 2002; Cupples & Iacono, 2000; Kennedy & Flynn, 2003; Snowling et al., 2002). Some general suggestions from this work are to use assessment tasks that allow the child to respond nonverbally, pictures to support auditory memory, vocabulary that is familiar to the child, and game-like assessment formats.

It is also a good idea to keep assessment sessions short to maximize the student's attention to the tasks. Specific examples of assessment tasks that have proved effective for students with moderate or severe disabilities are included in Figure 4.1.

Instruction   Most experts recommend that phonological awareness instruction be incorporated into an existing reading program and not taught in a separate *drill* manner. However, there are a number of high-quality published phonological awareness programs that may be helpful to teachers in planning a sequenced and comprehensive instructional program (see Resources for a list of such programs). The bottom instructional line is that phonological instruction must accompany visual letters to accomplish the most effective learning. Teachers can use the instructional sequence and teaching ideas in these programs and individualize activities based on their students' learning needs. Instruction on phonological awareness tasks should be explicit but not include more than 10–20 minutes across a school day.

Small groups seem to be the most effective setting for phonological awareness instruction (Boyle & Walker-Seibert, 1997; Ehri et al., 2001) because these settings allow students to learn by watching their peers model skills within the group and provide a motivating context for the students. Some students may also benefit from brief, one-to-one mini-lessons on particular skills. Instructional targets should be selected carefully, based on assessment information for each student. It is best not to teach multiple skills at the same time but rather to focus instruction on one or two skills at a time (Ehri et al.). Segmenting and blending are

For each task, be sure to use pictures or line drawings of words that are familiar to the student (i.e., in the student's listening vocabulary). Always model what you want the student to do and offer several opportunities to practice the task before beginning the actual assessment.

Some younger children may enjoy and be motivated if you use a puppet to model the tasks and provide the directions.

Rhyme—recognition that two or more words end with the same sounds (e.g., *cat, hat*)

- *Matching:* Give the student two to four pictures or line drawings of objects, verbally labeling each one or asking the student to do so. Then say a word and ask the student to indicate (e.g., point to) which picture rhymes with that word.
- *Oddity detection:* Give the student three pictures or line drawings and either verbally label each one or ask the student to do so. Then ask the student to indicate (verbally or by pointing) which of the three pictures does *not* rhyme with the others.
- *Generation:* Give the student a picture or line drawing and either verbally label the picture or ask the student to do so. Then ask the student to say a word that rhymes with the object depicted in the picture.

Alliteration—recognition that some words begin with the same sound (e.g., *hat, house*)

- Provide two or three pictures or line drawings of objects and either verbally label each picture or ask the student to to it.
- Say a word or phoneme and ask the student to point to the picture that begins with the same sound as the spoken word (or phoneme).
- Randomly change the position of the target picture on each trial to reduce the chance that the student will guess the correct answer.
- This activity can also be used to assess a student's awareness of ending or middle sounds by using the same format but asking the student to find the picture that *ends* with the same sound as the word spoken by the examiner or find the picture that has the same *middle* sound as the word spoken by the examiner.
- Use the procedures under Rhyme above to also assess *oddity detection* and *generation* of alliteration ("*Which picture does not have the same beginning sound as house?*" or "*Tell me a word that begins with the same sound as house.*").

Blending—putting together two or more sounds to say a word (e.g., /d/ /o/ /g/, *dog*)

- Show the student a picture or line drawing of a familiar item and ask him or her to listen while you say the name of the picture very slowly. (This is often called word stretching or word rubber banding. It may be helpful or motivating to the student for you to stretch out a large rubber band while modeling this task or use your arms to show how you are stretching out the word.)
- Slowly say each individual sound of the word represented by the picture.
- Next, give the student two or three pictures or line drawings and say the name of one of the pictures slowly, phoneme by phoneme.
- Ask the student to point to the picture whose name you said.
- Begin the assessment with words made up of two or three phonemes (CV or CVC); progress to longer words that require up to four phonemes (CVCV).

Segmentation—breaking words into individual sounds (e.g., *blue* /b/ /l/ /oo/). Keep in mind that this is the most difficult phonological task because it requires more memory than other tasks. Segmenting a word requires the student to hold the word in memory and at the same time break it down into separate sounds.

Syllable Segmentation (e.g., *ta-ble*)
- Show the student a familiar picture of a two-syllable word and say the first syllable of the word for him or her. Ask the student to supply the next syllable.
- An alternative is to provide the student with a spoken one-, two-, or three-syllable word and ask him or her to clap or tap for each syllable heard.

Phoneme Segmentation (e.g., *boy* /b/ /oi/)
- Show the student a familiar picture (using a word that has only two or three phonemes) and ask the student to "say the sounds very slowly" (say each individual phoneme).

Figure 4.1. Examples of informal assessment of phonological awareness tasks.

two skills, in particular, that are associated with enhanced reading skills, and research supports explicit instruction in these two areas for students with moderate or severe disabilities.

Many phonological awareness tasks can be taught in an informal, game-like format or incorporated into singing and wordplay activities (Kennedy & Flynn, 2003; Lane et al., 2002). Lane and her colleagues made the points that phonological awareness is an auditory skill and effective instruction requires active participation—not sitting at a desk completing worksheets! Engaging, lively instruction may be especially important when teaching students with moderate or severe disabilities. Active responses and instruction that involves manipulation of objects can help these students become aware of phonological units of speech. For example, students can be asked to sort objects or pictures by their rhyme/rime units (see Figure 4.2). Or, students can clap, stomp, or tap to represent each word in a sequence. This is a fun and useful way to help students become aware of and represent each of these spoken units (e.g., "Let's clap each word of the sentence: 'John went to school'"). These same active responses can also be used when working at the syllable, onset/rime, or phoneme level (e.g., "Stomp the floor for each of the syllables you hear in the word *refrigerator.*" It should be noted that while use of manipulatives and active response formats are essential for students with moderate or severe disabilities, they greatly enhance instruction for *all* students, those with and without disabilities.

A slightly more difficult activity is to have students move some type of marker to represent each word or sound they hear. Word boxes, based on the Elkonin box (Elkonin, 1973), have been used successfully to teach onset/rime and phoneme segmentation to students with moderate disabilities (e.g., Joseph, 2002). This can be done in individual lessons or in small group formats.

The teacher makes a frame out of cardstock that includes up to four empty squares. The students are each given a frame and a set of markers (e.g., small chips). The teacher shows the group a picture of something familiar and models how to say each sound in the word slowly while moving a marker into a square for each sound. Next, the students are asked to move a marker into a square for

Figure 4.2.   Example of a picture sort to work on awareness of rhyme/rime units.

each sound they hear in the word (or for the onset and rime they hear). It may be most effective to begin with onset/rimes and then move to segmenting words into individual sounds because detection of onset/rimes typically develops before segmentation of individual phonemes (Liberman et al., 1974; Yopp, 1988, 1992). An enjoyable variation is to use a photograph of the student or a classmate in place of a picture of a familiar object and work to segment this person's name in the activity. These names will be familiar words and may be very motivating for students to work with.

Figure 4.3 shows an example of a word box in which a student has represented each of the sounds in *book:* /b/ /oo/ /k/. As we mentioned before, segmenting is an especially difficult phonological task. Using pictures and frames helps with the memory load required by the task and can support the students with disabilities' understanding and success with this task.

Notice that at this stage students are not asked to use letters to represent sounds. Instead, they focus on hearing individual sounds in words that they then represent with markers. Later, as students are introduced to letter–sound knowledge, they can substitute letters for the makers in the same activity. In fact, research supports the practice of connecting phonological awareness instruction with letter knowledge, especially for students with disabilities (Ehri et al., 2001).

Boyle and Walker-Seibert (1997) developed instruction that illustrates these practices. They provided intensive phonological awareness instruction to elementary school students with mild intellectual disabilities that included teaching them to apply their newly acquired skills when they were reading both real and nonsense words. They taught the students a mnemonic, Stare-Tell-Open-Put (STOP), to help them learn and apply segmenting and blending skills directly to reading tasks. This mnemonic taught students to 1) look (Stare) at each letter of a novel word, 2) say (Tell) the sound of each letter in the word to themselves,

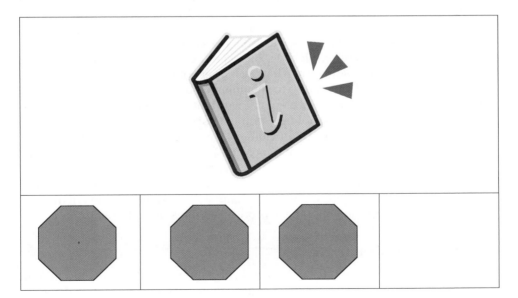

Figure 4.3.   Example of a word box for teaching segmenting.

3) say the word out loud (Open), and 4) blend the sounds of each letter together (Put) to say the new word. Students who learned this strategy improved their decoding of novel words and improved their tested phonological awareness skills. They were also able to generalize their newfound skills to short text passages that included new words.

PHONICS

Phonics is the explicit knowledge of letter–sound relationships. It is also reading instruction that teaches students to make the connections between phonemes (sounds) and the graphemes (letters) we use to represent these sounds. Phonics instruction teaches various letter combinations that represent spoken sounds in words; that is, it teaches students to "represent speech with letters" (O'Connor & Bell, 2004, p. 486). Once phonics knowledge is acquired, students can apply their knowledge to unfamiliar words to identify them or to spell words when creating a written text.

Decoding develops in predictable patterns of phonological (sound) and orthographic (spelling) recognition in reading (Calhoon & Leslie, 2002; Leslie & Calhoon, 1995). Initially, students appear not to be influenced by the number of times they've seen a specific word. However, once students have been exposed to instruction, they appear to develop a sight word recognition of high-frequency words with a large number of shared ending (rhyme neighborhood) units first, followed by high-frequency words with a moderate number of shared ending units. Once students have developed this level of sight word recognition, they can use these specific words to help them identify low-frequency words from large and moderate neighborhoods. Students also can use this knowledge to decode nonsense words. At the point when students have acquired a sight word vocabulary that includes high-frequency and low-frequency words with large numbers of ending units, and high-frequency words with medium numbers of ending units, they appear to no longer be influenced by the frequency words they encounter. They also appear to enter the decoding phase where they can use word-attack skills to figure out most new words they encounter.

However, being able to decode, or sound out a word involves more than simply knowing which sound each letter or letter combination represents. It also involves memory and the ability to manipulate sounds. To correctly decode a word, the student must first segment the word into the individual sounds represented by the word's letters, hold these in memory, and then blend these sounds together to pronounce the word. Blending places a demand on auditory memory, making decoding difficult (but not impossible) for many students with moderate or severe disabilities whose auditory memory may be compromised (Cupples & Iacono, 2000). Blending also requires some skill in articulation of sounds, which may be another area of difficulty for students with moderate or severe disabilities who have accompanying speech problems (Johnson et al., 1999).

Phonics Approaches

It is beyond the scope of this book to describe all the varied approaches used in phonics instruction and the accompanying debate surrounding each of these approaches. It may be useful for practitioners, however, to understand two general approaches for teaching phonics. One approach is often called *implicit/analytic phonics* or *whole-part phonics*. This method focuses on teaching students letter–sound relationships by analyzing sounds within familiar words instead of first isolating and then blending letter sounds. Students who are taught using this method first look at the whole word and then analyze the letter sounds found in that word. For example, a student might learn the sound of the letters by examining the word *sat* and recognizing that its beginning sound is /s/. Some experts argue that this approach is especially suited for students with moderate or severe disabilities because phonics knowledge is taught within a meaningful context that makes it less abstract for these learners (e.g., Katims, 2000).

Explicit/synthetic phonics, on the other hand, involves a part–whole approach. Students are first taught isolated letter–sound relationships and then taught to blend sounds to decode words. Put another way, they are taught to synthesize the parts (sounds) into a whole (the word). For example, a student learning the sound for *s* might be taught the individual sound for the letter *s* /s/ and then taught to blend this sound with the sounds for *a* /ă/, and *t* /t/ to read the word *sat*. This instructional method has been shown to be especially successful with students who have significant reading problems, including those with poor phonological awareness. However, students with auditory memory problems may struggle using this approach with longer words because of the memory load involved in blending. Isolating individual sounds also alters the sounds of some letters, especially *stop* consonants (those speech sounds in which the air flow is stopped such as /d/, /b/, /p/, /t/, /k/, and /g/), so students may not be able to recognize the word they are blending.

Phonics Research

Rather than be concerned about which of the two approaches described above is the right one to use, most experts agree that both are useful and can be combined within instruction, depending on the focus of the lesson or the individual learning needs of the students for whom the lesson is intended (Baer, 2003; Gunning, 2002a). Although relatively few researchers have examined the effect of phonics instruction on the reading skills of students with moderate or severe disabilities (Joseph & Seery, 2004), reviews of the available literature (e.g., Connors, 1992; Joseph & Seery) show clearly that students with moderate or severe disabilities can benefit from phonics instruction, even when complete mastery of all phonic generalizations does not occur. Al Otaiba and Hosp (2004), for example, studied the effects of a tutoring program that included phonological awareness, phonics, sight word fluency, and vocabulary instruction on the word identification and word-attack skills of four elementary school students with Down syndrome. Although the magnitude of skill improvement varied across students, most students showed increases in both decoding and word recognition skills.

Cupples and Iacono (2000) compared the effectiveness of a whole-word instructional approach to an analytic one in which they taught participants to use onset/rimes (word families) to learn new words. They found that children with Down syndrome who were taught some basic phonics skills (i.e., the analytic approach) were able to generalize their newly learned skills to read novel words, while children taught using the whole-word approach were not able to do so. This is an important finding because it indicates that learning even basic phonics skills can promote generalization of reading skills by children with intellectual disabilities.

Phonics Instruction

A common sequence of letter–sound instruction begins by teaching initial consonant correspondences, final consonants, short-vowel sounds, consonant diagraphs, consonant blends, and long-vowel patterns. A published phonics curriculum will provide a systematic sequence of instruction that teachers can use to plan instruction (see Resources for listings of available curricula and resources). Regardless of the phonics program followed, however, lessons for students with moderate or severe disabilities should include dynamic participation using game-like activities, manipulatives, and other instructional formats that involve active student participation (Mirenda, 2003).

Sound Cards   Students can create individual cards for each letter–sound correspondence they are learning by finding pictures of items that begin with these sounds (see Figure 4.4). These sound cards can be filed in a shoebox or other container for easy reference for other activities (Reutzel & Cooter, 2003). For example, students might use these to play a game to review and reinforce the letter–sound relationships they are learning. The cards are stacked on the table. The teacher and students take turns selecting a card, showing the picture side of the card, and asking "What sound does ___ begin with? What letter makes that sound?" If the student whose turn it is to answer correctly answers the question, she or he gets to keep the card, and play passes to the next student.

Making Words   Making Words activities, generally used as part of the Word Block in the Four Blocks literacy program (Cunningham, Moore, Cunningham, & Moore, 2004), are also an effective means of teaching phonics skills to students with moderate or severe disabilities. Hedrick, Katims, and Carr (1999), for example, successfully used Making Words as a part of a balanced literacy program for elementary students with cognitive disabilities. Students in their study all made gains in literacy skills, including phonic skills.

In a Making Words activity, students are given letter tiles, usually 6–9 tiles, which they manipulate to spell words the teacher calls out. The teacher gives the word, uses it in a sentence, and then calls the word out again. Lessons begin with the formation of two-letter words, progress to three-letter words, and so on. Stu-

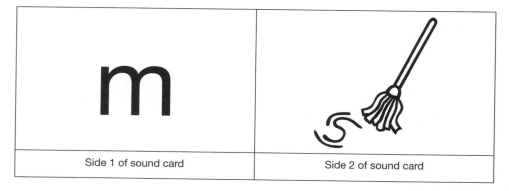

| Side 1 of sound card | Side 2 of sound card |

Figure 4.4.   Example of a sound card students create to learn and remember letter–sound correspondences. (From Reutzel & Cooter [2003]. *Strategies for reading assessment and instruction: Helping every child succeed* [3rd ed., p. 226]. Upper Saddle River, NJ: Prentice Hall.)

dents with more intensive needs can be paired with a partner such as a typically developing peer to provide additional support, and they can work together to create target words. Students who use ACC devices can have their devices programmed ahead of time with the letters needed for the activity, or eye-gaze boards can be equipped with the letters needed for a lesson so that the students need only to eye point to indicate which letters are required for each target word while a partner puts alphabet tiles in order as the student points to the letters she or he thinks make up the target word.

Often students in a Making Words lesson take turns coming to the front of the room to create the target word in a pocket chart so that students at their desks can check the word for accuracy. The final portion of the lesson involves sorting the words in various ways (e.g., initial letter, final letter, word families). Making Words lessons incorporate many of the components needed to facilitate the learning of students with intensive support needs. The pace of instruction moves fairly quickly, and students are actively involved in each step of the lesson rather than waiting for their turn while other students respond. In addition, each phonics element is taught systematically but it is also taught within a meaningful context (e.g., by using the target words within sentences).

Word Sort   A word sort activity is another method of reinforcing phonics skills that has been used successfully with students who have cognitive or severe disabilities (Bear, Invernizzi, Templeton, & Johnston, 1999; Joseph & McCachran, 2003). In word sort activities, students sort words by identifying common patterns among them. For example, students might be asked to sort words by initial sounds or by a spelling pattern (e.g., putting all the words with the rime *ot* together). Engaging in word sorts helps students begin to identify patterns within words and to become aware of letter–sound relationships. (See Figure 4.5 for an example of a word sort activity based on word families.) Word sorts may also be open, in which students define their own categories for sorting, or closed, in which the categories are preassigned or designated (Bear et al.).

Generally, words to be sorted are written on cards. The teacher explains the pattern the students should look for and models the activity. Then the students are given the cards and asked to place them in the correct categories. This can be done as an individual activity, or students can take turns in a small group sorting words in a pocket chart that has each target category labeled. Students should read the words aloud, either as they are sorting them or after the sorting is completed. The teacher should ask questions such as "Why did you put those

ship	shell	shop
skip	fell	top
lip	tell	lop
sip	well	mop
drip	sell	drop

Figure 4.5. Example of word sort activity based on word families.

cards in that stack?" to get the students to focus on what the patterns are. The teacher should ask the students about any words that are not sorted correctly to determine why the mistake was made. For example, the student may have mis-read the card or may be struggling with a particular spelling pattern.

Analogy Activities   Teaching students to recognize words using analogy (i.e., using onsets and rimes) has also been an effective means of instructing students who have moderate or severe disabilities. Calhoon (2001), for example, showed that children in her study with Down syndrome and autism successfully used knowledge of word families to decode words and nonsense words.

Oelwein (1995) suggested teaching onset/rime strategies (i.e., word families) to students with moderate or severe disabilities after they had learned at least some letters of the alphabet and mastered some sight words. She also suggested beginning instruction with short-vowel word families (e.g., *op*) and single-initial consonants before moving on to rimes with long vowels and onsets consisting of consonant blends and diagraphs.

The first step in using an analogy approach is to teach the student to pronounce the rime. Once he or she can do this consistently, add an initial consonant to the rime. For example, give the student a card on which is written *op*. Then place a card in front of the rime on which is written a consonant (e.g., *t*). Explain that you can make a new word by adding the *t* to *op*. As you move the consonant to the rime card, say the word *top*. Repeat this with other initial consonants (e.g., *m*, *c*, *p*, *b*). When the student has mastered reading all the words in one word family, introduce other word families.

These word recognition skills can be reinforced by using a variety of manipulatives (e.g., letter tiles, word wheels, slide-throughs). It is also important to create connected text for the students to read that incorporates words the students are learning through the word-family approach. Students can help to create books or silly poems based on a particular word family, or they can read published books such as those by Dr. Seuss. Another useful way to reinforce these skills is to create Word Walls (Gaskins, Ehri, Cress, O'Hara, & Donnelly, 1996, 1997). As new word families are mastered, the words in that family are placed on large cards and then on the walls of the classroom. The students can practice reading these words together and use the Word Wall as a handy reference when they want to incorporate one of the words in text they are writing.

Whichever phonics approach is selected and implemented, to be effective, it must incorporate frequent opportunities to apply skills learned to connected text and the students' own writing (Cunningham, Cunningham, & Allington, 2002). Without explicit instruction and support to do so, the students will not effectively generalize isolated skills (e.g., *t* makes the /t/ sound) to the actual tasks of reading and writing. It cannot be emphasized enough that teaching these skills must take place within meaningful contexts if the students are to truly understand the functions of literacy.

SIGHT WORD INSTRUCTION

Decoding is not always the best strategy for word recognition. There are a number of high-frequency words with irregular spellings that are easier for beginning readers to learn through memorization (sight word or automatic recognition) than by trying to apply their decoding skills (Gunning, 2002a). Every comprehensive literacy program for beginning readers (with and without disabilities) includes instruction in both phonics and sight word recognition so that the students gain proficiency in multiple-word identification approaches. Moreover, there are students with moderate or severe disabilities who will not acquire sufficient phonics skills to make decoding a practical strategy for identifying all novel words they may encounter. Practitioners must teach these students other word recognition methods. Indeed, sight word reading can form the foundation upon which more complex skills can be built. Some students who begin formal literacy instruction by learning sight words may be able to build upon these skills and learn phonics skills that will expand their reading abilities. For these reasons, it is critical that teachers and other practitioners become skilled at providing effective sight word instruction in addition to implementing effective phonics instruction.

The remainder of this section contains a discussion of considerations that must be made in designing sight word instruction and descriptions of some effective instructional strategies for teaching sight words to students with moderate or severe disabilities. Keep in mind, however, that sight word instruction must go beyond the students merely learning to name words. Comprehension of target words should be taught from the beginning. It is also critical that students be taught to recognize and comprehend words in connected text, beyond the word or sentence level. This is certainly appropriate for high-frequency words whose meanings may be abstract unless they are taught within the context of a sentence (e.g., *of*, *and*, *that*). Even functional sight words such as safety words are most effectively taught when students learn what the words mean and what the appropriate response is to words such as *exit*. This is addressed in more detail in Chapter 7, Vocabulary Instruction.

Selecting Sight Words and Planning Instruction

In general, sight word instruction involves directly teaching the association between the word and the thing or idea that the word represents. For example, a teacher may use flashcards presented in a drill format to teach a set of words by first modeling saying the word on each card and then asking a student to repeat the word. Or the teacher may pair a word with a picture to teach a sight word (e.g., the word *bus* is paired with a picture of a city bus).

But which words should be taught? This is especially important for students with significant disabilities. If a student is likely to master only a limited number of words, these words must be selected with care so that she or he learns words that are most meaningful and useful to him or her. For students who are developing more conventional reading and writing skills, it may be more important to teach high-frequency words that will facilitate reading textbooks, stories, newspapers, and so forth (e.g., Instant Words, Dolch Words).

In other words, using an ecological assessment approach to selecting target words is helpful. For example, examine the student's current environments, consider future environments, and consult the student and his or her family to generate a list of possible instructional items. Consider the student's age and home language, if different from English. It is also important to consider the written environmental print in a student's community. Sections of some communities may have many signs written in languages other than English, and it may be important to the student and his or her family that he or she learns to recognize these community words. Each of these strategies will provide useful information in determining which words to include in sight word instruction. Generally, try to choose words that are of interest to the student (e.g., TV words, car words); needed to increase participation in general education activities (e.g., classmates' and teachers' names, direction words, key content vocabulary such as science or social studies terms); found in the student's current environments (e.g., environmental print in the classroom or school); names of friends and family; product or laundry labels (for older students); useful in staying safe (i.e., safety words such as *exit* or *fire extinguisher*); or found in the student's employment site (for older students).

After determining which words to teach, and before actually beginning to teach, arrange the words in sets for instruction (usually four to ten words but this number should be matched to the learning characteristics of the student). Decide where to teach sight words; unfortunately, this often takes place in the classroom in a decontextualized instructional setting such as the flashcard instruction described above. Therefore, the next critical step is to give students opportunities to practice their sight word recognition in context, either within connected texts or for functional sight words, in the natural settings in which the words are found. This facilitates skill generalization and aids in developing students' understanding of literacy. Students with more significant cognitive challenges and those with less well-developed language skills will need more instruction in the natural settings in which the target words are used. Some students may even require that all of their sight word instruction take place within natural settings if it is to be effective.

Determining the instructional strategy that will be used to teach target words is another important consideration. (More information on various strategies is found later in this section.) Will words be taught using a prompting strategy? Using a computer program? Will a one-to-one format be used or will words be taught in a small-group format? Just as with other aspects of literacy learning, match the instructional strategy selected to the learning needs of the students.

Creating instructional materials is an additional consideration. To facilitate transfer of word recognition skills from the instructional setting to authentic literacy activities, sight word materials should be prepared using a variety of font sizes, typefaces, and print colors. However, all words in a teaching set should be written in the same manner to ensure that the students are focusing on differences in the words and not on some extraneous aspect such as font size. Doing so maximizes the likelihood that students will recognize target words in a variety of contexts.

Finally, plan from the beginning opportunities for students to practice and generalize the sight words they are learning. Some suggestions for activities to build fluency and facilitate generalization are to

- Have the students create word banks of the words they learn. They can write the word on one side of the card and on the other add a picture illustrating the word's meaning, or they could write a short sentence using the word (Reutzel & Cooter, 2003). The students could consult their word banks when using the sight words in writing activities or use the cards to do word sort activities.

- Create books with students based on the sight words they're learning and give them frequent opportunities to read these books.

- Add sight words to the Word Wall words in the classroom and practice daily as a whole class (Gaskins et al., 1996, 1997).

- Sing the words (Gunning, 2002a). Use published songs or create your own with words the students are learning. Be sure to provide the text as students sing and point to the words as they are sung to reinforce word recognition.

- Label items in the classroom and have the students *read* the classroom each day.

- Play games using sight word cards such as bingo, concentration, or go fish.

- Have a treasure hunt for environmental print or functional safety words. Assign students to small groups or pairs. Give them a list of environmental print/signs to locate on the school campus. Give a reward such as extra free time if the group/pair locates all the items on the list and can read and explain the meaning of each word. Or, ask the students to find and write down all the environmental print/signs they can find in the school in 15 minutes. They must return to the classroom and read each word they found and give its meaning to earn a point. Provide rewards for the most words found, written, read, and defined.

- Allow the students to use computer software programs to practice word recognition (see Resources for a list of companies offering word recognition software).

Teaching Sight Words

The research and practice literature describes a number of methods of teaching sight words to individuals with moderate or severe disabilities. Several of these are described below. In any case, select a strategy based on student learning characteristics but monitor the student's acquisition of words carefully and adjust instruction if a strategy does not appear to be working.

Pairing Pictures with Words   Although pairing pictures with the words they represent is popular with teachers, research findings comparing this procedure with other instructional strategies are mixed (Sheehy, 2002). There is evidence suggesting that students with more intensive support needs attend primarily to the picture rather than the word when these are paired. They make an association between the spoken word and the picture, not the spoken word and the printed word. Another way of saying this is that the picture *blocks* the student's identification of the word (Sheehy). When the picture is removed, the students often can't identify the word alone because they were attending to the picture and not the printed word during instruction and so made an incorrect association.

Despite these negative findings, researchers have identified several variations of the picture–word method that have been more effective than merely placing a word and picture together. One variation is a form of stimulus fading. A picture is paired with a word during initial instructional trials. Over time, the picture is gradually faded, finally leaving the word alone. (Figure 4.6 provides an

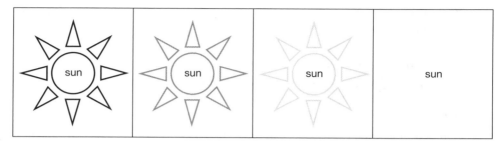

Figure 4.6. Example of using stimulus fading to teach sight word recognition.

illustration of this.) Embedding the word within the picture and then fading the picture seems even more effective, perhaps by focusing the student's attention more closely on the word instead of the picture.

Another variation of pairing words and pictures is embedding a picture or symbol within a word. Sheehy (2002) called this Integrated Picture Cueing (IPC). This strategy is different from the examples in Figure 4.6 in that the word is more prominent than the picture or symbol. Researchers believe that this approach is effective because the student must attend more closely to the figure to find the picture, requiring that she or he pays more attention to the word itself (Sheehy; see Figure 4.7 for an example of this technique).

Sheehy (2002) found that rather than using a predetermined symbol within a word, such as that shown in Figure 4.7, it was more effective to include a symbol that had meaning for an individual student. She asked the students with moderate and severe disabilities to tell her what they thought a list of words meant and then incorporated a symbol into each word that was unique to the understanding of each student. For example, if a student said "hot" when asked what sun means, then a picture of flames might be used in Figure 4.7 rather than a drawing of the sun itself. Students in Sheehy's study using these individualized cues acquired a larger number of sight words than did students using cues selected by the teacher. While there is little research available comparing these two approaches, it might be a helpful strategy to utilize in the classroom, particularly with students who have failed to learn sight words through other more traditional instruction.

Another variation of picture–word instruction also described by Sheehy (2002) is adding a mark of some kind that is related to the student's understanding of the word to the printed word. Sheehy referred to this as the Handle Technique because "it uses a non-pictorial, personal mnemonic cue (a handle) to prompt recall of the word's name and positively support a transfer to word recognition" (p. 50). These marks are more abstract than the pictures used in the IPC approach and are not as large (see Figure 4.8 for an example). However, the marks do indicate in some way the student's understanding of the word, making them uniquely individualized for each student. Another important characteristic of the Handle Technique is that words taught in this manner are selected from words the student actually uses—those in his or her speaking or signing vocabulary. This increases the meaningfulness of the instruction and makes it more likely that the student will grasp the word recognition skill being taught. Students in Sheehy's study learned more sight words using this approach than with the IPC or word alone strategies. Like IPC, there is little research available examining the

Figure 4.7.   Example of Integrated Picture Cue.

Handle Technique, but teachers might find it useful for students who are not successful with other methods.

It is probably apparent that as effective as the approaches described in this section are, preparing materials for these strategies takes a lot of effort on the part of practitioners. Nevertheless, the amount of work involved may be worth the effort if the end result is a student learning to read sight words. At least one company now publishes materials using the IPC method (see Resources for ordering information). Another option is having students draw their own picture illustrations and then gradually fading the illustrations over time. (Students could work with their typical age peers in the classroom to create illustrations. This may be highly motivating and thus add to the effectiveness of the approach.) Rivera, Koorland, and Gueyo (2002) used this approach successfully with a youngster who had learning disabilities. Again, while little research has been done to explore the efficacy of this strategy, it might prove useful for particular students. It is also less expensive for districts if teachers understand these principles and can individualize instruction using multiple strategies and teacher-made materials for students in their classes. Keep in mind that creating individualized materials is another strategy that is effective with *all* learners. For example, students learning English (English language learners—ELLs), students with mild disabilities, or students without disabilities who may be struggling with beginning reading skills can all benefit from this approach.

It is possible that students who are initially taught using one of the methods described in this section may be able to move on to more traditional instruction that doesn't involve extensive stimulus modification once they have experienced some success in word identification. Once they have grasped the underlying principle that printed words are associated with spoken words, they may be able to benefit from instruction that doesn't provide the level of support these picture–word approaches do.

Figure 4.8.   Example of an individualized Handle Technique.

Copy, Cover, and Compare   Copy, cover, and compare (CCC)—sometimes called cover, copy, and compare—is an instructional strategy that has been used successfully for students with disabilities in a variety of subject areas such as math, science, spelling, and geography (Murphy, Hern, Williams, & McLaughlin, 1990). Because one of the components of the strategy is that students check their own work, it is also useful in developing students' self-management skills (McLaughlin & Skinner, 1996). It can be done independently or with a teacher or peer. Conley, Derby, Roberts-Gwinn, Weber, and McLaughlin (2004) used a variation of this procedure to teach sight word recognition. These authors' general instructional procedures for this method of sight word instruction are described in this chapter.

In using the Copy, Cover, and Compare method of sight word instruction, the first decision is to determine which words will be taught and to arrange these target words in learning sets (Conley et al. [2004] used sets of five words). Next, the teacher divides a piece of paper into thirds (see Figure 4.9) and prints the target words in the first section. In the second section, words are printed using dashed or very light-colored lines, and the third section is left blank. For the next step in the instructional sequence, the teacher asks the students to say the name of the first word. After saying the name of the word, the students trace the first word, saying the letter names as they are traced (Copy). Then they cover the first two sections with a card or fold the sections so they cannot be seen (Cover) and write the word from memory, again saying the names of the letters as they are written. Finally, the students remove the card or open the paper and evaluate the word they wrote with the model in the first section (Compare). They repeat these steps with each target word.

Conley et al. (2004) also provided opportunities for students in their study to read the target words they had learned in several contexts such as singly on cards and in sentences within short stories. This is an important feature of effective sight word instruction because it allows students to practice words in different situations, facilitating generalization and understanding of word meaning.

An interesting finding from the Conley et al. (2004) study, which compared the CCC method of sight word acquisition with a picture-matching procedure, was that students taught to recognize sight words using a picture-matching strategy learned words more quickly than when using the CCC procedures. Nonetheless, students did not maintain recognition of these words across time. Words learned using the CCC procedures, however, were maintained. This finding has

the	*the*	
and	*and*	
all	*all*	
of	*of*	
that	*that*	

Figure 4.9. Example of the Copy, Cover, Compare strategy.

implications for practitioners who may be tempted to use a procedure that seems to take less instructional time. Nevertheless, if students can't remember the new sight words or recognize them in other contexts, the strategy is ultimately not useful and other instructional approaches, such as the CCC method, should be implemented.

Response Prompts   There is a large literature base supporting the use of response prompts to teach sight words to students with moderate or severe disabilities (Browder, 2001). Response prompts are any assistance or feedback the teacher gives a student that increases the likelihood that the student will respond correctly. For example, when a student is trying to find the word *apple* on a grocery list and the teacher says, "Look for a word that begins with *a*," she has just used a response prompt. Prompts may be verbal cues, gestures, modeling, or even full physical assistance. Prompts can be given before a student responds, such as with simultaneous prompting (see below), or they can be given in the form of feedback after a student responds (e.g., "That isn't correct. The word is *exit*").

Simultaneous prompting is a form of errorless learning. In this strategy the teacher presents a word, names the word, and tells the student to say the word. For example, the teacher shows the student the word *danger* while saying, "This word is *danger*. Read *danger*." In other words, the student is instantly provided with a model and therefore knows exactly how to respond. After several trials, the teacher assesses the student's performance by presenting the words but not giving the prompt. Errorless learning is an effective strategy for some students, especially those who get upset when they make a mistake (Browder, 2001).

The teacher may decide to wait a predetermined amount of time after showing a word to a student before providing a prompt. This is called *time delay*. This strategy allows the student time to respond before receiving a cue from the instructor. The teacher could decide to wait a predetermined number of seconds on each trial (constant time delay) or could vary the amount of time he waits within a teaching session (progressive time delay). Teachers using progressive time delay start with a 0–second delay and gradually move to a longer time period (e.g., 10 seconds) before providing a prompt. The benefit of the time delay procedure is that it discourages students from getting into the habit of relying on the teacher to give them a cue.

A final prompting strategy is the use of *stimulus shaping* (McCoy & Sundbye, 2001). This technique has been used successfully for many years to teach sight words to students with intensive support needs. In fact, the popular Edmark Reading Program is based on this strategy. When using stimulus shaping, the teacher presents the target word with at least two distracters. In the initial stages, the distracters are very different in appearance from the target word (see Figure 4.10 for an example). As the student gains more experience identifying the target word, the distracters become more similar to the target word, forcing the student to make finer and finer discriminations.

While stimulus shaping is very effective in teaching sight words, it must be supplemented with opportunities to read the newly learned words in connected text in a variety of situations. Otherwise, the students will learn *word calling* but may have little idea of what the words mean or how to engage in authentic literacy activities in all areas of their lives.

that	—	—
—	that	—
that	—	the
the	that	thin
the	thatch	that

Figure 4.10. Example of stimulus shaping used to teach sight words.

SUMMARY

Word recognition instruction for students with moderate or severe disabilities should encompass several approaches so that the students are equipped with multiple tools to use in identifying words. Instructional decisions should not be based on a student's label (e.g., not giving students opportunities to learn basic phonics skills because of a belief that students with cognitive disabilities cannot benefit from such instruction). Instead, practitioners must start with high expectations and provide quality instruction so that the students are not inadvertently limited in the literacy skills they acquire. Students' progress should be carefully monitored and teaching strategies changed based on actual student progress. Care must be taken to continually give students opportunities to apply newly learned skills within meaningful literacy activities and within connected text so that they can develop a fuller understanding of what literacy is and how it can enrich their lives.

Chapter 5

Fluency

Elizabeth B. Keefe

This chapter will examine the major approaches to reading fluency identified as effective by the literature and consider how these approaches might be implemented for students with moderate or severe disabilities. Reading fluency is the area of reading instruction that has received the least amount of attention from researchers (Allington, 2006; Rasinski, 2003). In particular, scant attention has been paid to reading fluency for students with moderate or severe disabilities. We believe that there are two major reasons for this omission—both related to the fact that, historically, fluency was defined and measured by oral reading rate (Rasinski, 2003). First, as noted in Chapter 1, students with moderate or severe disabilities have not been given the same opportunities to develop reading skills as their typically developing peers; therefore, it is not surprising that little attention has been paid to reading fluency, which depends on the ability of a student to recognize words. Second, students with moderate or severe disabilities often have difficulty with spoken language (see Chapter 3 for a fuller discussion) and therefore may have difficulty demonstrating reading fluency through measures of oral reading rate.

READING FLUENCY FOR STUDENTS WITH MODERATE OR SEVERE DISABILITIES

Reading fluency has not been given a low priority just by researchers. In 1983, Allington noted that fluency was the most neglected area of reading instruction in schools. He observed that silent reading had become the more prominent goal in our classrooms. Reading textbooks and curricula still devote the least amount of attention to reading fluency (Rasinski, 2003). Reading fluency is currently receiving increased awareness as a result of research demonstrating the importance of this area of reading to overall reading competence (e.g., Allington, 2006; National Reading Panel, 2000). The National Reading Panel has identified reading fluency as one of the areas of reading instruction critical to the development of competent readers.

Defining Reading Fluency

Although oral reading rate or speed of reading is the variable most commonly associated with reading fluency, current definitions of reading fluency go beyond rate of oral reading to include accuracy of reading, proper expression, and text phrasing (Allington, 2006; National Reading Panel, 2000; Reutzel & Cooter, 2003). *Accuracy* of reading depends on the ability to recognize and decode words correctly. *Speed* of reading depends on the ability to recognize words accurately and with automaticity. *Proper expression* and *text phrasing* are complex and depend on a number of factors. The use of proper expression depends on the ability to modulate the pitch and stress of one's voice. The use of proper expression and text phrasing also depends on the ability to understand grammar and punctuation. Finally, proper expression and text phrasing are closely related to the comprehension of the reading material.

Students with moderate or severe disabilities may have other factors that affect their ability to read fluently. All the elements of reading fluency described above are dependent on basic physical and sensory abilities such as the ability of the eyes to see and track print and symbols. We cannot assume that students with significant disabilities have these capacities. As a result, some students may have difficulty reading fluently for reasons that are not related to their potential reading ability. For example, some students with cerebral palsy and other physical disabilities may have impaired motor coordination of the muscles that control eye movement. Impaired motor coordination of the neck or trunk may restrict the area of sight for other students. Low vision or blindness may require accommodations or modifications to the format of text. In addition, demonstration of reading fluency most often depends on oral reading ability. Many students with moderate or severe disabilities do not have the expressive language to communicate what they really know (see Chapter 3). While it is true that these physical, sensory, and linguistic challenges present obstacles in the area of reading fluency, these challenges are not insurmountable. The use of low- and high-tech assistive devices can make text accessible for students with motor and sensory challenges (see Chapter 9). The design of instruction using brain-based learning, universal design, and the principle of partial participation will enable reading fluency to become a part of reading instruction for all students.

We believe the least dangerous assumption is that reading fluency is an important element of reading instruction for students with moderate or severe disabilities. The rest of this chapter will examine how to assess reading fluency and provide effective instruction for all students.

The Importance of Appropriate Assessment

As with all areas of instruction, it is critical to assess students to find out where they are functioning in order to design appropriate instruction. Each area of reading fluency needs to be assessed (i.e., reading rate, accuracy, expression, phrasing). Teachers must first assess students with moderate or severe disabilities to make sure they have the physical, sensory, and language skills to see and track print and express accurately what they are reading.

Print Access Skill Assessment   To ascertain whether a student will have trouble accessing print due to physical and sensory impairments, teachers should consult with related service providers such as occupational therapists, speech–language pathologists, assistive technology specialists, and physical therapists. Family members and family physicians are other good sources of information in this area. The students are also a good source of information about their own abilities, and their input is often overlooked. A simple print access checklist such as the one in Figure 5.1 can help guide teachers.

Student: _____   Age: _____

Teacher: _____   Date: _____

Assessed by: _____

Skill	Yes	No	Support needed
Maintains stable and comfortable body position to see print			
Visually discriminates print			
Focuses on printed text			
Tracks print from left to right			
Tracks print from top to bottom			
Manipulates reading material			

Other observations: _____

_____

_____

Figure 5.1.   Print access checklist.

Teachers need to consult with educational team members to decide how well the student is able to accurately demonstrate his or her reading skill through oral language. Students with moderate or severe disabilities are often presumed to be less competent when they have impaired expressive language. Students who have difficulty with oral reading should still receive instruction in reading fluency. The challenge is to find appropriate individually designed supports for students to accurately demonstrate their reading skills. As always, the least dangerous assumption is to presume competence and provide access to quality reading instruction.

Reading Rate and Accuracy   Chapter 4 described assessments for measuring accuracy of word recognition. Those assessments can be used in combination with reading rate measures. The measurement of words correct per minute (WCPM) combines information about reading rate and accuracy. There are curriculum-based oral fluency norms measured in WCPM by grade level (Hasbrouck & Tindal, 2006). Their norms for the beginning and end of grades 2–5 are shown in Figure 5.2. These figures are meant to be only a guideline. Individual student targets will vary as is made clear by the different WCPM rates by percentile. In particular, targets for students with moderate or severe disabilities should not be tied to grade level or age but instead to student readiness.

The assessment of WCPM should be carried out using text that the student can read with 96%–100% accuracy. Basal readers or leveled books have vocabulary controlled by grade level, so they provide good sources of text for this as-

Grade	Percentile	WCPM Fall	WCPM Spring
2	10	11	31
	25	25	61
	50	51	89
	75	79	117
3	10	21	48
	25	44	78
	50	71	107
	75	99	137
4	10	45	72
	25	68	98
	50	94	123
	75	119	152
5	10	61	83
	25	85	109
	50	110	139
	75	139	168

Figure 5.2. An example of curriculum-based fluency norms. (Table from Hasbrouck, J.E., & Tindal, G.A. [2006, April]. Oral reading fluency norms: A valuable assessment tool for reading teachers. *The Reading Teacher, 59*[7], 636–644.)

sessment. Teachers can assess WCPM using one of two basic approaches. One approach uses a predetermined number of words usually ranging from 100 to 300 words depending on grade level. Another approach uses a predetermined time frame, usually 1 or 2 minutes.

Measuring WCPM Using Text Length   To assess WCPM using a predetermined length of text, you will need the following materials:

- A cassette player and blank tape labeled with the student's name
- A stopwatch or timer
- A selection of text that the student can read with 96%–100% accuracy
- A dated photocopy of the text sample with a notation at the preselected number of words (100–300), which can also be used to document word recognition errors
- Graph paper that can be used by the student to document baseline and progress throughout the year
- WCPM data record form for teacher records (see Figure 5.3).

Once the materials have been gathered, you are ready to assess WCPM using the following steps:

1. Turn on the tape recorder.
2. Ask the student to read the preselected text; the student is not allowed to practice the selected text.

3.   Start the stopwatch or timer when the student starts reading.

4.   Mark any errors on your copy of the text as the student reads.

5.   Stop the timer at the end of the text sample (100–300 words) but let the student keep reading to the end of the passage.

6.   Turn off the tape recorder.

7.   (Optional) Ask two or three comprehension questions or ask the student to retell the story.

8.   Calculate the WCPM (total number of words read correctly divided by minutes taken to read). Share the WCPM with the student and have the student document progress on his or her individual graph. The teacher can assist students who need help completing this task.

9.   Document the WCPM in teacher files. We recommend stapling the WCPM form to the inside cover of a file folder and keeping the dated marked text samples in this file.

Although the purpose of this assessment is to evaluate reading rate, it is important to check periodically to make sure that the students understand what they are reading. Comprehension can be checked by asking two or three questions after the student has read the passage. Another alternative is to ask the student to retell what he or she just read.

Measuring WCPM Using Predetermined Time   The second major way to structure assessment of reading rate is to use the 1-minute reading probe (Rasinski, 2003). You could also use a 2-minute reading probe if the students have disabilities that make it slower for them to either access print or demonstrate their understanding of it. The materials needed are similar to the WCPM by predetermined length of text:

•   A cassette player and blank tape labeled with the student's name

•   A stopwatch or timer

•   A selection of text that the student can read with 96%–100% accuracy

•   A dated photocopy of the text sample with more than enough words to last 1 or 2 minutes for this student. We recommend using a sample that is a complete passage so that it makes sense to the student. This copy can also be used to document any word recognition errors.

•   Graph paper that can be used by the student to document baseline and progress throughout the year.

•   WCPM data record form for teacher records (see Figure 5.3).

The One-Minute Reading Probe requires the following steps (adapted from Rasinski, 2003):

1.   Turn on the tape recorder.

2.   Ask the student to orally read the preselected passage of text that is on his or her reading-proficient level. Students are not allowed to practice the text for this assessment.

3.   Turn on the stopwatch or timer as soon as the student starts to read.

4.   Record any word recognition errors on your copy of the text.

5. Ask the student to stop reading when the timer reaches 1 minute. Turn off the tape recorder. Mark on the passage how far the student read. Count the number of words read correctly—this will be the WCPM (remember to divide by 2 if you conducted a 2-minute probe).

6. (Optional) Ask two or three comprehension questions or ask the student to retell the story.

7. Share the WCPM with the student and have the student document progress on his or her individual graph. The teacher can assist students who need help completing this task.

8. Document the WCPM in teacher files. We recommend stapling the WCPM form to the inside cover of a file folder and keeping the dated marked text samples in this file.

These two approaches to measure WCPM using a predetermined length of text or time are quick and simple ways to document reading rate and accuracy. They require very few materials and no purchase of expensive programs. The two methods are appropriate for all students—with and without disabilities. Students could be pulled once a week for a WCPM reading probe during independent reading activities. Educational assistants, related service providers, and peer tutors could assist the teacher(s) in completing these assessments.

Assessing Proper Expression and Phrasing   As noted at the beginning of this chapter, reading fluency is not solely defined by oral reading rate, it also includes proper expression and phrasing. Measurement of these skills is much more subjective. These two areas may be negatively affected by speech and language disabilities for students with moderate or severe disabilities. Working on these areas of reading fluency may provide a great area of collaboration for related service providers and teachers. They also may provide an excellent opportunity for related service providers, particularly the speech–language pathologist, to integrate services into the general education classroom.

Student: _____   Age: _____

Teacher: _____

Date	Text	WCPM	Comments

Figure 5.3.   WCPM data record.

Fluency Rubrics   We recommend the use of fluency rubrics to assess proper expression and phrasing. There are some rubrics available in the literature that can provide a sample or guide for teachers to develop their own fluency rubrics. The U.S. Department of Education sponsors the National Assessment of Educational Progress (NAEP) to evaluate student achievement in academic areas, including reading. NAEP developed an Oral Reading Fluency Scale that does take into account phrasing and proper expression (see Figure 5.4). According to NAEP, a rating of 3–4 on this scale indicates fluent reading.

Another example of a fluency rubric is the Multidimensional Fluency Scale (MFS; Rasinski, 2003). This rubric has four sub-scales, and this allows the teacher to focus in on specific areas of reading fluency (see Figure 5.5).

To complete an assessment of reading fluency using a fluency rubric, you will need the following materials:

- A tape recorder and blank cassette labeled with the student's name
- One or two passages of text (200–300 words) that are at or one grade below the student's reading-proficient level (96%–100% word recognition accuracy)
- Reading fluency rubric

Once you have the materials, complete the reading fluency assessment using the following steps:

1. Let the student practice reading the selected text for the assessment.
2. Turn on the cassette recorder.
3. Ask the student to read the passages with his or her best voice and expression.
4. Turn off the recorder. Thank the student and give positive feedback for his or her reading and/or effort.
5. Listen to the tape later and rate according to one of the fluency rubrics in Figures 5.4 and 5.5 or your own fluency rubric.

The use of these rubrics will help you document fluency and target areas that need to be addressed through instruction.

Level 4	Reads primarily in larger, meaningful phrase groups. Although some regressions, repetitions, and deviations from text may be present, they do not appear to detract from the overall structure of the story. Preservation of the author's syntax is consistent. Some or most of the story is read with expressive interpretation.
Level 3	Reads primarily in three- or four-word phrase groups. Some smaller groupings may be present. However, the majority of phrasing seems appropriate and preserves the syntax of the author. Little or no expressive interpretation is present.
Level 2	Reads primarily in two-word phrases with some three- or four-word groupings. Some word-by-word reading may be present. Word groupings may seem awkward and unrelated to larger context of sentence or passage.
Level 1	Reads primarily word by word. Occasional two-word or three-word phrases may occur, but these are infrequent and/or do not preserve meaningful syntax.

Figure 5.4.   NAEP's oral reading fluency scale. (From U.S. Department of Education, National Center for Education Statistics [1995]. *Listening to children read aloud, 15.* Washington, DC: Author.)

A. Accuracy

   1) Word recognition accuracy is poor: generally below 85%. Reader clearly struggles decoding words. Makes multiple decoding attempts for many words, usually without success

   2) Word recognition is marginal: 86%–90%. Reader struggles with many words. Many unsuccessful attempts at self-correction

   3) Word recognition accuracy is good: 91%–95%. Self-corrects successfully

   4) Word recognition accuracy is excellent: 96%. Self-corrections are few and successful, as nearly all words are read correctly on initial attempt

B. Phrasing

   1) Monotonic, with little sense of phrase boundaries, frequent word-by-word reading; usually exhibits improper stress and intonation that fail to mark ends of sentences and clauses

   2) Frequent two- and three-word phrases giving the impression of choppy reading; lacks appropriate stress and intonation that mark ends of sentences and clauses

   3) Mixture of run-ons, mid-sentence pauses for breath, and possibly some choppiness; reasonable stress and intonation

   4) Generally well phrased; mostly in phrase, clause, and sentence units, with adequate attention to expression

C. Smoothness

   1) Frequent extended pauses, hesitations, false starts, sound-outs, repetitions, and/or multiple attempts

   2) Several rough spots in text where extended pauses, hesitations, and so forth, are more frequent and disruptive

   3) Occasional breaks in smoothness caused by difficulties with specific words and/or structures

   4) Generally smooth reading with minimal breaks, but word and structure difficulties are resolved quickly, usually through self-correction

D. Pace (during sections of minimal disruption)

   1) Slow and laborious

   2) Moderately slow (or overly and inappropriately fast)

   3) Uneven mixture of fast and slow reading

   4) Consistently conversational and appropriate

Figure 5.5.   The Multidimensional Fluency Scale. (From Rasinski, T.V. [2003]. *The fluent reader.* New York: Scholastic.)

Providing Effective Reading Fluency Instruction

Shared and guided reading, repeated reading, and silent reading have been shown to be effective in developing reading fluency (Allington, 2006; National Reading Panel, 2000; Rasinski, 2003; Reutzel & Cooter, 2003). This chapter will give examples of reading fluency instruction that implement best practices for all students, including those with moderate or severe disabilities. The lack of attention paid to reading fluency may actually make this area of reading instruction more open to meaningful participation by students with moderate or severe disabilities. There are no rigidly proscribed fluency programs requiring that a specific sequence of skills be taught in a specific time frame. In addition, reading fluency cannot be learned or developed passively; rather, reading fluency is, by its nature, active because it requires the students' participation. Reading fluency encompasses a range of reading instruction that can be used with individuals, pairs, and small and large groups. Reading fluency instruction can be designed with many degrees of student support. Finally, reading fluency is an area that naturally overlaps with oral language, word recognition, and comprehension, making it easy to meet different objectives with the same basic instructional activity (see Chapter 10).

The Importance of Read Alouds   Read alouds are important for all students regardless of age or ability. Although read alouds are not considered one of the research-based strategies for increasing reading fluency by the National Reading Panel (2000), there is considerable evidence that reading aloud to young children and students of all ages improves their literacy skills in general and their motivation to read (Fisher & Frey, 2003; Rasinski, 2003). Reading aloud benefits students by building motivation, providing exposure to varied genres and levels of text that students might not choose or be able to read on their own, improving comprehension, supporting language acquisition and vocabulary development, and improving content area mastery.

Reading aloud specifically contributes to reading fluency by providing a model of fluent reading for students. Teachers can model not only smooth, well-paced reading but also appropriate phrasing and expression. This modeling is particularly important for students with moderate or severe disabilities who may not have had a lot of experience hearing fluent reading due to low expectations and/or lack of exposure to literature at home and school. Students with significant disabilities who have been in segregated educational environments may also have been deprived of hearing fluent reading from their typical peers.

Read alouds demonstrate fluent reading and can be used as important elements of effective instruction such as providing an anticipatory set, enhancing literacy skills such as comprehension and vocabulary development, and communicating curriculum content. Reading aloud to students has been shown to be more effective when it is interactive (Fisher & Frey, 2003; Rasinski, 2003; Reutzel & Cooter, 2003). Read alouds need to be planned and prepared ahead of time by using the following steps:

1. *Choose the text for the read aloud.* Books that are favorites of the teacher and/or students are often good choices. School and public librarians can recommend appropriate books for grade level or topic. You should not limit read alouds to books. Other examples of great sources for read alouds are poetry, student writing, newspapers, magazines, and the Internet. Fiction and non-fiction are both appropriate. It is important to take into account how the text relates to students' interests and experiences and the content area curriculum.

2. *Practice reading the text fluently.* Read the selected text prior to reading for the students. Make sure you can read the words smoothly using correct phrasing, intonation, and expression. Look up the meaning of any words you do not understand. Anticipate words and concepts that you think your students may have difficulty understanding and think about ways you can help them make meaning out of the text.

3. *Prepare the environment.* Teachers need to consider what needs to be done to help the students maintain attention to the read aloud. Consider the following questions: Do you have a specific place in the classroom where students can sit comfortably to listen? Should the students clean off their desks?

Are students allowed to doodle or manipulate fidgets as they listen? Can students put their heads down on their desks or sit somewhere other than their assigned seats? Will the lights be dimmed? Can you put a sign on the door so no one interrupts the read aloud? Are you going to have any visuals or props to support the read aloud, for example, overheads of pictures from the book, posters, photographs, or costumes?

4. *Consider physical and sensory needs.* For students with moderate or severe disabilities, physical and sensory disabilities may need to be taken into account. Read alouds may provide a great opportunity for a student with physical disabilities to be taken out of his or her wheelchair. Students need to be positioned so they can maintain stability and pay attention to the read aloud. Students with sensory disabilities may have trouble hearing the text or seeing the reader and/or supporting visuals or props. Take seating, lighting, and acoustics into account and use any natural supports, manipulatives, assistive technology, and support personnel as appropriate to help provide access to the read aloud for all students.

5. *Read and think aloud.* Model fluent reading while reading the text. Use phrasing and expression to help the students understand the text. It is important not to read too fast or too slow. Communicate your enjoyment of reading through your behavior. As you read, it is important to monitor the students' reactions to see if you need to adjust your reading or stop to explain a word or concept. Rasinski (2003) also recommends occasionally thinking aloud so that students understand the processes of problem solving and meaning-making that occur while reading. Rasinski recommends being strategic about using thinking aloud and avoiding overuse of this technique.

6. *Engage students during the reading.* There are many ways to get the students involved in the reading. Teachers can use props and visuals to bring the reading to life and make concrete connections for students who have trouble with abstraction. Teachers can ask questions and encourage predications during the reading. Helping students connect the reading to their own prior knowledge or experiences will enable them to make meaning from the text.

7. *Provide opportunities to respond after the reading.* The act of responding to the read aloud is an important element of the experience (Beck & McKeown, 2001; Fisher & Frey, 2003; Rasinski, 2003). Teachers can lead a discussion after the read aloud. This discussion should be open-ended, and teachers should encourage students to think critically about the read aloud rather than just ask them to recall facts. The discussion can also be an opportunity to connect the read aloud to literacy development and/or related content areas. It does not have to occur in a large group only; teachers can use strategies such as think-pair-share or small-group discussions to enable more students to actively participate. Remember to think ahead of ways in which students with physical, sensory, or language impairments can participate in discussions; for example, making sure that appropriate responses are available on a communication device.

Students can also respond to the read aloud in other ways. Rasinksi (2003) suggested various creative methods teachers can use alone or in combination to give students opportunities to respond to text. For example, students could respond to a written prompt about the read aloud or keep a response journal, they could write a letter to the author or one of the characters in the book, they could respond with visual images prompted by the reading, or they could respond though physical movement by using drama or dance. Teachers can differentiate their instruction by offering students choices about how they respond to read alouds. By varying the format of responses, opportunities are opened up for students with moderate or severe disabilities to participate meaningfully in the read aloud while improving reading fluency for all students.

Shared Reading   Shared reading involves the teacher or other proficient reader reading with less proficient readers. The purpose of shared reading is to provide scaffolding or support for students to help them improve their fluency and general literacy skills. Shared reading is recognized as an excellent strategy to improve reading fluency (Fisher & Frey, 2003; Reutzel, Hollingsworth, & Eldredge, 1994). Although there is no research specifically demonstrating the effectiveness of shared reading on increasing the reading fluency of students with moderate or severe disabilities, the provision of supports and gradually fading the supports to teach independence is consistent with best teaching practices for these students (Snell & Brown, 2006). When implementing shared reading, it is critical to remember that some students may need extra support to access the text because of physical or sensory disabilities. Materials may need to be available in alternative formats such as Braille, large print, or assistive technology devices.

Shared Read Aloud/Shared Book Experience   A read aloud activity can be transformed into a shared reading activity by providing students access to the text. This can be done in multiple ways. Teachers can use a big book or a class set of books so that all students can read along. They can make overheads of the read aloud text and use an overhead projector to share the text with the class. Or they may read aloud the same text for a week, gradually encouraging the class to read the text with her. By the end of the week, many of the students may be able to read all the text independently while other students may be able to read parts of the text. The teacher can use student responses to the text to guide daily lessons based on the shared reading. Research has demonstrated that the shared book experience has a positive impact on reading ability, including fluency (Allington, 2006).

Choral Reading   Choral reading involves large or small groups of students reading the text in unison. There are many creative ways to implement choral reading. Students can read all or parts of the text in unison. As in the example of shared read aloud, the students can read more of the text together with the teacher each day until they are reading the whole text. Or they can use stories with repeated lines that they could read together such as Dr. Seuss's *Green Eggs and Ham* or fairy tales such as *The Gingerbread Man*. Students can be divided into different groups who then read different sections of the text in unison. Poetry and tongue twisters lend themselves well to choral reading activities. Choral reading can also be integrated into music through the use of songs as text. Movement can be built into choral reading activities to help students with meaning and interpretation.

Choral reading can be integrated into content areas and used with adolescent learners. Any text has the potential to be used for choral reading. A colleague, Kaia Tollefson, demonstrated an activity that involved reading a poem or narrative with the text visible so that the students could read along. The students then pick a line of text that they related to or liked, and the class rereads the text, with each student reading his or her line of text when he or she chooses. This results in a spontaneous, novel reading of the poem or narrative that does not follow the original order. It is important to choose a text that challenges the students to think or is a topic of current interest (e.g., racism). This is a creative way for teachers to get students involved in the shared reading. This activity is easily adapted for students with very diverse abilities. One student may *read* the text from their assistive technology device, another student may memorize a line, another student may sign a line, and another student may use Braille. With a little preparation ahead of time, every student can participate.

Another modification of choral reading is echo reading (Allington, 2006). Using this method, the teacher reads a portion of text, and then the students reread the same portion of text imitating the phrasing and expression. All types of choral reading can be done with small or large groups.

Peer or Paired Reading   Shared reading can occur with and without the teacher. Paired reading was developed by Topping (1987) as a way for parents to help their children with reading. Topping (1989) and others subsequently adapted the method for use with other pairs including teacher or other educator and student. Paired reading is a great way to actively engage all students in reading by having them read together as pairs. Paired reading can be more formal using a Preview-Pause-Prompt-Praise strategy as described by Allington (2006):

1. *Preview.* The peer tutor looks at the title and book cover with the tutee and they discuss what they think the book is about.

2. *Pause.* The pair begin reading the text together until the tutee feels comfortable reading alone. If the tutee misreads a word, the tutor will pause to allow the student to self-correct.

3. *Prompt.* If the tutee does not self-correct, the tutor will use prompting strategies to help the tutee read the word correctly. If the tutee needs help, the tutor will start reading with the tutee again until he or she indicates an ability to read alone again.

4. *Praise.* If the student self-corrects or gets the word correct after prompting, the tutor will praise the tutee. At the end of the reading, the tutor will praise the tutee for the good aspects of his or her reading performance.

Rasinski (2003) recommended that teachers document paired reading sessions whether they occur with parents, teachers, or peers by keeping track of the book read, the number of minutes read, and any other relevant comments.

Paired reading can also be less formal (Reutzel & Cooter, 2003). Students can choose their own text and work in pairs of similar ability. Pairs must be able to work well together and be willing to help each other. In this paired reading, the students read the text together for mutual support.

Peer reading can also occur between students of very different abilities and ages. The more proficient reader reads with the less proficient reader, providing a fluent reading model. The more proficient peer can support the less proficient reader as he or she attempts to read the text independently. Ideally, all students should have the opportunity to tutor less proficient readers. A student with significant disabilities may be able to be a peer tutor for a younger student. A less proficient reader may be able to be a peer tutor for a student with severe disabilities. Allington (2006) pointed out that by encouraging older students who are struggling readers to tutor younger students (or students with significant disabilities), they can read books at a grade level at which they are proficient without being embarrassed that they are reading *baby* books.

These forms of shared reading create opportunities for all students, including those with severe disabilities, to participate in reading instruction. They also are flexible and can be adapted to any age level and content area.

Repeated Reading   The National Reading Panel (2000) identified repeated reading as the major research-based strategy demonstrated to improve reading fluency. Research indicates that when students with severe reading difficulties reread a passage, they improve their reading fluency not only with the practiced passage but also with other passages of equal or greater difficulty (Samuels, 1979). Students with moderate or severe disabilities often need more repetition than students without disabilities in order to master and retain skills (Ryndak & Alper, 2003). The challenge for teachers is making repeated reading of text motivating and meaningful for students.

Allington (2006) recommended that students reread text to reach a target reading rate. One strategy Allington described to achieve this is Tape, Time, Chart. Materials needed are a stopwatch and a passage of text at the student's reading-proficient level (96%–100% accuracy). The student times and records how long it takes for each rereading of the passage and aims for a reading rate based on grade level standards (see Figure 5.2). This technique can be individualized for students with moderate or severe disabilities. The teacher can establish a standard based on the baseline reading rate of the individual student rather than the grade level standard. The teacher can then set a target based on a percentage improvement; for example, if the student can read 30 WCPM, an increase of 10% would result in a target of 33 WCPM. We recommend having the students record their own progress so they can visually see their improvement. The teacher can also keep a record of the students' reading rates using a simple recording form such as presented in Figure 5.3.

A modification of this technique is Skip and Drill (Carlene Van Etten, Personal Communication, 1983). To use this technique, choose a basal reader that is at the reading-proficient level of the student. Divide the basal reader into four parts. Determine a baseline reading rate from a 1-minute probe or a 100–200-word passage from the beginning of the basal reader. Set a target of a set % or number of words above baseline. Let the student practice reading a passage from the first quarter of the basal. When the student indicates that he or she is ready, time and chart the reading rate. When the student reaches the target rate, he or she gets to skip the rest of the first quarter of the basal and move to the second quarter. This procedure is highly motivating for students who feel successful as they rapidly move through the basal reader.

Repeated Reading Through Performance   Designing instruction that involves some type of performance provides many students with the motivation and purpose they need to reread text. Performance provides an authentic task for students to demonstrate their learning.

Readers' theater is a way to integrate performance into the classroom without the substantial demands of staging a formal play. In readers' theater, students perform using a script, but they do not have to memorize lines, build sets, or wear costumes. Scripts can be found at libraries, web sites, or commercial script sources. Scripts can be created by the teacher and/or students from books and poetry or in content areas such as science, math, and social studies. (Fisher & Frey, 2003; Rasinski, 2003). Or teachers can develop scripts with their students, modeling how to adapt a book for readers' theater. Allington (2006) recommended starting with a simple story that is familiar to students (e.g., a fairy tale). Once the script is developed, students need to have some time to practice their parts, which can be done in a day or across a week. Students with moderate or severe disabilities can participate in readers' theater with support and preparation. Students with sensory, physical, or speech and language disabilities may need adapted materials and assistive technology to access the text and participate in the performance. Remember the principle of partial participation from Chapter 10: If some students cannot participate in readers' theater independently, what support do they need to participate wholly or partially?

Puppet shows can provide another way to integrate performance into the classroom and provide an authentic reason for students to reread text. Puppet theater can follow the same format as readers' theater except that the students make simple puppets out of everyday materials such as socks, popsicle sticks, paper plates, and paper bags. The teacher and students write and practice the script as with readers' theater but perform it using the puppets.

Poetry readings are another way to encourage students to reread text. Poetry can include tongue twisters that provide a fun challenge to students. To read the poetry or tongue twister for the class, the students will need to practice. Poetry can be found at such varied levels that all students should be able to participate with support. Some teachers create Poetry Coffeehouse or Poetry Slam events, complete with refreshments, for the students to perform for their classmates, parents, and other school personnel (Rasinski, 2003).

Independent Reading   Providing time in school for independent reading is correlated with increased reading fluency (Allington, 2006; National Reading Panel, 2000). Although a causal connection has not been established, the assumption is that increasing the opportunities a student has to practice reading improves reading fluency. Many classrooms implement a period of Silent Sustained Reading (SSR) every day. While some students with moderate or severe disabilities will be able to participate in SSR in the same way as other students, technology can be used to provide support for independent reading for students who need assistance. Cassette recorders, CDs, TVs with closed captioning, assistive technology devices, and computers can provide access to written and spoken text. These technologies can support students with moderate or severe disabilities so that they can work independently in the general education classroom.

SUMMARY

This chapter discussed the importance of reading fluency instruction for all students. Lack of participation in reading fluency instruction may be the result of the presumption of incompetence for students with moderate or severe disabilities. Physical, sensory, speech, and language challenges may lead teachers to assume that reading fluency is not an appropriate area for instruction for students with severe disabilities. Ironically, the lack of participation and exposure to reading fluency instruction may increase the presumed incompetence of students with severe disabilities and consequently deny them instruction in this critical area of literacy. Reading fluency is closely related to oral language development, word recognition, vocabulary, and reading comprehension.

The chapter described strategies to assess reading fluency and instructional methods that could be modified for use with students who have significant disabilities. These methods provide an exciting opportunity to engage students with moderate or severe disabilities meaningfully in the general education curriculum. Reading fluency activities lend themselves well to differentiation and modification making them accessible to all students, regardless of reading level or disability. The methods used in this chapter are accessible to all teachers because they do not depend on expensive programs or materials or require additional professional development. The activities offered in this chapter are not intended to be prescriptions, but rather a catalyst for teachers to create engaging brain-friendly instruction to increase the reading fluency and related literacy skills for *all* students.

Chapter 6

Reading Comprehension

Susan R. Copeland

T he primary goal of learning to read is to make meaning out of text; that is, comprehending what you've read. Students with moderate or severe disabilities often struggle with this aspect of reading due to a number of factors. Too often, reading instruction for this group of students has focused on recognition of single words with little instruction devoted to reading and comprehending connected text. Limited exposure to connected text, in addition to underlying language and cognitive difficulties experienced by most of these students, make reading comprehension more difficult for them than for their typically developing peers. They may also have less experiential knowledge to apply when reading text because they have had fewer life experiences. For example, if all or most of their education has taken place within segregated settings, they may not have had an opportunity to participate in many of the typical academic and social experiences of their peers both in and out of school settings. This restricts the background knowledge they can use when trying to make meaningful connections between stories or educational materials they are reading and their prior knowledge and experience. Historically, teachers have had low expectations of these students' literacy abilities, and this may have resulted in the students being given significantly less exposure to important content knowledge and concepts and less experience working with various types of texts (e.g., narrative versus expository). All of these factors combine to contribute to difficulties in successfully comprehending reading material.

COMPONENTS OF READING COMPREHENSION

Successful comprehension of connected text involves active and simultaneous application of several component skills. First, the reader must recognize and understand the meaning of the individual words in the text. This involves either fluently decoding unfamiliar words and/or automatically (by sight) recognizing the words, and it requires accessing word meaning, necessitating a sufficiently well-developed listening and reading vocabulary. At the same time, the reader must activate any prior knowledge about the topic of the passage (i.e., relevant background knowledge) and knowledge of text structure and apply these to the text to facilitate comprehension. Frequently, readers must also use inference to fully understand the meaning of a passage. Finally, readers must constantly monitor their understanding as they read, adjusting that understanding as they notice something that doesn't make sense.

Given the multitude of skills necessary for successful reading comprehension, it is easy to see that the process can break down in several ways. It is also apparent that there is seldom a single cause of reading comprehension problems. Some of the most likely difficulties students may experience are underlying language impairments (e.g., difficulties with listening comprehension, semantics, vocabulary, grammar) that interfere with understanding, problems integrating incoming information with prior knowledge, poor (nonfluent) decoding skills, limited automatic word recognition, attentional problems that interfere with monitoring comprehension, limited knowledge of text structures, poor short-term (working) memory, and restricted experiential (background) knowledge (Erickson, 2003; Iacono, 2004; Kabrich & McCutchen, 1996; Morgan, Moni, & Jobling, 2004; O'Connor & Klein, 2004). Readers with significant physical challenges such as students with cerebral palsy may also experience eye movement problems that make scanning connected text difficult (Erickson, 2003). It is also important to remember that students who do not use speech may be limited in how they demonstrate comprehension. They may actually comprehend the text they've read but have very limited means to express their understanding, making it appear that they lack comprehension skills. Teachers' low expectations of students' abilities and/or a lack of appropriate technology to support communication can both contribute to this problem.

Rarely do students experience only one of the above challenges when trying to develop effective reading comprehension skills. More often, multiple problems affect students' success in comprehending what they read. Effective instruction generally must include intervention along several fronts—for example, working on underlying language difficulties *and* teaching specific strategies to facilitate comprehension.

As with other aspects of literacy development, there have been relatively few research studies examining instructional approaches targeting reading comprehension for students with moderate or severe disabilities such as those with cognitive disabilities or autism (Morgan et al., 2004; O'Connor & Klein, 2004). Fortunately, research examining reading comprehension instruction for students with other types of disabilities (e.g., learning disabilities) provides numerous instructional practices educators can use to teach and support the reading comprehension of students with moderate and severe disabilities. The remainder of the chapter will provide examples of these assessment and instructional strategies.

ASSESSING AND TEACHING READING COMPREHENSION SKILLS

Assessment is the first step in designing effective reading comprehension instruction. It is critical that teachers have a clear understanding of their students' reading comprehension skills before designing instruction. This includes knowing which (if any) strategies their students are trying to apply to comprehend text. Only after learning where their students' strengths and limitations are with regard to comprehending what they read can teachers design effective instruction.

Reading Comprehension Assessment

When assessing reading comprehension, educators can use standardized instruments, informal reading inventories, or classroom-based assessments that utilize reading material students are actually working with in class. It is most helpful to use several different types of assessment tasks. Doing so allows the practitioner to get a more complete picture of a student's current reading comprehension abilities and to more closely pinpoint areas of need (Carlisle & Rice, 2004). As mentioned earlier, it is rare for students to have just one problem area that affects their reading comprehension. The more information collected about students' reading comprehension skills, the more likely it is that the teacher will develop an effective, comprehensive instructional plan to improve their ability to read for meaning.

Running Records   If the student has sufficient skill to read a short passage, even at a very low reading level, then a simple running record can provide much useful information about reading comprehension. A running record assessment requires that a student reads aloud a short passage at his or her instructional reading level while the teacher notes any errors, substitutions, or self-corrections. This type of assessment allows the teacher to determine the kinds of decoding errors a student is making that may be interfering with comprehension as well as directly assessing the student's understanding of the text. After the student completes the reading, the passage is put away and the teacher asks the student comprehension questions about the passage or asks the student to retell the passage. The teacher can score the retelling by counting the number of content words the student uses or by counting the number and type of ideas in the student's retelling. The retelling could also be evaluated to see if it included the correct sequence of events, important information about characters, main ideas, key details, or evidence of inference, depending on the type of text that was read. Running records also have the advantage of being completed quickly—usually in 5 to 10 minutes—and requiring no special materials, making them something that can be easily repeated at regular intervals to monitor student progress.

Maze and Cloze Assessments   Another common assessment task utilizes a maze to examine a student's reading comprehension skills. A short passage is given to the student (again, at his or her reading level) with a word removed at regular intervals (e.g., every fifth word) and three words inserted from which the student can choose to complete each sentence. For example:

> *Jim went to the fair. He had to go through a big (car/gate/door) to get into the fair.*
> *Jim ate lots of good (food/mud/it) at the fair.*
> *He rode a Ferris wheel at the (dance/zoo/fair).*

Maze assessments may be timed if the teacher thinks this would be useful and can be scored by measuring the number of correct words selected. Cloze tasks are similar to maze tasks (i.e., the student is given a passage with a certain number of words omitted at regular intervals), but the passage does not include word choices from which to fill in the blanks. Instead, the student is asked to insert a word into each blank that he or she thinks would make sense. Cloze assessments are more difficult than mazes and would not be an effective measure for students with very low reading skills.

Picture Cards   Using picture cards as a part of reading comprehension assessment lessens the load placed on a student's expressive and receptive language. This can be especially important when assessing students with less well-developed language skills and those who do not use speech. The picture cards allow students to demonstrate their understanding of the meaning of a text even when they cannot express their ideas completely using speech. Picture cards also act as memory support. As mentioned elsewhere, many students with more significant disabilities have difficulty holding information in working memory. The picture cards can cue their memory of information they read, allowing them to demonstrate their understanding.

Picture cards can be used in several ways to allow students to demonstrate understanding of a reading passage. For example, the student can read a sentence or short passage and select from a group of pictures the one that best represents the main idea of the text or that best illustrates answers to comprehension questions that the teacher asks. If the student's knowledge of narrative is being assessed, he or she can be given a set of cards illustrating key events from the story and asked to put them in the order in which they took place. To assess prediction skills, the student might be asked to read a portion of a passage and then be given a selection of pictures. The teacher asks, "What do you think will happen next?," and the student selects the picture that best represents his or her prediction. The student can supplement picture selection with an explanation of why that prediction was made. Or, the student might be asked to draw his or her own pictures to retell the passage that was read.

The disadvantage of using picture cards as a part of assessment is that they are not as helpful in evaluating comprehension of more abstract ideas contained in the text that cannot be easily illustrated pictorially. Using picture cards may also require extensive preparation of materials prior to the assessment. These disadvantages may be outweighed, however, because use of pictures allows the teacher to obtain more detailed information on the student's understanding of text that might be lost using a more traditional comprehension assessment.

Multiple Choice Answers   A related assessment of comprehension is to provide students with multiple written choices from which to select an answer for comprehension questions about a selection. The multiple choice format provides some support for students with memory challenges while still assessing their understanding of what was read. For students who do not speak, possible answers can be affixed to an eye-gaze board or preprogrammed into the student's AAC device.

Acting Out Answers   Another way of assessing comprehension that decreases the load on expressive language is to ask students to act out the meaning of a sentence or piece of connected text. For example, a student can be asked to read the following sentence and then demonstrate to the teacher what it means: "Put the red ball in the blue box." This can be especially helpful in assessing reading comprehension of learners who are just beginning to read connected text and do not yet have sufficient skill to read a passage consisting of several sentences. This assessment task is easily incorporated into a game-like format, making it more motivating to students than traditional testing materials. See Figure 6.1 for an example of this.

Melanie Brawley, an elementary special education teacher, found a motivating and creative way to assess the reading comprehension of her young students with autism and give them opportunities to practice these skills. She placed individual sentences from a simple story on a series of cards. Melanie and her students then took turns drawing a card and role playing the sentences on the card. The sentences incorporated silly or unexpected actions such as "I put the hat on the dog." Students had to check the accuracy of each person's role play of the targeted sentence, in addition to reading and responding to their own sentences.

Figure 6.1.   Example of using active student participation to enhance and assess comprehension.

Reading Comprehension Instruction

As noted in the first section of this chapter, many factors affect an individual's ability to understand the meaning of text. Designing effective comprehension instruction requires teachers to carefully consider student assessment information and create an individualized, multifaceted intervention approach that addresses not only specific comprehension instruction but also other areas affecting comprehension. For example, if a student has limited decoding skills, reading comprehension is probably going to be affected because the student is putting so much effort and attention on decoding that he or she is not able to devote attention to understanding what is being read. One component of instruction for such a student would necessarily include explicit instruction in decoding skills. If language and vocabulary skills are weak, then an effective instructional plan would target these areas, in addition to specific comprehension instruction. It is easy to see, then, that successful reading comprehension instruction not only teaches specific comprehension strategies but also includes intervention in related areas that affect a student's ability to comprehend what is read. Since areas related to reading comprehension such as word recognition and language are addressed in other chapters in this book, the next section will focus specifically on strategies for comprehension instruction.

Before moving on, however, there are two other important points to consider when designing instruction. The first is the student's current reading level. Comprehension instruction is critical, even for students who are able to read only very short connected text. If the student has had little experience with comprehension instruction or seems to have extreme difficulty comprehending what is read, begin instruction using only a short sentence (two or three words) and gradually build to longer sentences or to several sentences within a passage as the student gains skill and confidence. Using even one short sentence at a time offers numerous possibilities for a student to develop comprehension skills. The teacher can, for example, use question words to facilitate comprehension development, as described below. Ask the student to role-play the sentence (as Ms. Brawley's class did) or draw a picture illustrating the sentence. Give the student a cut-apart sentence and ask him or her to reassemble it so that it makes sense. The main point to keep in mind is that reading comprehension should be a part of every lesson, no matter whether the student is working at the single word level or reading chapter books.

A second important point is to carefully consider the students' interests and select texts for instruction that relate to these interests. It is crucial for students to understand that reading is meaningful and enjoyable, not merely an exercise in solving a puzzle (i.e., decoding letter patterns). This won't happen if the reading material used is such that students can't relate to it, or if reading material on new topics is introduced in a way that prevents students from relating new information to their previous experiences.

It is up to practitioners to help students make the connections between what they are reading and their own experiences. One way to ensure that this occurs is to spend time finding out what students are interested in and then to locate numerous reading materials of various types and on various reading levels based on these topics. Materials should include both fiction (narrative) and nonfiction (expository) so that students can learn how to work with both types of text structures. Teachers can also use digital images to create personal books for students about family, friends, and hobbies. Figure 6.2 illustrates how one high school teacher used student interests to develop the reading comprehension skills of her students with moderate or severe disabilities.

Planning Instruction   When planning reading comprehension instruction, it is helpful to think about teaching strategies to use *before*, *during*, and *after* reading. Competent readers automatically do several things at each of these points in the reading process that help them make sense of what they read. Research on students struggling with comprehension supports teaching students specific things to do at each point in the reading process that will facilitate their understanding of what they are reading (Dowhower, 1999; Ehren, Lenz, & Deshler, 2004; Pressley, Symons, Snyder, & Cariglia-Bull, 1989; Vaughn & Klingner, 2004). The following sections include several strategies that students can use at each point in the reading process to improve comprehension.

MaryAnna Palmer, a local high school special education teacher, had a dilemma. Her students were in their late teens, but many of them had reading skills at or below the first-grade level. As she looked around her classroom, she realized that although the reading programs she used were appropriate for her students' current reading (word recognition) abilities, the stories and other texts that these programs used were not interesting to or age appropriate for these young men and women. Even though her students had very low reading skills, their interests were the same as their typically developing peers. No wonder they weren't engaged and excited during reading instruction!

MaryAnna decided to create stories and other materials that the students in her class could relate to. She thought carefully about each student. What did he or she enjoy doing? What did the students talk about? What kinds of reading materials did they gravitate to when given a choice? This led to the creation of multiple individualized books, each based on a student's particular interests. A book for one young man was based on wrestling, his current passion. The book contained simple text about famous wrestlers and used pictures the student and Mary-Anna had found in magazines and on the Internet. Another student's book was a story about himself and his girlfriend. It contained photographs of the student and his girlfriend participating in various activities on the high school campus. One of the girls in the class was an avid fan of a popular female rock star who was about her own age. Her individualized book was made up of pictures and text about the star's current music hits, clothes, makeup, and boyfriends.

These books were a tremendous hit with MaryAnna's students. Because they were based on topics that the students were passionate about, their motivation to read and understand them was very high. In creating the books with MaryAnna, they gained much valuable information about literacy, including the idea that reading could be fun and meaningful.

Figure 6.2.   Example of creating individualized books using images and simple text.

Before Reading

Skilled readers do several things before reading a story or expository (information) passage that assist their comprehension of the text. These include thinking about their goal for reading the selection (setting a purpose), thinking about any previous knowledge or experience they may have that relates to the passage (activating prior knowledge), and thinking about what might happen in the story or what the passage might be about (prediction). Readers with moderate or severe disabilities or other students struggling with comprehension don't do these things routinely and will likely need to be taught specific strategies to accomplish each of these actions.

Set a Purpose for Reading   One of the first things students can do to improve their comprehension is learn to set a goal or purpose for reading. For example, ask yourself why you are reading this book. What is it you want to know or find out by reading? Is it just for fun, or do you want to discover some specific information about something, such as how to more effectively teach comprehension strategies to students with moderate or severe disabilities? Chances are you deliberately selected this text for a specific reason—a reason that you constantly reflect on as you read through each chapter in the book and one that guides your understanding of the information you find as you read.

While it may seem obvious to you, a skilled reader, that reading is done with a specific purpose in mind, poor readers often don't realize why they are being asked to read a passage or how doing so might be helpful to them. As a consequence, they don't focus on critical information in the text that will lead to understanding what they have read. At the end of a reading, they may have successfully decoded the words but can't express the key ideas or concepts contained in the reading selection. These students need explicit instruction in determining what the purpose of a particular reading activity is and how that purpose can be useful to them.

Modeling the process of setting a goal through a think-aloud is an effective way to teach setting a purpose for reading. Deciding the reason for reading prior to actually reading a passage helps students activate any prior knowledge about that purpose and alerts them to key information or ideas within the text that will aid their understanding of the passage.

To get started, the teacher and students discuss possible reasons for reading different kinds of texts. The teacher then selects a particular type of text and thinks out loud about why she is reading that selection. She models for the students the kinds of self-talk to use to set a goal for the reading. For example, given a set of directions to the store, the teacher might say, "I need to go to the store to buy my groceries. The words tell me how to get to the store. I need to pay attention to the names of the streets as I read and the way I should turn on each street. That way I won't get lost. Reading this carefully will help me walk to the store by myself." After modeling a discussion, the teacher asks the students to practice self-talk before reading a similar type of passage, coaching them as they practice the process.

To be most effective, the purpose set for a reading should be explicitly linked to a follow-up activity done after the students complete their reading. An example of a follow-up activity for the illustration above might be to provide the students with a set of directions to a mystery location in the school. The students read and follow the directions to find the mystery site where they find a surprise such as bag of goodies to share with the class. The activity (finding a mystery site) is clearly linked to the purpose set for reading (following directions). It requires the active involvement of students in an enjoyable and meaningful way that helps them understand the usefulness of setting a purpose for reading.

It is important to repeat the think-aloud activity frequently with students, using different kinds of texts on topics that students will find interesting and relevant to their lives. These could include stories (e.g., narrative texts), content texts (e.g., social studies text), sets of directions (e.g., recipes), or informational texts (e.g., television guide, newspaper). Experience with many different types of texts helps students understand that reading can be done for numerous, important reasons.

Becoming familiar with the structural organization of different kinds of texts also facilitates comprehension. I saw this vividly illustrated when conducting a research project in a local high school. The students with moderate and severe disabilities in our project had received most of their education within segregated self-contained classrooms that focused primarily on functional academics and life skills. They were now taking some general education courses in elective and content areas. It quickly became clear that these students had very little experience working with textbooks and were unfamiliar with the typical organizational structures used in these types of books. This made it difficult for them to successfully complete the usual assignments given by their teachers such as answering chapter review questions. While most of their classmates used headings, diagrams, and other characteristic text structures to locate information, these students flipped randomly through chapters trying to locate needed information. Part of our intervention then became teaching them to locate some key structures such as headings and bolded vocabulary words to improve their participation in and understanding of the class assignments. Another simple support for students is using Post-It notes to mark key locations in the text.

Preteach New Vocabulary and Concepts

Preteaching is another effective strategy to apply before reading a piece of text. Teachers can preteach text-specific vocabulary that students must know to fully understand a reading selection. Preteaching can take place during individual or small-group instruction sessions prior to attending a general education class, or can be done within the classroom before work begins on a new text.

There are many ways to teach vocabulary (see Chapter 5 for a more thorough discussion). Use of a Word Wall, for example, is a common and effective strategy. Students learn meanings of words they will encounter in a new reading selection through a variety of activities. They write these words on large cards or strips of chart paper, adding a drawing, picture, or other graphic that illustrates the word's meaning. These cards are displayed on the Word Wall. The teacher refers to the words frequently as students work on the new text, using games such as Vocabulary Jeopardy to continually refresh students' memories of word meanings. Students can also put these words and their illustrations on small cards that are placed on a metal ring (Fisher & Frey, 2003). The ring of words becomes an individual and portable dictionary of words to which students can refer as needed when they are reading the assigned text.

Activate Prior Knowledge and Prediction   Activating students' prior knowledge relevant to a reading passage and teaching them to predict what the selected passage may be about are two other key components in skilled reading comprehension that take place before reading a selection. One effective approach for readers with cognitive or severe disabilities is to use question words that help the students remember information or experiences they have had that relate to the topic of the readings. After working with question words, students record their predictions about the passage using some type of graphic organizer (e.g., Morgan et al., 2004; Nation & Norbury, 2005).

To begin a question word activity, the teacher first introduces students to the question words *who, where, when, what,* and *why.* They discuss the meaning of these words and give examples of questions using the words. Teacher and students next preview the text to be read, looking at the title and the first few sentences and any pictures or graphics that might be included. After previewing, they make predictions about what the topic of the passage might be. The teacher uses the question words the students worked with previously to help them make predictions: "*Who* do you think the story is about?" "*Where* do you go to buy a fishing license?" "*What* do you think will happen in the story?" "*Why* do you think the story will be about a dog?" The students' predictions are listed on one side of a white board or piece of chart paper (see Figure 6.3). The teacher also uses the question words to activate any prior experiences the students may have that are relevant to the predicted topic, getting them ready to do the actual reading. For example, Morgan et al. (2004) described a student reading a story about fishing who was asked questions such as "What might you do at a lake?" to get the student thinking about activities and experiences associated with lakes that might help him better understand the story.

One helpful strategy to use with the question word activity in general education classrooms is to give students with significant disabilities the questions prior to beginning the activity. Many of these students need extended time to process the questions, decide on a response, and communicate that response. During group activities with their typically developing peers, the students may not have sufficient time to think through the questions and formulate a response before someone else jumps in with an answer. Working with students who need extended time prior to the activity allows them to have an answer ready when they are called on during the group activity. This increases their active, meaningful participation in the literacy activity and fosters social interaction with classmates. For example, a student who uses an AAC device can think of a response and have it programmed into his or her device. When she or he is called on in the group activity, the response is ready to transmit.

After the students have finished making and recording predictions about the text and discussing relevant prior experiences, they read the passage. The teacher then leads the discussion back to the students' initial predictions, and the students go back to the actual text to verify if their predictions were correct. They find story details in the text and record these on the right side of the chart paper (see Figure 6.3). They then compare and contrast their initial predictions with the actual details from the text.

As students become more proficient in using question words and making predictions, the strategy can be applied to longer texts. A longer story, for example, can be broken into smaller units or sections. Students can predict/ques-

| The Dog Show ||
Prediction (guess)	Story details
a dog	dog named Tag
bathing a dog	Jon took Tag to the dog show.
a boy	Jon gave Tag a bath.
a dog show	Tag ran away.
driving in the car	Tag rolled in the dirt.

Figure 6.3.   Example of questioning/prediction activity.

tion about one section, read that section to verify their predictions and adjust them, and then apply the process to the next section, and so on until the entire story or reading passage has been processed. Students can work as a whole group or can break into small groups or pairs to complete these activities.

A variation of the questioning/predicting process is to utilize a Directed-Listening-Thinking Activity (DL–TA) with texts that are read aloud by the teacher (Gunning, 2002a). (Components of a DL–TA actually take place before, during, *and* after reading, but for ease of organization, I will discuss it in this section.) In this activity, the teacher begins by previewing the title, headings, pictures, and other important text structures of a reading selection with a group of students. The group discusses their ideas about what the reading selection may be about based on their review of this information. Their predictions are recorded in a graphic organizer on the board or on a chart.

The teacher then reviews the purpose for reading (i.e., to verify the group's predictions) and begins to read the text. She stops at logical points to have the students summarize the information or story line contained in the selection thus far, ask questions about the material, discuss the plot or any information they have gained, and modify their predictions based on what they've heard. The graphic organizer is used to record these modified predictions as the students work through the selection. The teacher continues the process until the book or reading selection is completed. After the teacher finishes reading, the students engage in a final discussion of the book, describing how their predictions changed along the way and any connections they made between what the text says and their own experiences, and clarifying any confusing concepts about which they may still have questions. The teacher may then have the group dictate a summary of the reading selection that is recorded on the chart or board for the students to copy into their learning logs (Gunning, 2002a).

A DL–TA allows teachers and students another opportunity to think aloud about strategies they are using to understand a text. It offers teachers insight into approaches students are using to try and make meaning of a text. The activity provides models for students of effective questions to ask as they read or as they listen to text, key text structures to focus on to gain meaning, and instruction on how to use actual details from a text to modify their understanding as they read.

The structure of a DL–TA also encourages all students to participate. Since predictions are just that, predictions, there are no right or wrong answers. Even predictions that are not ultimately supported by the text offer opportunities to learn how to verify predictions by getting information from the text. This characteristic reduces anxiety that the students may have about giving a wrong answer in front of their peers. Predictions may also be very simple ideas or very complex ones. This, too, allows students who are at different skill levels to meaningfully participate in a group literacy activity.

Because in a DL–TA the teacher reads aloud instead of the students, this type of literacy instruction allows use of texts that may be highly interesting to students but above their current reading (word recognition) abilities. Using higher-level materials can be very motivating to students. Higher-level texts help students develop a more sophisticated understanding of concepts and ideas than they would gain from a text written on their independent reading level.

During Reading

Reading comprehension, as we have seen, is an active process. Skilled readers constantly monitor their comprehension of a passage as they read and go back to reread and repair any breakdowns in understanding. Students with moderate or severe disabilities may not know to engage in this self-monitoring behavior and benefit greatly from strategies that teach them to do this. For example, one difficulty students with poor comprehension often face is not understanding to whom pronouns refer within a reading passage. They are not clear about the referent for pronouns, but rather than go back and clarify this relationship, they continue reading. Confusion about the correct referents can easily break down their comprehension of events within the passage they read.

Anaphoric Cuing   Anaphoric cuing (O'Connor & Klein, 2004) is a strategy that can be used to remind students to monitor their comprehension and to go back and reread to clarify any breakdowns in their understanding. In teaching anaphoric cuing, the teacher gives the students a passage of text in which the pronouns are underlined. Under each underlined pronoun, a list of three possible referents is listed: one that is not appropriate; one that fits the sentence, but not the story; and one that fits both the sentence and the story. Students read the passage and mark the appropriate referent under each pronoun as they read. The list of possible referents seems to act as a kind of antecedent cue for students to go back and reread to clarify any misunderstandings about what they have read. This rereading helps them better understand the meaning of what they are reading (see Figure 6.4 for an example).

Cloze Exercises   Cloze exercises are another way in which students can work to improve comprehension skills. O'Connor & Klein (2004), for example, taught students with autism spectrum disorders to complete cloze exercises to improve their comprehension of short reading passages. In a cloze activity, the teacher gives students a short passage in which words at regular intervals (e.g., every fifth word) have been replaced with a blank. Students read the passage, inserting a word in each blank that would make sense in the given sentence. Students can complete the cloze either verbally when reading aloud or by writing a word in the blank if they are working independently. Completing a cloze activity successfully requires students to closely and continually monitor their under-

The bus driver walked to his bus. *He* opened the door and walked up the steps.

> police officer
> Juan
> bus driver

The bus's two-way radio made a loud noise. The driver picked *it* up. He said, "Hello. This is Mike. What do you need?"

> two-way radio
> key
> cup

The two-way radio operator said, "There is some road work on Main Street. *You* will need to leave soon or you will be late picking up the passengers."

> cab driver
> Mike
> Steve

Figure 6.4.   Example of anaphoric cuing.

standing of what they are reading. It also requires students to use any relevant background knowledge or experience they have and to use their knowledge of language (e.g., vocabulary, syntax, grammar) to select words. After students have completed the exercise, the teacher and students discuss the word choices the students made. The discussion allows students an opportunity to explain their word choices and receive feedback on why their word choices were or were not appropriate. It also provides an opportunity for instruction in language skills such as grammar or syntax.

The teacher can create cloze exercises to focus on particular types of words (e.g., content words such as nouns), depending on the focus of the lesson. He can vary the difficulty of the exercise by inserting more or fewer blanks and by controlling the length of the passage. Cloze exercises are not generally as effective for students with lower reading levels (below second or third grade; Gunning, 2002a). However, for less advanced readers, teachers can adapt a cloze exercise and turn it into a maze. The maze, as described earlier in the chapter, provides a list of three word choices for each blank within the reading passage. This adaptation provides support to students with word-finding problems and eliminates problems students may have with spelling words. Moreover, changing a cloze activity to a maze makes the activity more accessible for students who do not use speech, because these students can point or use eye gaze to select an answer for each blank.

After Reading

Effective comprehension instruction also includes activities students engage in after reading. These activities may take many forms but all facilitate students' understanding of what they've read and help them organize and synthesize new information. The following sections describe several types of after-reading instructional activities.

Story Mapping   Most narratives have similar structural components called story grammar elements. These include one or more characters, a setting, a problem the character(s) must solve, details of attempts to solve the problem, and a resolution of the problem. Narratives may also include a moral or theme.

Students struggling with comprehension are often unaware of story grammar components, and this lack of awareness negatively affects their understanding of what they have read. Research supports explicitly teaching story grammar to students with and without disabilities to improve reading comprehension (e.g., Gardill & Jitendra, 1999; Mathes & Fuchs, 1997). Teaching students to construct story maps is one way to assist them in learning to apply story grammar to facilitate comprehension. Story maps are visual representations of each grammar element of the story (see Figure 6.5). They help students identify and make connections between key elements of a story as well as cuing them to formulate questions to ask themselves as they read (Gardill & Jitendra).

Story mapping can be done individually, but working in cooperative, mixed-ability groups allows students to work with peers to expand and deepen their comprehension of a given text (Mathes & Fuchs, 1997). A small-group format is often more motivating to students than working individually and provides them with multiple models of how to think about and apply comprehension strategies. Mathes and Fuchs described an effective cooperative story mapping procedure they used to improve the comprehension of students with and without disabilities. Following is an adaptation of their procedures and recommendations.

The first step is to introduce and teach story grammar elements. The teacher selects a story with a clear story grammar structure to use for the initial teaching. Fairy tales or fables, for example, generally contain each element of story grammar. It is important to remember, however, to select age-appropriate materials when working with older learners. This can present difficulties because

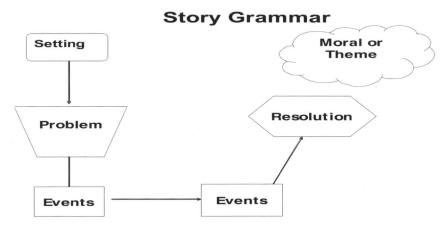

Figure 6.5.   Example of a story map.

many stories for older individuals are too complex for the initial learning of story grammar elements. However, even older readers enjoy some of the alternative versions of well-known fairy tales and fables available today (e.g., *The True Story of the Three Little Pigs*), so it is possible to use one of these simple, familiar stories in an age-appropriate manner as the initial teaching example.

After selecting an appropriate book, the teacher uses a shared reading activity to introduce students to the concept of story grammar. In shared reading, the teacher reads aloud to the students while they follow along using a copy of the text, or the teacher might project the text onto a screen so that all the students can see it. Before beginning to read, the teacher sets the purpose for reading. She explains that most stories have the same key components (story grammar) and that identifying these story elements helps readers better understand what is happening in the story. She instructs the students to be on the lookout for each story grammar component as they read along with her: main character, setting, problem, major events, resolution, and, possibly, a moral or theme.

After reading the story, the teacher and students use a story map to identify and record each story grammar element. This part of the lesson is highly interactive. The students must give their opinions about why they selected particular events as key story grammar components and then go back to the story to find the actual text that supports their opinions. Once students have had several opportunities to practice story mapping with the teacher, the teacher moves on to cooperative story mapping with small groups.

To begin cooperative story mapping, the teacher selects a story that has very clear story grammar elements and that is written at a level that most of the class can work with independently. The students read the story either independently or with a buddy. When engaging in buddy reading, each reader takes turns reading and summarizing sections of the text. They clarify questions each may have, provide support in decoding difficult words, and take turns predicting what will happen next in the story. (Please note that if the class includes students who are not conventional readers, a buddy or another adult can read the story to the student. This allows the student to participate in the story grammar group work and benefit from the group interaction, discussion, and modeling of comprehension strategies.)

On a following day, the students work in cooperative groups of four and quickly reread the assigned story. They are instructed to think as they read about the major elements of the story and where information about these elements is in the text. After rereading, the group members discuss each of the selection's important story elements. Mathes and Fuchs (1997) suggested that each group member take on the role of leader for one story element and one major event. Thus, one student is in charge of discussing the main character and an important event, another for the setting and an important event, another for the major problem and an important event, and the fourth student for the story resolution and an important event. (If the story has a moral or theme, another student role could be added for this element.) The students rotate jobs routinely so that they gain experience with all story elements.

Mathes and Fuchs (1997) recommended a five-step procedure to help leaders perform their roles. Leaders are responsible for

1. Telling: They tell their group the answer about the story element for which they are responsible and why they think this answer is correct.

2. Asking: They ask their group members what answers they came up with for this story element and to support their opinions using details from the text.

3. Discussing: They discuss the various answers with their group, trying to help them come to an agreement about the answer. If the group cannot reach a consensus, the leader's answer becomes the final answer.

4. Recording: They record their answer for that story element on a story map.

5. Reporting: They report to the whole class their group's answer for that story element.

In the final step in cooperative story mapping, all groups come back together for a whole-class discussion. The teacher asks one group to report on a story element (e.g., main character) and restates the group's answer and asks if other groups came up with a different answer. Any disagreements that arise are opportunities for additional discussion of how groups arrived at different answers that may also be correct (they must be able to support their answers by going back to the details in the story). Such discussions can deepen students' understanding of the story and how others can arrive at different conclusions, even when reading the same text. After all story grammar elements have been discussed, the teacher wraps up the lesson by summarizing the story grammar for the assigned story and reviewing why story grammar is helpful in improving understanding when reading a story.

A related story grammar strategy is *schema stories*. In this activity the teacher selects a story with clear sections; in other words, he chooses a story that has a clearly defined beginning, middle, and end. The teacher photocopies the story and cuts it into sections that contain at least one main idea. (Alternatively, the various sections can be written on large cards or sentence strips.)

The teacher divides the students into small groups and gives a section of the selected story to each group. One student is chosen to read the section to the rest of the group. (If a group includes a student who uses an AAC device, the teacher might preprogram that student's device with the text section so that the student can be the group's reader.) After each group of students has read their section, the teacher asks which group thinks they may have the section of the story that comes at the beginning. Any group that responds must explain why they think they have the beginning section. The entire class listens and then discusses whether they agree or not with the group's reasoning. After they come to a consensus, the teacher takes the card or strip with that section of the story and displays it in a chart holder or attaches it to a blank wall. He then asks which group thinks they have the next section of the story. The process continues until the entire story has been reconstructed.

Story schema activities can also be done in pairs or can be adapted as literacy center activities (Reutzel & Cooter, 2003). In this format, the story is cut into sections and placed in an envelope. Students visiting the center read each piece and then assemble the pieces in the order they think is correct. After they're satisfied with the order they've selected, they look at a key that shows the correct order. For young students or those with physical challenges that make manipulation of story strips difficult, story sections can be laminated and Velcro attached to the backs of each strip. Pieces of Velcro are attached to a laminated file folder and the students affix the story pieces to the Velcro. This keeps the strips from sliding out of place if they are accidentally bumped.

Story Retellings   Another effective method of enhancing comprehension after reading is to have students engage in story retellings, which can be utilized in several ways. Colasent and Griffith (1998) described a project in which they successfully used a variation of story retelling to improve the comprehension skills of three students with autism and cognitive disabilities. In this approach, the authors initially provided information to the students about the theme the students would be studying over the next few days. They did this to activate the students' prior knowledge about the topics of stories they would be reading. For several days the authors read a series of three different stories about the same theme to their students. During each reading, the authors stopped to ask the students to predict what might happen next in the stories.

After reading each story, the authors asked the students to retell the story. They used an interview format to ask the students a series of questions to cue their memories of the stories. In this format, the students pretended to be interviewed by a radio station and responded to the authors' questions using a microphone. The authors also asked students to write and/or draw something about the stories they had heard.

After engaging in the interview and drawing activities, the students' scores on recalling correct story details improved. Opportunities to respond both orally and through writing and drawing increased student recall of key story information even more than the oral only opportunity. The authors saw improvements in the students' written language (e.g., longer written samples) and in their oral language (e.g., a reduction in echolalia) after the intervention. These findings suggest that this might be an effective strategy for other learners with autism or cognitive disabilities.

Readers' theater is another variation of story retelling to assist comprehension after reading. Narratives, poetry, or even picture books can be used as the basis for this activity. After reading a selection, students develop a script based on the reading that they will act out for others. Key ideas, dialogue, and events from the reading are incorporated into the script so that the meaning of the piece is clearly illustrated.

When performing the script during the readers' theater, participants can read directly from the script the group has developed, or they can act out roles that don't require verbalization but that illustrate important events or ideas from the selection. Because of its versatility, readers' theater is ideal for groups of students with mixed literacy abilities. It offers active involvement that facilitates comprehension for all students and offers opportunities to develop additional literacy skills such as fluency.

SUMMARY

Reading comprehension is a complex process that requires active participation by the reader. Although comprehension of written text can be challenging for learners with moderate or severe disabilities, there are many effective ways to build the comprehension skills of these individuals and help them to understand and enjoy the reading process. An important key to successful comprehension instruction is giving learners opportunities to work with a variety of texts within authentic literacy activities. Including typically developing peers in these activities can be especially helpful by providing models of successful application of comprehension strategies.

Chapter 7

Vocabulary Development

Elizabeth B. Keefe

Vocabulary development is often viewed as a subset of comprehension. However, research has demonstrated that vocabulary development plays a prominent role in the reading process in general, and this has prompted consideration of vocabulary development as a critical area of literacy instruction in its own right (Beck, McKeown, & Kucan, 2002; Fisher & Frey, 2003; National Reading Panel, 2000; Reutzel & Cooter, 2003).

THE IMPORTANCE OF VOCABULARY

We believe that vocabulary development is of great importance to students with moderate or severe disabilities. We also believe that best practices in vocabulary development for students without disabilities lend themselves particularly well to differentiation and modification for diverse learners. This chapter will discuss the various definitions and types of vocabulary, the assessment of vocabulary, and effective instructional approaches for improving the vocabulary development of all students.

Vocabulary Definitions

There are generally four types of vocabulary recognized in the literature. All of the types of vocabulary are related and all are important to the development of effective literacy skills for all students.

Listening Vocabulary   Listening vocabulary is the largest vocabulary. It includes the words an individual can hear and understand, although he or she may not be able to use the words in speech. This would include individuals who receive words through signing. Think of the infant who clearly understands many words before she or he is able to say or sign them. Many people learn a second language and are typically able to understand more vocabulary words than they are able to generate—even when they have not taken instruction in the language for many years. Listening vocabulary functions as an information receiver and is categorized as receptive vocabulary (Cooter & Flynt, 1996).

Speaking Vocabulary   Speaking vocabulary is considered an expressive vocabulary; its function is to produce vocabulary. This is typically the second largest vocabulary and includes all the words an individual can hear, understand, and use in speech. For students with sensory, physical, speech, and/or language impairments, this could also include words that the individual can understand and use in sign or through the use of alternative augmentative communication (AAC). For most students, the gap between listening and speaking vocabularies is greatest at younger ages, with the gap narrowing as the student reaches adulthood. However, the gap may not narrow for students with severe disabilities as they get older; in fact, the opposite may be true. Students with severe disabilities may understand more and more words, but because of sensory, physical, speech, and/or language impairments, they may still not able to express their knowledge of vocabulary though oral language. For these students, speaking vocabulary may be their smallest vocabulary.

Reading Vocabulary   This vocabulary consists of all the words a student can read and understand. For students with vision impairments, this includes reading and understanding through the use of Braille. Like listening vocabulary, reading vocabulary functions as an information receiver and is categorized as receptive vocabulary.

Writing Vocabulary   Writing vocabulary consists of all the words that a student can understand and reproduce when writing. It is typically the smallest of the four types and includes writing through the use of assistive technology devices and word processing. Writing is categorized as expressive vocabulary.

Note: For typically developing students, the four types of vocabulary described above are considered subsets of one another. Speaking vocabulary is a subset of listening vocabulary, reading vocabulary is a subset of speaking and listening vocabularies, and writing vocabulary is a subset of speaking, listening, and reading vocabularies. This hierarchical conception does not work for students with sensory, physical, speech, and/or language impairments. We must be careful not to deny access to instruction in reading and writing vocabularies because some individuals with moderate or severe disabilities cannot demonstrate their true knowledge and ability through speaking or signing vocabulary.

Vocabulary Assessment

Assessment of vocabulary is challenging for a number of reasons. Beck and colleagues noted that "What it means to know a word is clearly a complicated, multifaceted matter, and one that has serious implications for how words are taught and how word knowledge is measured" (2002, p. 11) and that "Knowing a word is not an all-or-nothing proposition" (p. 9). There are many ways in which to *know* a word. Dale D. Johnson (1965, cited in Beck et al., 2002, p. 9) conceptualized word knowledge as passing through the following four stages:

1.   Never saw it before.
2.   Heard it but doesn't know what it means.
3.   Recognize it in context as having something to do with _____.
4.   Know it well.

When assessing students with sensory, physical, speech, and/or language impairments the task of determining how well a student *knows* a word becomes even more challenging. Assessment can occur through formal and informal procedures.

Formal Testing   Gunning (2002a) noted that additional testing for vocabulary knowledge may not be necessary. Some indication of vocabulary knowledge may be gained from formal testing that has already been given. Students with disabilities have usually been given multiple tests to determine eligibility for special education services. Examples of formal assessments that might yield information about a student's vocabulary knowledge are

- Peabody Picture Vocabulary Test
- Vocabulary portions of IQ tests
- The Diagnostic Assessments of Reading with Trial Teaching Strategies (DARTTS; Riverside)
- The Stanford Reading Test (Harcourt)

It is important to remember that there are many reasons that students do not perform to their ability in a formal testing situation, so results should be used as just one source of information about vocabulary knowledge, not the sole source.

The most reliable and common form of assessing vocabulary knowledge is done through teacher observation and teacher-made assessments (Beck et al., 2002; National Reading Panel, 2000; Reutzel & Cooter, 2003). Teachers also may gain insight into vocabulary words that cause difficulty for a student through assessments carried out for word recognition and/or fluency as described in Chapters 4 and 5 of this book.

Teacher Observation   Teacher observation involves paying attention to the vocabulary words the students seem able to understand and use in the classroom and other school environments. Anecdotal records can be used to document these observations. Gunning (2002a) recommended recording anecdotal information on sticky notes, and then later transferring the information to the student's file or a notebook.

Teacher-Created Assessments   These can include checklists, quizzes, or tests that document the student's mastery of target vocabulary words. These words may apply to literacy instruction and/or content area. There are a number of word lists relating to beginning reading proficiency (e.g., Instant Words and Dolch Words) that can help teachers identify high-frequency reading vocabulary words. Environmental print is a great source of target vocabulary for young students and students with severe disabilities.

Target vocabulary words can also be selected from stories, poetry, newspapers, textbooks, and/or any other text-based curriculum material. The selection and assessment of target vocabulary words can be individualized for students of differing abilities. For example, Beck et al. (2002) recommended vocabulary words to target for many books (see Figure 7.1). We have added the fourth column to demonstrate how simpler words could be selected as appropriate for students with more severe disabilities. Teachers could select one or more of these words as vocabulary targets.

Content area textbooks often identify target vocabulary for teachers. For example, in *The American Nation* (Davidson, 2005), a textbook used in eight-grade social studies, key terms are identified for each section. Teachers can simplify these key terms or add other related vocabulary from the section that students with moderate or severe disabilities can learn (see Figure 7.2).

Book/author	Publisher	Vocabulary words	Alternate vocabulary words
Curious George Takes a Job By H.A. Rey	Houghton Mifflin	curious cozy mischief	big little yellow hat zoo bus monkey

Figure 7.1.   Target vocabulary words from a storybook. (From Beck, I.L., McKeown, M.G., & Kucan, L. [2002]. *Bringing words to life.* New York: Guilford Press.)

The principle of simplifying vocabulary can be applied to any grade level and any content area. Figure 7.3 shows the way in which a high school lecture in science can be modified for diverse learners.

Assessing Students with Moderate or Severe Disabilities   Ascertaining whether students with moderate or severe disabilities understand and can use vocabulary words may be difficult when students have physical, sensory, speech, and/or language challenges. Some students can use Braille, sign, AAC, or other assistive technology devices to demonstrate their knowledge. However, we are frequently faced with teachers who suspect that one of their students with severe disabilities is more capable than he or she has been given credit for using standardized testing. These teachers have to be very creative in figuring out how to individualize assessment for these students. For example, flashcards are a very common means of assessing vocabulary knowledge (Reutzel & Cooter, 2003). Usually the assessment involves demonstrating knowledge by saying the word. The following are some simple suggestions for assessing vocabulary for students with physical, sensory, speech, and/or language challenges:

- Ask the student to point, gesture, or eye gaze to indicate the target vocabulary word. You can ask the student to choose from a choice of two or more

Textbook/section	Publisher	Key terms	Alternate key terms
The American Nation Chapter 8, section 2	Prentice Hall	House of Representatives Senate bill electoral college appeal unconstitutional override impeach	president White House state country white house year two four six

Figure 7.2.   Target vocabulary words from a textbook.

Subject area/ grade level	Lecture topic	Target vocabulary	Alternate target vocabulary
life science ninth grade	Structure of the Earth	geology atmosphere hydrosphere lithosphere crust mantle asthenosphere outer core inner core	Earth core mantle crust sun moon inside outside air

Figure 7.3. Target vocabulary words from a lecture.

words. It is important to make sure you vary the position of the target word and the distracters. For example, some students may have limited mobility and it is easier for them to point, gesture, or gaze at a word using one side of their bodies.

- Give the student the definition of the target vocabulary word and ask him or her to identify the correct word from a choice of two or more, using pointing, gesturing, or eye gazing.

- Ask the student to physically match the target word to the definition.

- Ask the student to indicate yes or no when asked the definition of a vocabulary word or whether a vocabulary word is the correct choice in a sentence.

- Read a sentence with the target vocabulary word missing. Ask the student to select the appropriate word from a choice of two or more using pointing, gesturing, or eye gazing.

These are just some ideas of how you can assess the vocabulary knowledge of students with physical, sensory, speech, and/or language challenges. Don't ever give up! It often takes trial and error, along with creativity and persistence, to get an accurate picture of the true abilities and potential of students with moderate or severe disabilities. You will be rewarded for your efforts as students with moderate or severe disabilities finally get access to engaging literacy instruction.

Importance of Collaboration

The sections above on assessment demonstrate that teachers can identify various levels of vocabulary to assess the vocabulary knowledge of their students to create opportunities for active participation. It should be noted that these multi-level assessments should occur with the collaboration of a general education teacher, a special education teacher, related services personnel, paraprofessionals, and family members, as appropriate. In addition, the assessments included in this section are just examples. Students with severe disabilities often display unique combinations of characteristics that require creative thinking from the educational team. Our lack of knowledge should not create an additional barrier to literacy; it is our challenge is to make sure we find out what these students really know.

Effective Vocabulary Instruction

Vocabulary development is closely related to word recognition, reading fluency, and comprehension. As a result, many of the instructional strategies in Chapters 4, 5, and 6 can also be used to increase vocabulary development (e.g., Making Words, word families, word banks, word sorts, shared book experience, readers' theater, cloze exercises, DL–TA). Similarly, many of the strategies in this chapter designed to increase vocabulary will also assist in word recognition, comprehension, and reading fluency.

There are two major elements of vocabulary instruction: how to select appropriate words for instruction and how to teach these words. A general caution applies, however, to the choice of instructional goals for students with moderate or severe disabilities.

Research into Effective Vocabulary Instruction   Very little research has been done in the past two decades specifically on vocabulary development for students with moderate or severe disabilities apart from the research on word recognition strategies that were summarized in Chapter 4 of this book (See Figure 4.1). See Figure 7.4 for a summary of current available research into best practices specifically for vocabulary instruction.

Johnson (2001) made the following general recommendations based on his review of the research:

- Set aside time for reading in the classroom and increase reading volume.
- Use direct instruction.
- Use methods that involve active learning by the students.
- Provide opportunities for repetition and repeated exposure to targeted vocabulary words.
- Encourage students to develop their own strategies to learn vocabulary.

Avoid **Potato** *Goals*   The most consistent recommendation from the research into vocabulary instruction is that it should be active and engaging (see Figure 7.4). Unfortunately, students with physical, sensory, speech, and/or language disabilities present considerable challenges to teachers in this area. The extent of the disabilities can lead teachers to focus on the challenges rather than the possibilities. As a result, students with moderate or severe disabilities are often limited to passive participation in classrooms. Even worse, educators sometimes think it is okay for these students just to be present. This has been true in both segregated and inclusive settings and is an example of teachers having what we call *potato* goals for some of their students. The potato test is simple: If a *potato* can achieve a certain goal, then that should not be a student goal. For example, a potato can *sit* in class, but we should always be looking for active class participation from students. See Figure 7.5 for examples of common potato goals and examples of active student counterparts. Time and time again, we have seen students get so excited when they are able to finally actively show their

The National Reading Panel (2000) summarizes research into vocabulary instruction and recommends the following components:

1. Vocabulary taught both directly and indirectly.

2. Repetition and multiple exposures to vocabulary words.

3. Learning in rich contexts.

4. Active engagement in learning tasks.

5. Use of computer technology.

6. Effective assessment and evaluation.

7. Use of multiple instructional methods.

Figure 7.4. Summary of available research into vocabulary instruction. (From National Reading Panel [2000]. *Report of the National Reading Panel: Teaching Children to Read. Report of the Subgroups.* Washington, DC: National Institute of Child Health and Human Development.)

knowledge and participate. Teachers often catch the excitement of the students and are almost always surprised by what students *can* do instead of focusing on what they *cannot* do.

Choosing Words for Instruction   It does not matter how effective your instructional methods are if the choice of vocabulary words for instruction is flawed. Beck et al. (2002, p. 8) propose conceptualizing words in three tiers:

- Tier 1: The most basic words that rarely require attention to their meaning for most students (e.g., *clock, baby, happy, walk*)

- Tier 2: Words that occur at high frequency and are found across many domains (e.g., *coincidence, absurd, industrious, fortunate*)

- Tier 3: Words that occur with low frequency and are usually related to a specific discipline (e.g., *isotope, lathe, peninsula, refinery*)

Potato goals	Active goals
Student will listen to a story.	When asked a vocabulary question, student will choose the target word from a choice of three.
Student will sit in science class.	Student will match three target vocabulary words taken from the lecture.
Student will observe peers in language arts.	Student will participate in cooperative groups by indicating choice of words to include in group story.
Student will be placed in prone stander for 20 minutes.	Student will assist teacher in handing out materials to class from the stander.
	Student will use AAC device to greet each student and acknowledge each thank-you.

Figure 7.5. *Potato* versus active goals in vocabulary instruction.

Beck et al. (2002) recommended a process to determine which words fit which tier for any specific text. The identification of words in each tier will vary by grade level and the readiness of specific groups of students.

For students with moderate or severe disabilities, we can utilize a similar conceptual framework, but the scale will have to be adjusted because these students will typically have a much more limited vocabulary. This makes the choice of words for instruction even more critical. We offer the following three tiers for students with moderate or severe disabilities:

- Tier 1: Basic words that occur in high frequency in the student's immediate environment (e.g., *home, school, community*). Attention may still need to be paid to the meaning of the words for some students but most students will understand the words receptively (e.g., *Mom, Dad*, student's name, *Walgreens, Pepsi, chair, door, home, school*)

- Tier 2: Words that occur at high frequency across multiple environments and may facilitate access and meaningful participation in home, school, and community (e.g., names of teacher and therapist, subject areas, classmate names, *push, pull, in, out, office, cafeteria, library, computer;* may include high-frequency sight words)

- Tier 3: Words with abstract meanings that are taught in academic settings but that also can be used in home, school, and community environments (e.g., high-frequency sight words, target vocabulary from general education classes [see Figures 7.1–7.3])

The vocabulary words for the tiers will not be drawn solely from text, but many words will be drawn from the home, school, and community environment. The challenge is that these three tiers will vary from student to student. You will have to determine individually the three tiers for each student on your caseload. It is important to note that these tiers are not a strict hierarchy of vocabulary. Vocabulary words will be chosen from all three tiers, but the highest priority should be given to the words in Tiers 1 and 2.

Using Ecological Inventories

Brown et al. (1979) suggested that teachers conduct informal assessments of school, home, and community domains to identify functional skills on which to focus for individual students. They called these assessments *ecological inventories*. Their work in this area has subsequently been built on by many experts in the field of moderate or severe disabilities and remains a critical assessment and instructional planning tool (e.g., Downing, 2002, 2005; Ryndak & Alper, 2003; Snell & Brown, 2006). We suggest that an environmental vocabulary inventory be completed to help you identify appropriate Tier 1–3 vocabulary for students with moderate or severe disabilities across home, school, and community environments. You will need to collaborate with other educators and family members to identify important words in your students' environments. You may also have to visit community settings such as the grocery store or restaurant a student visits the most and other recreational settings and/or vocational settings.

The number of words selected for instruction for each student will be individualized. You will need to identify whether you are targeting listening, speaking, reading, and/or written vocabulary for each word (see Figure 7.6 for an ex-

Student: Meg Brown   Age: 10   Date of assessment: 8/30/05

Parent(s): Andrew Brown and Rachel Finley

Teachers: Maria Sandoval (special ed.), Peggy Alford (general ed.), Bill White (SLP)

Word(s)	School	Home	Community	Type*	Tier
Meg	X	X	X	L, S, R, W	1
Mom	X	X		L, S, R	1
Dad	X	X		L, S, R	1
Ms. Sandoval	X	X		L, S	2
Ms. Alford	X	X		L, S	2
Days: Mon–Fri	X	X	X	L, S	2
A, and, the	X	X	X	R, W	2
Earth	X			L, S, R	3
Sun	X			L, S, R	3
Moon	X			L, S, R	3

*L: Listening, S: Speaking, R: Reading, W: Writing

Figure 7.6.   Example of environmental vocabulary inventory.

ample). The environmental vocabulary inventory should be a dynamic assessment and adjusted as needed depending on student progress and changing environments and curriculum.

Print- and Language-Rich Environments

In Chapter 3, Scherba de Valenzuela and Tracey emphasized the critical importance of language-rich environments to the development of oral language skills for students with moderate or severe disabilities. A rich language and print environment is also critical to the development of all the types of vocabulary from spoken to written (Allington, 2006; Beck et al., 2002; Reutzel & Cooter, 2003). A print-rich environment encourages the incidental learning of vocabulary and can be used to support the direct instruction of vocabulary.

Inadequate exposure to print is cited by Allington (2006) as one factor contributing to poor vocabulary development. We believe that access to language- and print-rich environments is negatively affected by the segregation of students with moderate or severe disabilities from their general education peers and settings. We have found that when students with moderate or severe disabilities are placed in community-based classrooms or intensive-support classrooms, their instruction tends to be limited to the deficit-based goals and objectives on their individualized education program (IEP). Because all students in the class have moderate or severe disabilities, they suffer from a lack of speaking, reading, and writing role models. Further, the low expectations teachers have for students with moderate or severe disabilities leads to a dearth of high-quality, engaging, and challenging literacy materials. Chapter 3 addressed the creation of a culturally responsive, language-rich environment. In this chapter, we will focus on the creation of print-rich environments in the classroom and school. In general, a print-rich environment is characterized by easy access to the printed word in multiple formats and genres together with ways to engage actively with the printed word. Every classroom should have plenty of books, magazines, posters, and other printed material at various reading levels. Every classroom should also have literacy tools, including computers and other technology, so that students can make and interact with printed materials. The print materials and literacy tools should not be haphazardly assembled and organized. Teachers need to think carefully about the print in their classroom and organize the classroom environment so that the students know how to access and use the materials (Reutzel & Cooter, 2003). This may require direct instruction about how to use specific equipment or learning centers. Finally, teachers need to think about ways in which the print in the classroom can reinforce target vocabulary and expose students to additional vocabulary in meaningful ways.

Reading *the Classroom* One way to be strategic about print in the classroom environment for students with moderate or severe disabilities is to label common objects in the room (e.g., chairs, doors, windows, computers, tables). This strategy can be used for incidental and direct instruction. The idea is that the students will see these words frequently and associate them with the objects. The words also can be incorporated into direct instruction in a number of ways, including

- Sight word instruction using the environmental words
- Walking around the classroom and saying, reading, or matching the words using index cards, labels, symbols, or photographs
- Making a book using labels for the words; for example, a student named Deborah Huggins suggested writing a book about looking for a spider hiding in the classroom
- Classifying or sorting the words into categories
- Alphabetizing the words
- Completing sentences using the words; for example, "I sit on the *chair.*" "I like to play Math Munchers on the *computer.*"
- Matching the words with pictures or definitions

This strategy can be expanded to include labeling photographs, pictures, and posters around the classroom and school environment. Ultimately, the strategy can be coordinated with the Word Wall strategy common in elementary school classrooms (see Chapter 4). Although the classroom-labeling strategy is designed to help students with moderate or severe disabilities, all students may benefit from the labeling and frequent exposure to common printed words (e.g., English language learners [ELLs], students who are poor spellers).

Environmental Print The concept of print richness should not be confined to the classroom or school environment. Naturally occurring environmental print is a great source of vocabulary instruction for students and particularly for students with moderate or severe disabilities. Environmental print consists of high-frequency print also found in the home and community environments. This may include common signs (e.g., stop, exit, in, out), business signs (e.g., Kmart, Wendy's, Car Wash), and products (e.g., Coke, Pepsi, Fruit Loops, Starburst). Using environmental print builds upon the prior knowledge students have about the world around them and their ability to associate symbols consistently with an object. Some examples of activities using environmental print to increase vocabulary are

- Including environmental print words on the Word Wall
- Classifying and sorting environmental print words (e.g., for drinks, food, toys)
- Putting environmental print words on flashcards to teach as sight words
- Making sentences out of environmental print words
- Finishing sentences with environmental print words (e.g., "I like to drink Coke")
- Matching environmental print to flashcards of the same word
- Cutting up the individual letters in environmental print words and asking the students to put the letters back in the correct order
- Making word families out of the letters in environmental print (with thanks to my students Sandra Crowell and Gail Baxter)
- Making an alphabet chart with an environmental print vocabulary word for each letter
- Using environmental print to help with instructions for class activities such as cooking

Environmental print has potential beyond the classroom and can be used in the wider school environment, home, and community. By learning common signs such as stop, poison, and exit, students increase their vocabulary and become personally safer and more independent.

Modified Sight Word Approaches   Sometimes students have difficulty learning targeted vocabulary with traditional sight word approaches. To enhance the acquisition and comprehension of new vocabulary, we suggest pairing the vocabulary word with something that is known by the student (e.g., object, symbol, or photograph). As mentioned in Chapter 4, it is important to fade the stimulus when the purpose is teaching decoding. When teaching the meaning of words, students ideally will progress to learn the meaning of the word apart from the stimulus. This won't always be possible, but that does not mean that we should abandon vocabulary instruction if the student cannot understand the word apart from the stimulus. It is appropriate instruction to teach students to use words to refer to objects, people, and other items that are in their immediate environment.

If a student cannot understand a word in isolation, pair the word with a more concrete stimulus and then gradually fade that stimulus. The sequence may proceed through the following stages:

- Stage 1: Vocabulary word paired with an object

- Stage 2: Vocabulary word paired with a specific photograph
- Stage 3: Vocabulary word paired with a generic picture
- Stage 4: Vocabulary word paired with an icon
- Stage 5: Vocabulary word paired with the written word

These stages can be used to teach target vocabulary that is identified for individual students in any content area. Not all students with moderate or severe disabilities will need any or all of these stimulus prompts. Some students will consistently need the maximum level of prompting. The result is that all students will be participating meaningfully in classroom instruction and developing vocabulary at their own levels.

Word Sorts   Word sorts were originally presented in Chapter 4 as a strategy to increase word recognition. A way in which word sorts can be modified to aid in building vocabulary comprehension is to vary the way in which the students are asked to sort words. Students can learn and demonstrate understanding of words by sorting/classifying. For example, they can

- Sort by similarities
- Sort by opposites
- Sort by which word does not belong
- Sort by a feature (e.g., size, color, function)
- Sort in the order in which words occur in a lecture or film

Word sorts are a good way to get repeated exposure to words and to help students develop a deeper understanding of meaning.

Vocabulary Cards   Index cards and book or binder rings are the only materials needed for a variety of engaging activities that encourage students to learn the meaning of words through repetition. This activity is similar to the sound card activity in Chapter 4. The difference is that in these activities the emphasis is on the meaning of the word rather than on decoding the word. Fisher and Frey (2003) shared two examples of vocabulary card activities for adolescent learners. We have found these strategies to adapt perfectly well to elementary school settings and for students with moderate or severe disabilities.

Quiz Me Cards   Quiz Me Cards can be made from index cards or cardstock. As students learn new vocabulary, they write the vocabulary word and the definition on the front of the card. On the back of the card the students draw five lines for five signatures. Cards are kept together by punching a hole in one corner of the cards and stringing them together with a book or binder ring. In the example given by Fisher & Frey (2003), the music teacher introduces vocabulary words and their definitions. After the students record the word and definition on their Quiz Me Cards, they are required to ask five adults from outside their class to quiz them on the word and sign the back of the card if the student gets the definition correct. This provides an opportunity for meaningful practice of the vocabulary words and has the bonus of encouraging the students to interact with adults around campus.

Quiz Me Cards are easily adapted by grade level, content area, and ability. Not all students in the class need to have the same vocabulary words for this strategy to be successful. In addition, you could complete the activity within class by having the students quiz one another and sign the vocabulary cards. You could also adapt this activity so that the signatures could be from a variety of sources, including family or community members. This activity can be used appropriately with students with and without disabilities as well as English language learners. As with all activities, this could be adapted for students with physical, sensory, speech, and language disabilities by using pointing, gesturing, eye gazing, Braille, assistive technology devices, and peer support.

Definition Cards   Fisher and Frey (2003) described the use of vocabulary cards to enhance understanding through visual representation and application. The basic idea is to help the students come up with their own meaning of words rather than passively copying down the teacher's definition. The activity as described by Fisher and Frey involved asking the students to draw a line down the middle of the index card horizontally and vertically, resulting in four quadrants (see Figure 7.7). The students are asked to fill in the quadrants as follows:

- First quadrant: The vocabulary word
- Second quadrant: The definition in the student's own words. Students should not be required to find definitions in a dictionary with no guidance. Beck et al. (2002) shared research indicating that when students used dictionaries to find definitions of words, the definitions were frequently incorrect or incomplete. They suggested providing *student-friendly* explanations of words by giving examples of how the words are usually used in everyday language.
- Third quadrant: A graphic or picture to represent the word
- Fourth quadrant: A sentence using the word

The cards are then hole punched and kept together with a book or binder ring. The cards can later be used by the students to practice their words individually or with a partner.

As with the Quiz Me Cards, this activity can be varied so that the quadrants match the purpose of instruction for any grade or ability level and content area. Index cards come in different sizes to allow for the larger writing and drawing of younger children or children with disabilities. The information in each quadrant can also be adapted as needed. For example, for a student with moderate or severe disabilities who has a goal of recognizing and using environmental words

Quadrant 1 Name of food or drink e.g., MILK	Quadrant 2 Classification e.g., DRINK
Quadrant 3 Paste word, icon, or picture from environmental print	Quadrant 4 Complete the sentence e.g., I LIKE TO DRINK MILK.

Figure 7.7.   Vocabulary card activity using environmental print.

and differentiating between drink and food, a vocabulary card template as shown in Figure 7.7 could be designed.

These environmental print vocabulary cards could then be used for word sorts and other practice activities. As with the Quiz Me Cards, this activity can be used successfully for students with and without disabilities as well as for English language learners. As with all activities, this could be adapted for students with physical, sensory, speech, and language disabilities by using pointing, gesturing, eye gazing, Braille, assistive technology devices, and peer support.

SUMMARY

This chapter has discussed the assessment and design of effective instructional strategies to develop vocabulary for all students. One of the most important elements of vocabulary instruction is that it needs to be active and engaging for students. We believe this makes vocabulary instruction one of the easiest areas of instruction to modify for students with moderate or severe disabilities in general education. This chapter included specific strategies and examples to help teachers accomplish meaningful instruction in inclusive settings. Including students with moderate or severe disabilities may benefit all students by providing the general education teacher with the impetus to implement differentiated hands-on vocabulary strategies for all students with the collaboration of special education support staff.

Chapter 8

Written Communication

Susan R. Copeland

N o literacy program is complete unless it offers students daily opportunities to write (compose written text). Learning to express thoughts and ideas in written form has many benefits and is important in developing students' overall literacy knowledge and skills. Participation in even basic writing activities deepens individuals with disabilities' understanding of literacy and the uses of print (Pierce & Porter, 1996). Indeed, writing and reading are related processes whereby engaging in one enhances the development of the other (Langer & Flihan, 2000). For example, creating written texts gives students opportunities to practice the sound–symbol relationships needed to decode words, to recognize letter patterns within words (e.g., word families), to develop vocabulary, and to enhance understanding of grammar and syntax.

Sturm and Koppenhaver (2000) defined writing as "a holistic and authentic process of communicating by construction of a meaningful text" (p. 75). Using this definition allows a broader interpretation of writing. Meaningful text might include pictures, graphics, letters, single words, sentences, or a combination of all of them. This definition opens up the role of writer to individuals who may be at the emergent writing stage and who may never move on to more conventional writing stages. Figures 8.1 and 8.2 show examples of the writings of individuals with significant disabilities using varied forms of expression. The individual in Figure 8.1 is in the emergent stage of writing and uses strings of letters, numbers, and scribbles to express his thoughts. The individual in Figure 8.2 uses words and sentences combined with pictures to construct his message.

It is important to remember that putting thoughts or ideas in written form does not necessarily require the author to actually hand write the words. The author can type the words using a keyboard or use specialized software programs that employ pictures or symbols to represent words (e.g., Writing with Symbols 2000). Software that utilizes prediction (i.e., offers a menu of word choices when composing a text) is also available for students who need this type of support. Or the author could dictate thoughts to someone who writes them down or use a combination of written words and pictures to get his or her message across. These and similar options open up the writing process to individuals with more intensive support needs, many of whom have never been seen by teachers or other adults as capable of composing meaningful text. When viewing the examples and ideas in this chapter, keep in mind that they may be modified using any of the above access strategies or others that are individualized for students' needs.

Figure 8.1. Example of writing by an adult with intellectual disabilities in the emergent stage of writing. He used letters, numbers, and shapes to create a text about his visit to a doctor.

COMPONENTS OF THE WRITING PROCESS

Writing is a complex process involving multiple activities that take place in a recursive versus a sequential manner (Singer & Bashir, 2004). Writers do not necessarily progress linearly from one activity to the next and so on until their text is completed. Rather, they may shift back and forth between activities in the writing process as they compose, edit, and polish their work. To successfully compose conventional text, writers must use their knowledge of language structure (e.g., syntax, grammar, vocabulary) and phonics (e.g., spelling words) as well as apply planning and organizational skills. Writers must know writing conventions (e.g., punctuation, capitalization) and apply them correctly to their texts. They also must have sufficiently well-developed fine motor skills to form the letters within words fluently if writing by hand or know how to quickly and efficiently locate letter keys if using a keyboard to compose text. Finally, and, most important, they must have something to talk about.

Figure 8.2. A piece constructed by a young man to describe his feelings for his caregiver.

Motivation, wanting to communicate a message to someone else, is an integral part of the writing process. An environment that provides stimulating activities connected to topics students find meaningful and interesting is one of the most effective means of enhancing students' motivation to write. Inclusive classrooms provide such an environment making them effective settings for the types of instruction and activities that enhance motivation to write. These classrooms provide numerous examples of and opportunities for engaging in writing for authentic, varied purposes. Typical age peers model writing behaviors thereby providing motivation for students with disabilities to want to communicate in written form.

Although there are numerous conceptualizations of the writing process (e.g., Hayes & Flower, 1980; Singer & Bashir, 2004), the process can generally be divided into three phases: planning, composing, and revising. In this chapter the writing process is discussed as a series of sequential tasks, but a successful writer actually moves back and forth between each of these processes as the text is developed. Indeed, part of what makes writing so complex is this need to move recursively between processes.

Planning, the first phase of the writing process, involves clarifying the purpose or goal of the proposed text and identifying its intended audience, deciding on the specific topic, selecting relevant ideas, and choosing an organizational framework for the proposed text. This process ranges from something as straightforward as deciding what to say in a message to your mother to let her know you are at a friend's house to planning a short story with numerous complicated plot twists and turns. Skill in creating a plan for writing and successfully applying it improves with age (Singer & Bashir, 2004) and with instruction (Sturm & Koppenhaver, 2000). Younger children and those with disabilities tend to write as they speak rather than use more complex structures. Their texts are typically shorter, and they often use a *stream of consciousness* style of composition in which they write down thoughts as they occur rather than use some type of organizational structure (Singer & Bashir).

In the next phase, *composing*, the writer actually creates the text based on the earlier decisions made during the planning process. Here, knowledge of grammar, syntax, vocabulary, the conventions of writing, and organizational skills come in to play. The writer must continually monitor what he or she writes, comparing the composition's content to the original purpose and plan and applying correct rules of grammar, syntax, phonics, and mechanics.

Then comes the final phase of the writing process, *revising*. In this stage the writer reviews the text and makes changes as needed to ensure that the content of the piece is communicated clearly, completely, and as planned. Correcting errors in writing conventions is also accomplished at this stage.

Writing and Individuals with Moderate or Severe Disabilities

Given the complexity of the writing process, it is not surprising that many individuals with moderate or severe disabilities experience difficulty in putting their thoughts and ideas in written form. Some of these difficulties may stem directly from their disabilities (e.g., problems with working memory) while others may arise from the types of writing instruction and experiences they've been provided or from a lack of any instruction at all. Some of the factors potentially affecting the writing skills of these individuals include

- Lack of opportunities to develop writing skills due to low expectations from teachers or other adults

- Provision of age inappropriate literacy instruction or instruction limited to recognizing sight words

- Underlying language problems such as limited vocabulary or incomplete understanding of grammar that makes it difficult to express ideas and thoughts in written form

- Limitations in working memory that affect planning, organizing, and composing text

- Difficulty with fine motor skills that makes handwriting laborious and time consuming and, for some individuals with physical disabilities, impossible

- Limited knowledge of phonics that affects the ability to spell words that the writer wishes to use in a composition

- Lack of technology and supports that would provide access to the writing process (Singer & Bashir, 2004; Sturm & Koppenhaver, 2000)

In contrast, some individuals with disabilities such as some persons with autism may actually find it easier to work with written text than to use oral language (Kluth, 2003). Please keep in mind, however, that this characteristic is not necessarily descriptive of all individuals with autism spectrum disorders. Calhoon (2001), for example, noted in her research study examining rime use in word recognition by children with cognitive disabilities that one child with an autism spectrum disorder refused to respond to any directions unless they were in written form. Although such students should be supported and encouraged to use other communication forms, their reliance on written language can be used as a starting point for developing other literacy and communication skills as well as for developing social skills (e.g., use of social stories).

Value of Writing Instruction

Despite the difficulties that students with cognitive or severe disabilities may experience with written language, engaging in the writing process offers unique opportunities to these individuals to develop literacy skills. Sturm and Koppenhaver (2000) stated that "writing can be a particularly effective means of transportation for individuals with disabilities because of two characteristics of texts . . . written texts are more lasting than oral language and are able to be reshaped in context, form, or uses" (p. 74). Unlike oral language, a written text is permanent and doesn't "disappear" after the words are recorded. This characteristic allows ideas to be recorded and then reorganized over time as the individual revisits the text and continues to refine what he or she wants to communicate. It also allows an individual to reread a written message as many times as needed to understand it (Farrell & Elkins, 1995). Creating and working with written text thus offers numerous opportunities to develop language, communication, and formal literacy skills.

ASSESSING WRITING

Assessing students' writing can be accomplished in many different ways. Each method of assessment has its own strengths and weaknesses. Selection of an assessment is best done by keeping in mind the purpose for which it is intended and the learning characteristics of the student being assessed. Formal standardized assessments are available (e.g., *Test of Written Language-3* [TOWL-3; Hammill & Larsen, 1996). However, these may not be as useful as more informal, classroom-based assessments (e.g., checklists, rubrics) in monitoring and planning daily instruction.

The process of writing text involves many aspects (e.g., selecting content, organizing text, using correct grammar and punctuation), which makes assessment of written text complex. A thorough evaluation of a student's writing should examine several dimensions. These might include content (e.g., a clearly articulated main idea, coherence throughout the text), organization (e.g., ideas presented in a logical sequence), vocabulary or word choice, mechanics (e.g., correct use of punctuation), and fluency and sentence structure (e.g., complete sentences that follow grammar rules). For students in the early stages of writing, informal observations of students may be the most useful way to evaluate writing. For example, is a student's writing composed of scribbles, drawings, or scribbles with occasional letters? Is there evidence that the student is trying to apply sound–symbol knowledge indicating that she or he is in the early alphabetic stage of understanding? Does the student indicate a purpose for his or her writing such as saying that the writing is a letter to a friend? Does the student *read* back what he or she has written when requested? These and similar questions can provide rich information about a student's current understanding of the use of written language and conventional writing skills. Collecting the writings of students in this early stage across time is helpful in tracking changes in their understanding and skill levels (see the section below on portfolios).

The texts of students who are able to use more conventional writing skills can also be assessed in several ways. Some of these might include examining the types of sentences a student used (simple, compound, or complex fragments) or examining spelling patterns to provide information on students' understanding of phonic patterns. Determining average sentence length is helpful in assessing fluency (total number of words used/total number of sentences). The diversity of words used can be evaluated to examine students' vocabulary usage. Examining use of punctuation and capitalization also provides a picture of students' understanding of writing mechanics.

Portfolios

Portfolios are an increasingly popular means of assessing students' progress in writing. They are essentially a collection of a student's work across time. Teachers, students, and parents can use them to evaluate student growth as the school year progresses. Portfolios can be organized around a particular skill area (e.g., correct use of mechanics, developing a narrative) and the work in them evaluated using a rubric individualized for that skill area. Often the teacher and the student meet together at regular intervals to review the student's work and decide what will go into the portfolio as examples of student progress. Used in this way, the portfolio is especially useful in developing students' ability to evaluate their own work. Learning self-evaluation skills will help them become more skilled writers.

It may also be helpful for the teacher to write an explanatory note on the items included in a student's portfolio indicating why the piece was selected and how it demonstrates development of a particular skill. This is particularly useful if the portfolio contains the writing of students in the early stages of writing-skill development who do not use conventional writing skills. The teacher's notes point out to parents and others key features of each piece and how these writing artifacts demonstrate progress in developing written language skills.

Organization is critical to successful use of portfolios. Managing multiple students' work can become overwhelming as more and more pieces are added to the portfolio throughout the school year. It is important to develop a simple, clear system to organize each student's writing samples. Portfolios are not synonymous with scrapbooks. In other words, not every piece a student writes should go into the portfolio; only those pieces the teacher and student have decided are representative of the student's progress in a particular skill area should be included.

Rubrics

Rubrics are a common method of assessing writing skills. These assessments can be created to meet the learning needs of a particular student and task situation (Schirmer & Bailey, 2000). For example, one rubric might be written to focus on use of organization in writing a story while another assesses sentence structure and use of varied word choices. In general, rubrics are created by specifying the qualities (dimensions) the teacher wants to examine, selecting a scale to represent different levels of each quality, and describing the characteristics of each quality at each selected level. Students' texts are scored on each dimension included in the rubric. Student scores are then used to pinpoint areas for instruction and support. Figure 8.3 shows a sample rubric for evaluating paragraph writing.

TEACHING WRITING

There are four important points to keep in mind when teaching students with moderate or severe disabilities to create *meaningful texts*. First, begin with high expectations. Start with the belief that the students have something to communicate through written language/symbols. Ensure that they have rich experiences that motivate them to want to communicate their ideas, thoughts, and impressions to others. Second, act on these high expectations by providing meaningful opportunities for the students to write across each and every day. This is an important but often overlooked aspect of writing instruction. It sounds simple, but because of the struggles these students have with writing, they (and their teachers) may avoid writing tasks, making it even less likely that the students will acquire basic skills in composing written texts (Millar, Light, & McNaughton, 2004). Writing skills will only develop and improve if the students engage in writing.

Third, make access and support available for the students as they tackle the writing process. Supports might be as simple as providing a range of writing instruments with adaptive grips or as complex as having computer software or specialized keyboards available for the students. Access to the tasks involved in writing can be provided by carefully selecting the means and level of support a student requires (see Chapter 10). Finally, provide effective instruction geared to the students' learning needs and strengths. Utilize evidence-based instructional practices and monitor student progress closely so that adjustments can be made as needed. As with other aspects of literacy instruction for students with cogni-

	Score			
Writing quality/ dimension	4	3	2	1
Content	Well-developed main idea clearly supported with three details	Contains a main idea; has three details but they aren't all clearly related to main idea	Contains a main idea but includes fewer than three supporting details, or details are not related to main idea	Main idea is not clear; does not include supporting details
Organization	Has a clear organizational structure; each supporting detail is arranged in proper sequence to support main idea	Has a discernable organizational structure; supporting details are not arranged in a logical sequence	Some organizational structure is apparent; not clear how supporting details relate to the main idea	No apparent organizational structure
Mechanics (punctuation, capitalization, spelling)	Very few or no errors	Only a few minor errors	Some errors in either punctuation, capitalization, or spelling	Multiple errors in all three aspects of mechanics

Figure 8.3. Example of rubric used to assess paragraph writing. (From Gunning T. [2002]. *Assessing and correcting reading and writing difficulties* [pp. 133–135]. Boston: Allyn & Bacon.)

tive or severe disabilities, there is little research on effective writing instruction for these students (Bedrosian, Lasker, Speidel, & Politsch, 2003; Millar et al., 2004). There is, however, considerable research on teaching writing to typically developing individuals and much of this work can be applied to students with more intensive support needs (Millar et al.; Polloway, Smith, & Miller, 2004; Sturm & Koppenhaver, 2000).

Current research suggests that using both instruction in process writing and direct instruction in writing strategies can be effective in developing the writing skills of students with cognitive or severe disabilities (e.g., Bedrosian et al., 2003; Millar et al., 2004; Sturm & Koppenhaver, 2000). Process-writing approaches are student centered and allow students to be actively engaged in each stage of writing (Sturm & Koppenhaver). Strategy instruction is useful because particular areas of need can be targeted and students can be taught specific tactics to address these areas of weakness. Following are writing instruction activities that incorporate aspects of these approaches and that have been used effectively with students who have cognitive or severe disabilities.

Journaling

Many students begin their school day by writing in a journal. Sometimes the teacher gives students a specific writing prompt (e.g., "Write about what you saw on the way to school this morning"). Other times the students are allowed to select their own topics. Teachers review the students' journals periodically as a way to assess their growth as writers.

Journaling is an effective way for students with moderate or severe disabilities to develop written language skills (e.g., Foley & Staples, 2003). Some students will be able to use the same format for journal writing as their typically developing peers; others may require simple modifications that will allow them to participate in this valuable writing activity.

One possible modification to journal writing is to have the students draw a picture in response to the day's writing prompt or select a picture from a magazine and then dictate a caption to a peer to record under the drawing. Students can use stickers or stamps to create their responses (Foley & Staples, 2003). Another option is to allow the students to dictate the journal entry to a peer or adult who records it in the students' journals. If desired and appropriate, the students can trace over the entry or type it into a computer to gain practice in handwriting or keyboarding skills. Students in the pre- or early alphabetic stage may want to respond to the journal prompt on their own using squiggles or letter strings as illustrated in Figure 8.1. This should be encouraged because it gives the students opportunities to develop critical understandings about written language (e.g., working from left to right, representing speech or ideas with symbols). The teacher can always ask a student to read aloud what he or she wrote and then write the student's oral interpretation on a sticky note and attach it to the journal page.

Some students may respond to the journal topic using a program that combines words and symbols (e.g., Writing with Symbols 2000). Another option is to provide students with a fill-in-the-blank journal form that they can complete independently or with peer support. (Figure 8.4 describes how one special education teacher used this approach in developing written language with students who had significant support needs, and Figure 8.5 shows an example of the family checklist and journal format.)

Writing Conversations

As mentioned earlier, students' writing abilities will improve more rapidly if they are given multiple, authentic opportunities to write across the school day. A simple but fun way to encourage students to create written text is to have them

---

Kay Osborn, a veteran special education teacher and supervisor for the Albuquerque Public Schools-University of New Mexico Intern Program, modified the "Weekend Report" designed by Mayer-Johnson, Inc. to fit the needs of her students with severe disabilities and their families. She used a checklist sent home each Friday that asked families to mark the activities their child participated in over the weekend. (The checklist and an example of the fill-in-the-blank journal format are included in Figure 8.5. The form uses a menu of choices and takes only a couple of minutes for busy families to complete.) The families returned the form on Mondays, and Kay used the information as a basis for the students' journals for that day. Some students completed a fill-in-the-blank form, either by tracing the answer after Kay wrote it or by writing it independently or with a model. Other students selected picture symbols from a menu of choices to complete the same questions. The activity was valuable in maintaining home–school communication and allowed students with the most intensive support needs to participate in creating a message using written communication.

Figure 8.4.   Description of how one teacher used a fill-in-the-blank journal for students with moderate or severe disabilities.

Family Checklist for Fill-in-the-Blank Journal Writing

Name:_____

Parents: To help your child tell the class what she or he did over the weekend, please check off the child's weekend activities. Additional information can be noted on the back. Please send this to school on Monday morning. Thank you!

This weekend I went to

__ the mall	__ Kmart	__ grocery store	__ park
__ toy store	__ church	__ bowling	__ movies
__ grandparents	__ hospital/doctor	__ playground	__ post office
__ lake	__ friend's house	__ party	__ zoo

__ other _____

I went with

__ mom	__ dad	__ family	__ friend
__ grandmother	__ grandfather	__ brother	__ sister
__ aunt/uncle	__ cousin	__ other _____	

I ate at

__ McDonald's	__ Burger King	__ Wendy's	__ Taco Bell
__ Pizza Hut	__ KFC	__ Denny's	__ Sonic

__ other _____

Fill-in-the-Blank Journal format (filled in by the student based on the information from the Family Checklist above):

Name: _____   Date: _____

I went to _____

_____

I went with _____

I had a _____

Figure 8.5.   Example of family checklist and fill-in-the-blank journal format.

engage in written *conversations* with the teacher or with a peer on a regular basis (Gunning, 2002b; Kluth, 2003). This can be done in several ways. One simple method is to schedule a short block of time several times a week for the activity. Explain to the students that during that block of time no one is allowed to talk out loud. Instead of talking to each other, the students and teacher must write notes to a writing partner to express what they want to say. For example, the teacher might start off by writing a note asking a student about something she or he is interested in (e.g., "What did you think about the new *Harry Potter* movie?"). The student reads the note and replies in written form to the question. The teacher replies to that note, also in written form, and so the *conversation* continues.

Students' notes can contain words or pictures or a combination of both. To keep students from laboring too long over writing conventions instead of focusing on the content of the note, assure students that their notes won't be graded. Encourage them to use correct grammar and writing conventions but remind them that the point is to get their thoughts down on paper in a manner that is comprehensible to their writing partner, not to have a perfect paper. This facilitates fluency and assists students in learning to put their thoughts into written form.

A logical extension of this activity is creating situations in which students write letters to friends or other individuals. Having an actual audience for writing (e.g., a pen pal) is motivating to students and may help them plan and generate ideas (Stanford & Siders, 2001). Many teachers have successfully used a pen pal strategy in which they team their class up with students in another teacher's class. The two groups write back and forth at regular intervals. Sometimes students team with a class in another state or another part of the world. This gives students a chance to get to know peers who may have very different experiences from their own. Doing so offers numerous opportunities to integrate writing with other content areas such as geography, social studies, economics, and math.

Pen pal teaming can also be done with classes in the same school or district. Partners can be same-age peers or peers who are older or younger. Veronica Moore and Frances Duff, teachers in an inclusive classroom in a local high school, teamed their students (with and without disabilities) with students at a nearby elementary school (also with and without disabilities; Moore, Metzler, & Pearson, 2006). The two groups corresponded regularly across the school year, providing numerous opportunities to practice written language skills. At the end of the year, the high school students visited the classroom of their pen pals and had a party celebrating their experiences. This activity gave all the students opportunities to develop and refine their written communication skills. It allowed older students with and without disabilities to fulfill a mentor role for the younger students who benefited from an opportunity to get to know older students and to use their developing literacy skills.

E-mailing is rapidly becoming the modern version of letter writing and the pen pal activity is easily modified to allow students to correspond with partners through e-mail. E-mailing is a highly motivating activity for students and can be an effective means of enhancing written language skills (e.g., Stanford & Siders, 2001). Before beginning an e-mail activity, however, it is critical to discover what your school district policies are with regard to Internet use and to provide close supervision to students to ensure that your students use Internet sites in a responsible and safe manner. It may also be necessary to consider access issues because some students will require specialized keyboards or e-mail software programs to facilitate their participation in the activity. Assistive technology staff or speech–language pathologists are often great resources for solving these types of access issues.

Shared Writing

Struggling writers, particularly those with moderate or severe disabilities, often have great difficulty generating ideas and putting them down in written form (Sturm & Koppenhaver, 2000). One of the most powerful means of facilitating these students' writing skills is to uncover and model the writing process for them. Shared writing, in which the teacher and students engage in the writing process together, provides this opportunity. Shared writing begins with the teacher modeling how to move through the writing process to create a written text. The teacher uses think-alouds (see Chapter 6) to demonstrate how she determines what she will write and how it will be organized (planning), how to put her plan down in writing (composing), and finally, how to revise and edit a completed piece of writing. Students actively participate in the process with the teacher (another key feature of successful instruction for students with intensive support needs), who gradually fades her support as the students acquire more independence in the process. There are many ways in which shared writing can be incorporated into a literacy program. What follows are some instructional activities that are particularly relevant for learners with cognitive or severe disabilities.

Morning Message   A morning message is a widely used activity to enhance the writing skills of students with and without disabilities. It has numerous variations but in general the teacher sets aside a separate chart or section of the board that is used daily to write a short message for the class. The teacher begins this whole-group activity by creating the message herself, thinking aloud as she writes it on the board or chart so that the students can *see* how she makes decisions about what to write and how to record it in written form. The content of the message can vary widely. It might simply state the date and describe the day's weather or it might relate a funny incident that occurred in the class or in the school. See Figure 8.6 for examples of morning messages.

The teacher composes the morning message aloud and then writes it in the designated space. She rereads it, using finger pointing to demonstrate the relationship between her spoken words and the written words on the chart. Students sometimes use choral reading to read the message aloud together or the teacher may ask individual students to find a particular word or letter within the message. At times the teacher may deliberately make a mistake in spelling or in mechanics and encourage the students to find and correct it. The teacher may also use specific questioning to help students understand why she selected a particular word or used a specific punctuation mark (e.g., "Why did I put a period after Mr.?"; Reutzel & Cooter, 2004). Some teachers have beginning writers copy the morning message into a notebook to practice handwriting and mechanics. As the students gain more proficiency with the writing process, the teacher may ask individual students to dictate the morning message or ask specific students to come up and actually write the message on the chart or board.

Today is Monday, October 28. The wind is blowing. The leaves are falling from the trees. It is cold! Did you wear your coat today?

Good morning, class. Today, two visitors will come to our class. One wears a special uniform and drives a special car. The other visitor rides in the car, but he can't drive. His job is to find things for his partner. Can you guess who the visitors might be?

Figure 8.6.   Two examples of a morning message.

Language Experience Stories   Language experience stories combined with shared writing are another effective way to help students gain proficiency in written language. This activity is effective because it combines both the interests and actual experiences of the students with the modeling of and active student participation in the writing process. The activity is often used with younger students but can be used successfully with older readers and writers as well. The activity works well within inclusive classrooms because its structure allows participation by students with varying skill levels. More proficient readers and writers provide models for students whose skills are not as advanced, but the activity allows everyone to participate at some level.

One of the other strengths of the language experience approach is that the teacher can introduce many different types of writing (genres) to students. For example, the students might write a story about their classroom pet, create a recipe for a snack they have all enjoyed, write directions for a game the class played, write a letter to the principal about an issue the students are concerned about, or summarize information on content they are learning in a science unit about the solar system. Ideas for potential topics are endless but should be selected based on activities and experiences in which all students have participated in some manner.

The first step in using language experience/shared writing is to create a shared experience for the students that forms the basis for the writing process. The experience might be a field trip the class has taken, a response to a text the class has read (or a text the teacher has read to the class), or any other activity in which all students have participated. After the activity, the teacher works with the whole class or a small group of students to create some type of written composition related to the experience. Throughout the instructional process the teacher models the writing process using think-alouds and solicits student participation in creating and editing the story. As the students gain proficiency in planning, composing, and revising, the teacher fades the amount of support he or she provides, allowing the students to gradually assume full responsibility for the writing process.

To begin the instruction, the teacher states the purpose of the proposed writing activity (e.g., creating a story about the class trip to the local theater to see *Cinderella*). The teacher asks the students to dictate what they want the story (or other writing piece) to say and writes the students' suggestions on a white board or chart paper. The teacher uses prompts to elicit additional details or clarify content. The teacher also may use the activity as an opportunity to reinforce other aspects of literacy instruction such as asking the students to identify the letters needed to spell a particular sound within a word. The lesson could be structured around a specific writing skill, such as organizing story events sequentially or working on use of writing mechanics, or it can be a more general model of the writing process as a whole.

The teacher continues the lesson until the students judge the story complete. During the next lesson, teacher and students begin the revision and editing process. They reread the story and decide if it meets the purpose of the writing activity and if it needs additional content or detail. Once the students are satisfied with the content, they move on to editing. They review the story carefully, looking for errors in mechanics or spelling. The teacher can use this portion of the lesson as an opportunity to reinforce prior lessons on writing mechanics (e.g., use of commas).

After the story is judged complete and correct, the students move to publishing. They handwrite or type the story and add illustrations or graphics to the pages, and when that is finished to their satisfaction, they place the completed work in the class library. The students can choose to read these language experience compositions during self-selected reading time. Students with moderate or severe disabilities may especially enjoy reading these stories because they are based on the students' own experiences. Additional stories can be added across the school year. These stories provide a history of class activities that can be copied and given to each student at the end of the year as a keepsake. If the class has a web site, language experience stories can be added to the site for students, families, and others to enjoy.

Creating Books

Students enjoy creating books that they can read during self-selected reading time or that they can share with others. The process of creating books teaches many literacy skills, including those associated with composing and utilizing written language. Ray (2006) noted that "When we invite students to *make* something with writing instead of just asking them to write, they go about their work differently" (p. 14). Seeing oneself as a book author assists students in deepening their understanding of the purpose of the writing process and encourages them to expand their skills (Ray).

Student-created books can take many forms. They may be based on the students' own experiences (see previous discussion on language experience stories). A motivating activity is having older students create books to share with younger students. Although these books contain low-level text, the process of creating them gives students many age-appropriate opportunities to acquire and practice important literacy skills. The use of low-level text allows the students who are in the early stages of literacy to participate in the activity and is also helpful to students with more advanced literacy skills.

Constructing children's books requires students to engage in each step of the writing process including planning and organizing the content, composing the text, providing supporting illustrations or photographs, and then revising and editing their stories until they are completed. The students can practice reading their newly created books, and when they have mastered them, they can share the books with younger students. The format of these books could be wordless picture books, books with predictable text, simple fairy tales, or other formats appropriate for young children.

An interesting variation in creating a children's book is to use the simple format together with content that is appropriate for older students. For example, a teacher in a local school worked with a group of fellow teachers to create a book targeted for teenagers with moderate or severe disabilities on the dangers of drug abuse. The content was age appropriate but the format used predictable text and simple illustrations to convey the dangers of drug use. This same type of activity could be done by groups of learners with mixed skill levels. They can work together to create books on age-appropriate topics using higher-level concepts in a simple format. Students of all ability levels benefit from these types of activities, which offer opportunities to learn content and develop literacy skills.

The PowerPoint software program offers an innovative yet simple way to create books that are accessible to students who do not use speech or those with physical challenges. PowerPoint software has several characteristics that make it ideal for this purpose. It is widely available, fairly simple to learn and use, permits graphics or photographs to be inserted easily into presentations, and allows a spoken narration to be recorded for each slide. A student who doesn't read print can use the computer to move through each page of a PowerPoint book while the computer reads the story. Students who cannot use a keyboard to manipulate the PowerPoint slides can use a switch (individualized to their particular motor challenges) to advance the slides. This feature offers them independence and allows them to use technology, placing them in a socially valued role. A student with significant support needs, for example, might use this program to read a story to his typically developing classmate during the self-selected reading period.

PowerPoint software activities offer other ways to develop students' written language skills. Books can be created in PowerPoint using a published text or a book created by the teacher and students that is then put in the PowerPoint format (see Figure 8.7 for an outline of the steps needed to create a PowerPoint book with students). A local teacher, for example, scanned in selected pictures from his students' favorite fairy tale. The students recorded the text for each picture, creating an interactive book that all could enjoy. Another teacher and her students created a story about a class outing using predictable text. The students drew pictures to illustrate the story. The teacher scanned the text and illustrations into the computer, and then she and the class created a PowerPoint book from these images.

Story Grammar

As mentioned previously, planning is a crucial part of creating written text. All students can benefit from instruction in how to effectively plan a writing task, but students with more intensive support needs typically need more explicit instruction and support in learning to plan writing projects. One way to teach and support the planning process is to instruct the students to use story grammar elements to plan a simple story that they will write. This activity also has the advantage of reinforcing the writing process approach because it incorporates each element of process writing in the instruction: planning, composing, revising, and publishing. Bedrosian and colleagues (2003), for example, taught two junior

---

Creating a Book Using PowerPoint

You will need a scanner and a computer with

- a sound card
- a microphone (internal or external)
- speakers

1. Select or create a book with the class. Tip: Choose books with simple illustrations unless you have a computer with a large amount of memory.
2. Scan the book's illustrations into the computer. (Remember to save the file!) Keep in mind that you don't have to use every picture—select illustrations that provide the most meaning for the story.
3. Open up a new presentation in the PowerPoint program. Use the Insert function to insert each image into a separate slide. (Remember to save the file!)

Recording the Voice Narration

1. Open the PowerPoint presentation in which the illustrations were saved. If using a computer with an external microphone, be sure the microphone is plugged in and turned on. On the Outline tab or Slides tab in normal view, select the slide icon or thumbnail on which you want to start the recording.
2. On the Slide Menu, click Record Narration. Click Set Microphone Level. Follow the directions to set the microphone level. When this is completed, click OK.
3. In the Slide Show View, speak the narrative text for the first slide into the microphone and click in the slide to advance to the second slide. Speak the narrative text for that slide, advance to the next slide, and so on. If you want to pause and resume the narration, right-click in the slide, and on the Shortcut Menu click Pause Narration or Resume Narration.
4. Repeat these steps until the narration for each slide is complete.
5. When you come to the black Exit Screen, click to automatically save the narration.

Figure 8.7. Steps in creating a book using PowerPoint software.

high-age students (one with autism and one with a cognitive disability) to answer seven story grammar questions prior to creating the narrative. These questions formed a story map. The students then used this story map as an outline when creating their stories. Both students' ability to write a narrative that included all story grammar elements improved after they learned to use story maps. In addition, they both used more accurate writing conventions and made fewer syntactic and grammatical errors in writing stories.

To use story maps to teach the writing process, the teacher begins instruction by showing students a blank story map that includes key questions for each story grammar element (see Figure 8.8 for an example). The teacher and students brainstorm ideas to answer each question, selecting the ideas they like best for each element and writing down their responses in sentence form. (All students should contribute ideas so that all feel joint ownership of the story.) Next, the students, with modeling and support from the teacher, take turns composing the story using their answers to the story grammar questions as an outline. The students can take turns writing the sentences or they can dictate sentences that the teacher records on an overhead transparency or a white board, or by using an LCD (Liquid Crystal Display) projector so that all students in the group can see the story taking shape.

Title of the Story: _____

1. Who is the story about? (Characters) _____

_____

2. Where does the story take place? (Setting) _____

_____

3. What happens first? (Problem) _____

   Then what happens? _____

   What happens next? _____

4. How does the story end? (Resolution) _____

_____

Figure 8.8.   Story grammar questions to help with planning. *Source:* Bedrosian, Lasker, Speidel, & Politsch (2003).

After each story grammar element has been incorporated into the group's story, the teacher models the revision process. She reads the story aloud and uses the think-aloud process to ask herself if the story is complete or if there are additional elements to add that might improve the story and to check for correct use of writing conventions. She encourages the students to engage in the revising and editing process with her, adding their ideas and making any corrections they see as necessary. When the group is satisfied with the story, the students take turns typing the story into a computer and adding any illustrations or graphics they desire. The finished product is printed and placed in the classroom library for the students to read. After repeating the process several times as a group with the teacher, the students can work in small groups or pairs using the story maps to create their own stories.

Poetry

"Poetry instruction with students with cognitive or severe disabilities? You've got to be kidding! You don't know the students in my class or you wouldn't even suggest that!"

This comment is typical of those received from teachers in a graduate class on literacy instruction for students with severe disabilities when they learned that they would be required to work with their students, including those with cognitive disabilities, to create a poem to share with their colleagues. Many of these teachers were working with students who had significant cognitive disabilities, physical challenges, or severe autism. When we suggested that they create poetry with their students, many did not believe that such a thing was possible. Can poetry truly be an effective tool in developing students' literacy skills? The answer is a resounding "Yes!" Creating poetry can be a highly effective way to develop students' language and literacy abilities, and it is fun for both students and teachers (e.g., Kahn-Freedman, 2001; Sturm & Koppenhaver, 2000).

The first step in developing a writing lesson using poetry is to remember that poetry doesn't need to consist of complex rhyme schemes; iambic pentameter is not required for a successful poem. What is required is creative thinking from teachers and students. Poetry is about language—enjoying and using it in imaginative ways. So often instruction in written language for students with disabilities is structured, predictable, and, frankly, sometimes boring! Struggling writers frequently become frustrated and overwhelmed with the writing process and many give up. Poetry, because of its flexibility, allows students with widely varying skill levels to experience success, express their creativity, *and* learn new skills. Students can begin to see themselves as writers and find new motivation to hone their written language skills.

As with other types of literacy activities, start a poetry lesson using topics of interest to the students or topics that directly relate to their life experiences. Begin by first reading various types of poems to students around these topics. This illustrates for students what poetry is and the various forms it can take. It will also be easier for students to begin creating poetry by adapting the form and structure of a poem they enjoy rather than having to generate both an organizational structure and content at the same time. Figure 8.9 recounts how one teacher used this approach effectively with a student who had intellectual disabilities.

Another way to help students begin this type of writing activity is to provide an intriguing picture or photograph that sparks the student's interest. Give the student a phrase (i.e., a structure) related to the photograph and let him or her brainstorm ways to fill in blanks in the phrase. For example, one elementary student with severe disabilities composed a poem about pizza, one of her favorite foods, with support from her teacher. The teacher gave the student a basic form (Pizza is_____), and the student generated words to complete the blanks. The words selected by the student are not those often thought of as being in the vocabulary of someone with a severe disability (e.g., *gooey, yummy, cheesy*). Her poem illustrated the power of having high expectations for students with moderate or severe disabilities and providing those students with opportunities to engage in authentic, creative literacy experiences.

Acrostics are another way to introduce the idea of poetry to students with moderate or severe disabilities. Students can use the letters in their name to generate a list of adjectives to describe themselves or use a word that represents a topic they find interesting. Poems that focus on sensory stimuli are another option. Focusing on the sounds, smells, sights, or tastes of favorite events is a wonderful way to elicit creativity, expand word usage, and express feelings and emotions (Kahn-Freedman, 2001). Sturm and Koppenhaver (2000) related Koch's (1971) description of a poem created by a young man with a cognitive disability that was based on sounds. The poem begins with a starting phrase ("At a football game one thing you can hear is . . . " [p. 82]) and then recounts sounds the young man overheard at a football game (e.g., "french fries cooking in grease and hot dogs boiling" [p. 82]). The poem illustrates the power of starting with the student's own experiences as the basis for writing. It also demonstrates the flexibility poetry allows in constructing written text. Because writing conventions are not as strictly followed in poetry as in other literary forms, students can focus on

Frances Farrah, a teacher of middle-school students with intensive support needs, describes how she and one of her students created a poem together.

In creating this poem, I used materials available in the classroom. I tried to explain the nature of poetry [to Jesus], but he was unable to grasp the concept, so I explained that a poem can tell a story, much like a book. We browsed through a collection of Shel Silverstein poetry, but my student was obviously losing interest, so we turned to another anthology containing poems about food, people, and school. Since Jesus loves to eat, we went to the food section and finally read the poem about eating worms. He laughed and so I used that as a starting point. I asked him questions about whether or not he would (or ever had!) eat worms, and he exploded with imagination. I wrote everything he said, and then typed and printed the phrases. I cut them into strips, and we arranged the strips in a way we both found pleasing, with Jesus being the final boss. He then chose black paper to mount the poem; he would not have it simply typed and printed. Finally he signed it and was very proud of it. When I thanked him, he said "You're welcome!" with a big smile.

Frances Farrah
Polk Middle School

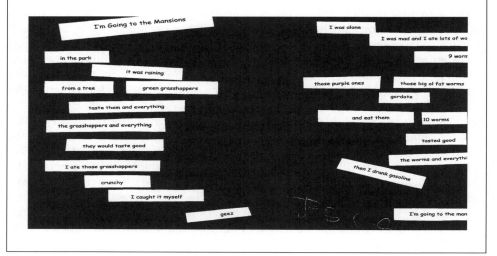

Figure 8.9.   The experience of one teacher and student in writing poetry.

generating content rather than on worrying about mechanics. This can assist students who have had little or no experience in expressing themselves in written form to practice putting their ideas down on paper.

SUMMARY

Students with moderate or severe disabilities can create meaningful texts if given individualized supports and authentic opportunities to develop and practice their skills. The first step is for us, practitioners and caregivers, to deepen our understanding of what the writing process is and to view these individuals as authentic writers with messages to communicate. Their capabilities are more often hampered by our lack of vision than by their own challenges.

Chapter 9

Supporting Literacy Development with Assistive Technology

Beth E. Foley and Amy Staples

INTRODUCTION

In previous chapters, we learned about the importance of providing students who have significant disabilities with the print-rich environments and comprehensive literacy instruction typically found in general education classrooms. We know, however, that children with severe disabilities are often excluded from high-quality literacy learning experiences (Foley & Pollatsek, 1999; Foley & Staples, 2003; Hedrick et al., 1999; Katims, 1996; Koppenhaver, 2000) despite the fact that balanced literacy instruction develops essential skills such as phonemic awareness, vocabulary development, reading comprehension, and communication fluency. No Child Left Behind (NCLB) and IDEA legislation mandates explicit, systematic, and research-based instruction for *all* students, as well as increased access to the general education curriculum for those with significant disabilities. However, such children often face significant barriers to literacy learning that compromise the instructional opportunities afforded them by NCLB. Because they may have difficulty communicating effectively, understanding spoken language, and accessing and producing written text independently, many require assistive technology (AT) tools and strategies to participate in and benefit from high-quality literacy instruction.

In this chapter, we examine the ways that AT can improve literacy outcomes for individuals with significant disabilities, mainly by minimizing the barriers to their active participation in the general education curriculum. We will define AT, including augmentative and alternative communication (AAC) technology, explain how to assess literacy-related AT/AAC needs, and provide examples of how AT/AAC use can be integrated into the learning contexts and activities commonly associated with balanced literacy instruction.

ASSISTIVE TECHNOLOGY BACKGROUND

Ever since 1975, AT devices and services have technically been within the scope of the Individuals with Disabilities Education Act (IDEA) of 1990. However, the incorporation of these devices and services into students' educational programs significantly predates by more than a decade the congressional coining of the phrase *assistive technology*. The specific terms *assistive technology devices* and *assistive technology services* were first used in the Technology-Related Assistance for Individuals with Disabilities Act of 1988 (PL 100-407), which clarified existing legislation regarding technology access for Americans with disabilities. In 1990, the terms were incorporated into IDEA, and in 1992, into its regulations to further specify the role of AT in public education. *Assistive technology device* was defined as "any item, piece of equipment, or product system, whether acquired commercially, modified, or customized, that is used to increase, maintain, or improve functional capabilities of individuals with disabilities." (*Federal Register*, August 19, 1991). Within this inclusive definition are AT options ranging from no-tech to high-tech (see Table 9.1 for the general categories of AT and examples of each). No-tech strategies (e.g., providing sign language interpreters to students who are deaf) and low-tech adaptations and devices (e.g., enlarged pencil grips or magnifiers) are every bit as important as high-tech solutions (e.g., a Braille Notetaker or battery-powered wheelchair) if an individual's functional capabilities are improved, increased, or maintained through their use.

The purpose of all of these AT devices, whether simple or electronically complex, is to empower individuals with disabilities to break through the barriers that exclude them from participating in appropriate social, educational, and vocational experiences, thereby increasing their independence.

In addition to AT devices, related support services are a necessary component of AT implementation. *Assistive technology services* are specified in the federal regulations as those activities that assist individuals in selecting, acquiring, and using appropriate technology, including

- evaluation of a person's need for AT devices
- purchasing or leasing AT devices
- designing and fabricating devices
- coordinating services offered by those who provide AT services
- providing training or technical assistance to a person who uses AT
- training and technical assistance to those who work with people who use AT devices such as teachers or employers

By including specific reference to AT services, the law recognizes the importance not only of providing assistive devices, but also of ensuring professional support for successful implementation of AT solutions.

In the years since the 1990 IDEA amendments were enacted, AT use in the public schools has expanded. However, the pace of this growth has been slow, and many students with significant disabilities have not had access to appropriate technology, often because of unlawful restrictions related to cost. The 1997 IDEA Amendments were developed to strengthen the foundations of AT provision in the public schools, and, as a result, AT is no longer a school system option. Simply put, if a student requires AT devices and services to obtain a free and appropriate education, then public schools *must* provide it at no cost to parents. The language of the Individuals with Disabilities Education Improvement Act of 2004 (PL 108-446) is even stronger, requiring that AT be considered as part of *every* individualized education program (IEP). This legislation emphasizes that such devices and services must support the general education curriculum.

Table 9.1.   General categories of assistive technology

Categories of assistive technology	Examples (low, medium, high tech)
Communication	Communication board with pictures AAC device with digitized speech output Computer-based AAC system
Writing—mechanics	Pencil/pen with adapted grip Adapted paper (e.g., raised lines) Portable word processor
Writing—composition	Word bank/word wall Electronic talking dictionary/thesaurus Multimedia software for expression of ideas
Alternate computer access	Arm support Track ball with onscreen keyboard Voice-recognition software
Reading	Changes in text size, spacing, color Books adapted for easier page-turning Electronic books
Learning/studying	Print or picture schedule Voice output reminders for assignments Software for organizing ideas and studying
Activities of daily living	Non-slip materials to hold things in place Adaptive eating utensils Adaptive dressing equipment
Math	Number line/abacus Talking calculator Tactile/voice output ruler
Recreation and leisure	Adapted toys and games Universal cuff to hold crayons and paints Drawing/graphic program on computer
Positioning and seating	Adapted chair Prone stander Custom-fitted wheelchair seat cushion
Mobility	Walker Manual wheelchair Powered wheelchair with sip/puff control
Environmental control	Light-switch extension Powerlink and switch to turn on electrical appliances Radio/remote-controlled door opener
Vision	Magnifier Screen/text reader Braille keyboard and note taker
Hearing	Pen and paper Real-time captioning Personal amplification system

Operating under the mandates of IDEA and NCLB, public schools today are held accountable for the progress of students with significant disabilities toward achieving academic content goals. It is the intent of the law that all students, regardless of ability, have access to the general curriculum. Access may encompass inclusion in the general education classroom and/or adapting or modifying the existing curriculum to allow participation by the student with special learning needs. As NCLB is implemented, the use of AT will be essential. To participate fully in general education classroom activities, students need to see, hear, speak, write, and process information. When a student has a significant disability in one or more of these areas, AT bridges the gap between the student's functional skills and his or her ability to participate in the educational process. To be effective, AT use must be aligned with the performance requirements of the general education curriculum, and IEP goals and objectives must reflect that integration.

Selecting Appropriate Assistive Technology

Thousands of commercially available AT products and software applications are now used in educational settings, and the number is growing rapidly as students with significant disabilities receive part or all of their instruction in inclusive general education settings. The challenge to the IEP teams serving such students is to select the AT options that will most effectively support the learning needs of these students. Team members must have some knowledge of available AT options, and, more important, a framework that enables them to match AT devices and services to students' individual needs, abilities, and learning contexts.

The SETT framework offers an organizational tool to help IEP teams in school settings assess the needs of individual students and identify appropriate AT tools they can use for identified needs (Zabala, 1995). Because the needs of students with significant disabilities are often complex, AT assessment teams are typically multidisciplinary, including participation by the student, family members and/or caregivers, and appropriate educational and related-services professionals such as speech-language pathologists, occupational and physical therapists, special and general educators, psychologists, and administrators. The premise of the SETT framework is that teams must first gather information about the **S**tudents, the **E**nvironments in which the students spend their time, the **T**asks required for the students to be active participants in teaching/learning processes, and the **T**ools needed to complete those tasks successfully. The SETT framework links the expectations of the general education curriculum with AT solutions and offers a mechanism for assessing the effectiveness of AT interventions. Denham and Zabala (1999) developed an AT consideration guide for IEP teams that utilizes the SETT framework. This and other AT assessment guidelines, materials, and resources can be found at web sites for Joy Zabala (http://sweb.uky.edu/~jszaba0/JoyZabala.html), the Georgia Project for Assistive Technology (www.gpat.org), and the Wisconsin AT Initiative (www.wati.org). The GPAT and WATI web sites contain downloadable checklists of potential AT solutions that can be useful to IEP teams who are unsure of what AT is available for specific tasks like communication, reading, writing, and math. While there are many AT assessment tools to choose from, all share a common focus on gathering information about student abilities, specifying the academic tasks to be completed and the contexts or environments in which they occur, and then using that information to identify potential AT solutions.

Later in this chapter, as we consider literacy instruction for students with severe disabilities, we will apply a similar approach to the selection and use of AT. Before we do that, however, we will discuss the complex communication needs of students with severe disabilities, and the importance of integrating a specific category of AT referred to as augmentative and alternative communication (AAC) within literacy interventions.

Augmentative and Alternative Communication Technology

Engaging effectively in literacy instruction depends on the communication skills that students bring to the learning process. To benefit from such instruction, students must be able to communicate for various purposes in a range of natural contexts. For example, general education core curriculum standards for literacy specify that students develop the skills needed to

- Interact socially
- Retell, reenact, or dramatize stories, including personal events
- Use a variety of sentence patterns
- Select and use new vocabulary and language structures
- Use oral communication to identify, organize, and analyze information
- Explain and describe new concepts and information in their own words

As discussed in Chapter 3, these spoken language skills provide a foundation for reading and writing abilities, but are typically poorly developed in students who have complex communication needs secondary to intellectual, physical, sensory, and/or neurological impairments (Berninger & Gans, 1986a, 1986b; Foley, 1993; Foley & Pollatsek, 1999; Smith, 1989, 2005). Students who are unable to speak, have speech that is difficult to understand, or have severe deficits in language comprehension are unlikely to make progress toward the performance standards listed above unless they are provided with AAC supports for expressive and receptive language development. In this chapter, the term *AAC* will be used to refer to communication techniques an individual uses either *in addition to* (i.e., augmentative) or *instead of* (i.e., alternative) whatever naturally acquired speech, gestures, or vocalizations he or she may have.

For students with limited verbal skills, a common misconception is that AAC will interfere with natural speech development and decrease their motivation to communicate. Professionals (and many parents) who operate under this erroneous assumption will consider AAC supports only after efforts to develop natural speech have failed. However, current research indicates that early and consistent AAC supports have a facilitating effect on speech and language development in persons with severe disabilities, including children (Bondy & Frost, 1995; Romski & Sevcik, 1996) and adults with developmental disabilities (Foley & Staples, 2003). AAC supports may include teaching strategies such as providing adequate wait time for processing and responding to spoken language (Light & Binger, 1998), augmenting spoken language input with visual supports (Miranda, 2001), or engineering the classroom environment to encourage and reinforce communication (Elder & Goossens, 1996). AAC supports also include communication options such as manual sign language, as well as non-electronic and electronic communication devices and software solutions.

An example of a low-tech, non-electronic AAC system is a communication board containing pictures that a student can use to convey intended messages during a reading activity. Pointing to a picture of a book might indicate the student's desire to choose a book to read, while pointing to the thumbs up symbol might mean that the student enjoyed the book his teacher just read aloud. There are a variety of simple voice output communication aids (VOCAs) that can be employed in similar ways with students who have limited vocabulary needs. Low-tech or single-level VOCAs are designed to deliver a limited number of messages, usually not more than 20, and have the advantage of being inexpensive, simple to program, and easy to use for communicative purposes such as commenting (I like it/I don't like it), directing (Turn the page), terminating (I'm all done), or perhaps providing a repeated line during a read-aloud activity (I'll huff and I'll puff and I'll blow your house down). Examples of single-level devices include the BIGmack® communicator (AbleNet, Inc.), the Wrist Talker™ (Enabling Devices), the MessageMate™ (Words +, Inc.), and the LITTLE Step-by-Step communicator™ (AbleNet, Inc.; see Figure 9.1). Mid-tech or multilevel AAC devices are fairly easy to program and vary in price depending on specific features and vocabulary storage capacity. Messages are recorded via digitized speech and accessed by selecting symbols from either fixed or dynamic displays. These visual displays correspond to *levels* of storage in the device. Multilevel devices with *static* displays have overlays and levels that must be changed manually, making

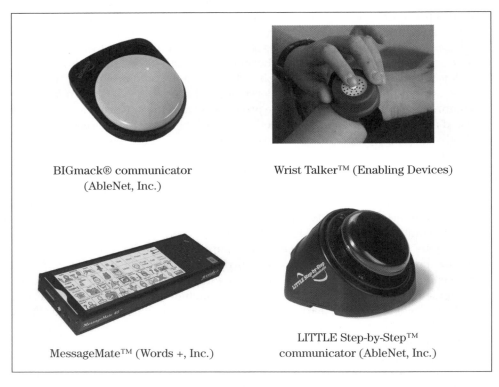

BIGmack® communicator (AbleNet, Inc.)

Wrist Talker™ (Enabling Devices)

MessageMate™ (Words +, Inc.)

LITTLE Step-by-Step™ communicator (AbleNet, Inc.)

Figure 9.1.   Examples of low-tech or single-level AAC devices.

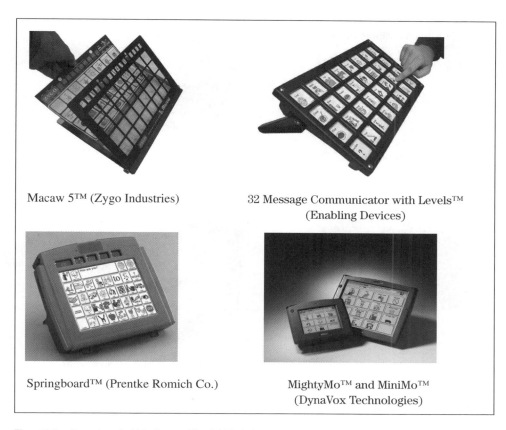

Macaw 5™ (Zygo Industries)

32 Message Communicator with Levels™
(Enabling Devices)

Springboard™ (Prentke Romich Co.)

MightyMo™ and MiniMo™
(DynaVox Technologies)

Figure 9.2.   Examples of mid-tech or multilevel AAC devices.

them difficult for many students with physical disabilities to access independently. Although the vocabulary storage capacity of these devices is greater than that of single-level options, it is still quite limited (e.g., if a static display device has 32 targets and 8 levels, then 256 different words or messages can be stored). Multilevel devices with *dynamic* displays, on the other hand, allow users to access a much more extensive vocabulary without manually changing symbol displays. For example, a device display containing generic category symbols (e.g., food, places, feelings) can provide automatic links to screens containing specific items from those categories. The device display changes based on selections made by the user. Because mid-tech or multilevel devices employ preprogrammed and/or prerecorded words and phrases, they can be used very effectively during predictable instructional routines or scripted communicative interactions. A student's ability to generate novel utterances with such devices, however, is somewhat constrained by the amount and type of preprogrammed vocabulary that is available. Some popular multilevel AAC systems include the Macaw 5™ (Zygo Industries), the 32 Message Communicator with Levels™ (Enabling Devices), the Springboard™ (Prentke Romich Co.), and the MightyMo™ (DynaVox Technologies).

High-tech, comprehensive AAC devices (see Figure 9.3) are computer driven and most offer a combination of output options including high-quality dig-

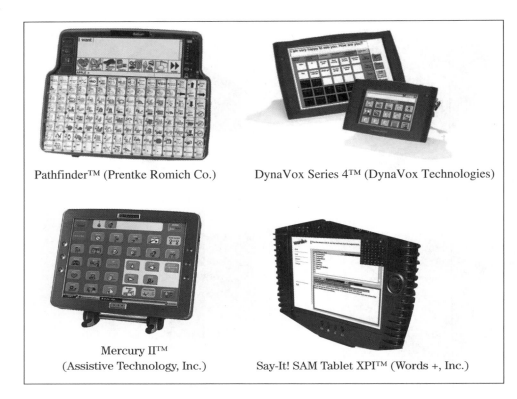

Pathfinder™ (Prentke Romich Co.)   DynaVox Series 4™ (DynaVox Technologies)

Mercury II™
(Assistive Technology, Inc.)   Say-It! SAM Tablet XPI™ (Words +, Inc.)

Figure 9.3.   Examples of high-tech or comprehensive AAC devices.

itized or recorded speech, synthesized speech, and printed output. These devices have the advantage of large memory capacities that allow for production of both preprogrammed and generative utterances. This allows for quick access to pre-stored high-frequency, generic messages (e.g., "I need some help." or "How was your weekend?") or personal stories, as well as the possibility of constructing novel messages as needed. These AAC devices provide users with a wide range of input options (e.g., touch, joystick, mouse, single switch, Morse code) and customization features that make them accessible to individuals with even the most severe motor impairments.

Most high-tech devices also offer word-processing and word-prediction functions, so access to language is limited only by the user's literacy abilities. High-tech AAC options are much more difficult to program and significantly more expensive than low- or mid-tech AAC options, but they are a necessity for individuals who are expected to develop and use conventional language and literacy skills. Some examples of comprehensive AAC systems are the Pathfinder™ (Prentke Romich Co.), the DynaVox Series 4™ (DynaVox Technologies), the Mercury II™ (Assistive Technology, Inc.) and Say-It! SAM Tablet XP1™ (Words +, Inc.).

Whatever the level of sophistication of a particular AAC system or the ability level of the user, the primary purpose of AAC use within literacy instruction is to enable individuals to communicate for a variety of purposes (e.g., commenting, labeling, describing, asking and answering questions, explaining, relating personal information, storytelling, and social interaction) in a range of naturally occurring literacy-learning contexts.

Selecting Appropriate AAC   AAC assessment involves gathering critical information about a student's cognitive, linguistic, motor, fine motor, and behavioral characteristics followed by a discussion of his or her current communication abilities and needs. Information about current communication status can be obtained using the SETT framework discussed earlier or the Participation Model described by Beukelman and Mirenda (2005). In addition, interviews with teachers and caregivers, a communication needs survey (Beukelman & Mirenda), systematic classroom observations, and other formal and informal assessment approaches provide the information needed to develop communication goals and appropriate AAC systems (see, for example, ACE: a tool for Analyzing the Communication Environment [Rowland & Schweigert, 1993]).

Educators interested in engineering their classrooms to support the language and literacy development of students with complex communication needs may benefit from collaboration with school speech-language pathologists whose professional roles and responsibilities in AAC service provision include

- assessment of AAC users, their communication partners, and the various environments in which communication occurs

- development and implementation of intervention plans that maximize effective and successful communication between individuals who use AAC and their conversational partners

- use of evidence-based practice to evaluate the functional outcomes of AAC

- coordination of AAC services, including those related to literacy learning (ASHA, 2004)

Collaboration among general and special educators, speech-language pathologists, and other related-service professionals in school settings will help ensure that students with complex communication needs have a means of understanding and using language in the classroom. At times, low-tech AAC supports will be most effective because they are simple and quick; at other times, only a high-tech AAC system with spoken or printed output will suffice. Students should not be restricted to the use of one type of AAC support or the other, but instead should be encouraged to develop a multimodal repertoire of communication skills and strategies to assist language and literacy learning.

AT/AAC AND BALANCED LITERACY INSTRUCTION

In previous chapters, authors discussed the importance of providing comprehensive, research-based literacy instruction to *all* students and described the essential elements of this instruction. Although specific organizational structures vary from teacher to teacher, balanced literacy instruction is often parsed into four main components: *guided reading*, which exposes students to a wide range of literature experiences with a focus on building comprehension; *word study*, which includes phonemic awareness, phonics, and vocabulary instruction; *self-selected reading*, which provides students with daily opportunities to read independently for sustained periods of time; and *writing*, which focuses not only on the mechanics of composition, but, more important, on communicating effectively for a variety of purposes. Each of these four components is offered on a daily basis and, when taken together, satisfy the National Reading Panel's (2000) recommendations for breadth and depth of literacy instruction.

An understanding of the key components of general education literacy instruction helps IEP teams identify potential barriers to participation for students with disabilities as well as a range of appropriate AT/AAC supports. In the next section of this chapter, we will examine each of these components (guided reading, word study, self-selected reading, and writing), related instructional access barriers, and ways to circumvent those barriers through the use of AT/AAC supports.

The Role of AT/AAC in Guided Reading

Guided reading instruction helps readers understand that reading is a meaning-making activity. Teachers typically read aloud to students to model how good readers approach text, how they make sense of it, and how they figure out unfamiliar words in connected text. As described in Chapter 4, teachers often employ a variety of pre-reading, during-reading, and post-reading strategies to activate background knowledge, maintain student interest, and provide opportunities for processing the text at deeper levels. Guided reading activities occur in both whole-class and small-group contexts, and in homogeneous and heterogeneous configurations.

During guided reading, most teachers choose texts for their students to read that are at their instructional level, meaning that children can decode 95%–97% of the text without error and comprehend at a level of at least 75%–80% (Betts, 1946). This standard is important because during guided reading there is a focus on processing the text, learning comprehension strategies to apply to other texts, and considering text content in a critical way. If children devote all of their attention to decoding the text, they have few cognitive resources for focusing on other tasks.

Barriers to participation in guided reading activities for students with severe disabilities can include physical barriers (e.g., inability to turn the pages of a book), communication barriers (e.g., not having a means to ask/answer questions or participate in discussions about books), and cognitive barriers (e.g., poor decoding skills or comprehension difficulties). AT/AAC devices and services can minimize or eliminate many of these obstacles.

Physical Barriers to Participation in Guided Reading   For students with significant disabilities who cannot manipulate conventional books, AT devices offer physical access to the text. Teachers can utilize a range of AT options to make text accessible. A simple no-tech strategy would be to read text aloud to the person with a disability. Paired reading activities, during which a peer reads the text aloud and the student with the disability follows along, provide another no-tech strategy for text access. However, reading aloud is not always feasible or desired, and it is important that students with disabilities have opportunities to read text independently.

Low-tech solutions to this kind of access problem include adapting books to make the pages easier to turn. This can be done by placing separators or *fluffers* between the pages, or by removing the binding of a book, laminating the pages, and placing them in 3-ring binders. Making tape recordings of books read aloud by peers who are competent readers can provide another simple, low-tech alternative to standard texts. One of the drawbacks of using taped books, especially with longer reading selections, is that it can be difficult for students to maintain the synchronization of voice and text. Similarly, if students must complete assignments that involve responding to information in the text, rewinding audio-tapes to a particular place in the book can be challenging.

Other AT options provide a greater measure of control for students with physical access problems. One such device is the BookWorm™ (AbleNet), which enables students to access books via switches. Information is recorded onto the BookWorm cartridge, and the student advances through the book by either pressing buttons on the BookWorm or activating a switch. A similar but less expensive option would be to use a computer, scanner, and PowerPoint software to create books that students can access page by page by hitting the spacebar or a switch.

Digitized texts represent another point of access. These are electronic texts that can be read by a computer, either using a recorded human voice or a synthesized computer-generated voice. Many publishers of leveled texts (e.g., Scholastic and Steck-Vaughn) have multimedia electronic companions of their print texts available for purchase. For example, Wiggleworks™ (Scholastic), a popular leveled-reading program, includes digital versions of each of its titles. A student who cannot physically manipulate a book can click a mouse to turn pages or have some or all of the text read aloud. Pair-It Books™ (Steck-Vaughn) have similar features and offer collections of thematically related fiction and non-fiction titles that can be made accessible through a variety of alternative access devices (e.g., enlarged keyboard, trackball).

The Internet is another rich source of electronic text. Popular sites for children such as the Public Broadcasting System (www.pbs.org) have areas that enable children to read and have stories read to them. Another web site providing text online is Tumblebooks (www.tumblebooks.com), which has multimedia books with features similar to the WiggleWorks and Pair-It Books. Students choose which book they would like to read and that book comes up in a reader window. By clicking, the students can have all or part of the text read to them. Tumblebooks is a fee-for-service program where users pay for the books they read. Schools can purchase annual subscriptions to the service so that all students have access. A range of companies catering to the special education field also offer electronic books or electronic access to books (see Resources).

Like motor impairments, sensory impairments can make participation in guided reading activities difficult unless AT supports are provided. Students who are visually impaired, for example, may need magnifiers, large print books, books on tape, and/or electronic text readers. They can also make use of standard computer-accessibility features that enable them to customize the computer's visual display by changing text size, spacing, background colors, and contrasts as needed. Students who are blind may need access to Braille books, screen reader software, or Braille translation software in order to participate in guided reading activities. Students with hearing impairments may benefit from the use of visual supports (e.g., pictures, graphic organizers), personal amplification systems, and/or classroom FM systems to augment spoken language input. Students who are deaf may need sign language interpreting services in the classroom if they are to benefit from guided reading activities.

Communication Barriers to Participation in Guided Reading   As

discussed earlier in this chapter, many students with severe disabilities have complex communication needs that necessitate the use of AAC supports. These supports enable students to communicate in meaningful ways for a variety of purposes during guided reading activities. During pre-reading activities, for example, when new vocabulary words essential for story comprehension are typically introduced, the teacher can relate them to symbol sets familiar to the AAC users. For example, the word *delighted* could be related to the symbol for *happy* on a communication board or AAC device. In addition, AAC symbols can be added to graphic organizers like semantic maps, storyboards, and KWL charts to highlight and organize critical information (see Figure 9.4 for an example of an adapted semantic map constructed using Inspiration software).

During read alouds, the teacher can support students with complex communication needs by stopping at various points in the story or informational text to paraphrase and/or summarize information using simple language. As events occur and/or characters are introduced in a story, he can provide visual support in the form of pictures of major events and characters or related AAC symbols. He can write questions generated during the read aloud on sticky notes (e.g., "What is a baleen whale?" "What do whales eat?"). When peers are reading on their own to find out and share the answers to these questions, students with communication impairments can put the sticky notes on the pages of their books to indicate where they located the information.

Post-reading, low-tech AT/AAC supports can provide a means for students to respond to texts in a variety of ways, depending upon the type of text and the

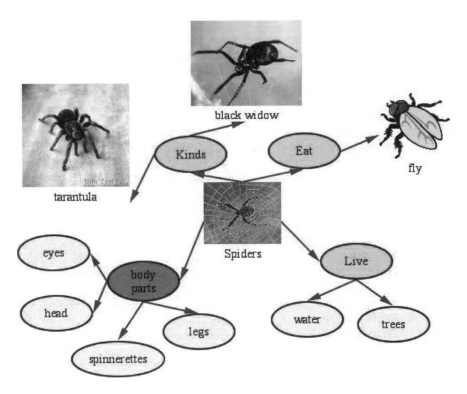

Figure 9.4.   Example of a semantic map.

purposes set for a particular reading selection. For example, students can *retell* a story with pictures, use AAC symbols to complete a story map, rate a story (thumbs up or thumbs down), act out the story with props, organize story vocabulary by adding AAC symbols to a semantic map, or put symbol-sentence strips in order to demonstrate knowledge of the story sequence. These AAC supports give students repeated opportunities for understanding and communicating about given topics and assist them in internalizing their knowledge of different text structures. Individuals with significant communication impairments may require a high level of teacher scaffolding initially, but most will demonstrate increasing levels of independence during guided reading activities over time when appropriate AT/AAC supports are provided (Foley & Staples, 2003; Hedrick, Katims, & Carr, 1999).

High-tech AAC devices hold the greatest promise for independence during guided reading because they provide users with access to a large and varied vocabulary as well as the potential for more complex, generative, and spontaneous language use. Students who learn to communicate effectively with comprehensive AAC systems are neither limited to a set of scripted utterances selected by someone else, nor forced to rely on others to anticipate their expressive language needs.

Cognitive Barriers to Participation in Guided Reading

Many students with severe disabilities, particularly those who use AAC, have reading levels that are much lower than would be predicted based on their cognitive and/or linguistic abilities. For some, poor decoding skills are the chief barrier to reading at higher levels. There are several electronic AT devices available that can help them bypass decoding difficulties to access text at their listening comprehension levels. The Readingpen® by WizCom Technologies, for example, allows the reader to scan individual words or lines of text and have them spoken. The Aspire-Reader (CAST Universal Design for Learning) is a handheld electronic reader that enables the user to download electronic books, have some or all of the text read to him or her via human-recorded or computer-generated speech, regulate the reading rate as needed, highlight important parts of the text, and take notes that can be sent to a graphic organizer.

Inspiration® and Kidspiration® (Inspiration Software) or Draft:Builder® (Don Johnston) can help students organize and categorize pertinent information during guided reading activities. Teachers can create semantic maps, graphic organizers, and/or templates of narrative and expository text structures. As students read through text, they can fill in the templates. Both Draft:Builder and Inspiration products have text-to-speech features that can be activated to support struggling readers. Inspiration software has an added benefit of a library of graphics and digital photos that can provide additional support to students with cognitive impairments and limited reading skills.

The Internet should again be considered as an important tool to support comprehension. Because of its combination of video, image, and text-based content, plus the relative ease with which the text can become audible to poorer readers, the Internet offers teachers an effective means of building background knowledge prior to reading a text, exploring an element of a text more deeply, or accessing original texts. For example, if students are completing a unit on arachnids and the teacher plans to have them read a nonfiction book on spiders, she could easily locate websites that provide information about spiders in multimedia formats. She could have students view the sites singly or in small groups, learn about spiders, and share what they've learned with the class before reading the targeted nonfiction book. For students with severe disabilities who often have limited world knowledge and experience, this type of Internet-based *virtual* experience can build the critical background knowledge needed for text comprehension. Technology in this case is available to anyone with access to a computer. While it is not specialized in any way, it becomes assistive when it provides key cognitive supports to students with disabilities.

AT/AAC and Guided Reading: A Case Example

Jake's first-grade class is getting ready to read the book *Dear Zoo.* His teacher reads the title of the book and asks whether anyone in the class has ever been to a zoo. Using a high-tech AAC device called a DynaVox, Jake relates a recent personal experience involving a trip to the zoo. He selects symbols for *I + go,* and then adds a past tense marker to change *go* to *went.* Next, he selects symbols representing *to* and *the,* followed by a symbol labeled *places.* When *places* is selected, the screen changes to a page of symbols representing different places; here Jake finds the symbol for *zoo.* He then speaks his completed message through the synthesized speech output of the device. When his teacher asks him for more details, Jake navigates to an *animals* page and tells his classmates which animals he saw on his trip. Later, when students are practicing reading the predictable book in a standard print format, Jake uses his device to read the text aloud to himself or a partner. Although participation in guided reading activities obviously takes longer for Jake than it would for a typically developing peer, his teacher provides him with adequate wait time because she feels that the benefits of giving Jake an independent voice outweigh the drawbacks associated with his slow rate. Jake's peers are typically patient as well. They are accustomed to his use of the DynaVox and seem to view it not as an oddity but as an extension of who Jake is.

AT/AAC and Word Study

The focus of the *word study* component of balanced literacy instruction varies according to the literacy levels of the students. Some of the most common core curriculum expectations addressed through word study are that students will

- demonstrate phonemic awareness and knowledge of alphabetic principles
- demonstrate decoding and word recognition strategies
- use word identification strategies appropriately to decode unknown words (e.g., *graphophonic, syntactic, semantic*)
- use pronunciation, sentence meaning, story meaning, and syntax to confirm accurate decoding

As described in Chapter 5, some of the instructional activities commonly used in general education classrooms are Word Walls, Making Words, Round Up the Rhymes, Guess the Covered Word, and Odd One Out. When students with severe disabilities have physical, communication, or cognitive access issues that prevent them from participating in these activities in a typical manner, they may benefit from a variety of AT solutions.

Physical Barriers to Participation in Word Study   Simple low-tech AT options for students with physical access issues include personal Word Walls, magnetic letters or alphabet blocks that can be easily manipulated during Making Words activities, and tape-recorded music or rhymes that enable students to engage in word play. More sophisticated technology also can be used such as text-to-speech word processing programs that allow students to hear the words or nonwords they make (e.g., Write:OutLoud and Intellitalk). Wiggleworks, the program discussed in the guided reading section of this chapter, includes an accessible onscreen magnetic word board feature that enables students to select letters, combine letters into words, and see/hear what happens when beginning or ending sounds are changed or prefixes and/or suffixes are added. Commercially available software programs like Bailey's Book House (Edmark) can offer students with motor impairments switch-accessible letter identification, rhyming, and word-building activities.

Communication Barriers to Participation in Word Study   Many commonly used word study activities involve speech production. For example, students are asked to say the sounds associated with letters and letter combinations, blend and segment words orally, sound out unfamiliar words, and develop automatic sight word recognition that they demonstrate by reading words aloud fluently. Students with moderate to severe speech impairments benefit from adaptations to word study activities because they are unable to perform these tasks in a typical manner. An alternative to a rhyme production task for such a student, for example, is to provide a display of pictures and ask the student to point to a word that rhymes with a target word supplied by the teacher. An Odd One Out activity can be modified by providing four AAC symbols (e.g., *fish*, *fan*, *man*, and *fat*) and having the student point to or look at the one that doesn't belong.

Additional support for development of word analysis skills can be provided via voice output communication devices. Mid-tech AAC devices can be used to *chant* during Word Wall activities. During Round Up the Rhyme activities, they can be programmed with displays of symbols representing rhyming words from a predictable book. Students can select pairs of symbols from the display, have the names of the symbols spoken, and decide whether they rhyme. They can also use AAC devices to recite nursery rhymes or fill in missing words (e.g., Humpty Dumpty sat on a ____). Displays can be programmed with individual sounds so that a student can participate when the teacher asks students to identify individual sounds in words (e.g., "What is the first sound in *mat?*" "The last sound?").

With high-tech AAC devices, alphabet dictionaries can be created so that when a letter is selected, the name of the letter is spoken and a page of words beginning with that letter is displayed. These devices can also be programmed with phoneme pages that enable students to experiment with letter combinations and to hear resulting words (or nonwords) pronounced by the device. The speech support provided by high-tech devices during word study may help students with complex communication needs strengthen their ability to store and retrieve phonological representations they access via print (Foley, 1993; Foley & Pollatsek, 1999; Foley & Staples, 2003).

Cognitive Barriers to Participation in Word Study   Students with severe disabilities typically develop word-level reading and spelling skills much more slowly than their peers. Without these skills it is difficult for such students to advance beyond a mid-second-grade reading level. Opportunities for individualized instruction and repeated practice can be provided via accessible speech-supported computer software designed for that purpose. Examples of software programs that can be used to support word study in students with cognitive impairments include Leap Into Phonics (Scholastic), Simon Sounds It Out and WordMaker (Don Johnston Co.), and Balanced Literacy (Intellitools, Inc.).

AT/AAC and Word Study: Two Case Examples

Cara is a kindergarten student who has a severe speech impairment secondary to muscular dystrophy. During phonemic awareness activities requiring speech, she uses a mid-tech AAC device with digitized or recorded speech output. For example, when Cara is asked by her teacher to say the first sound in *fish* she selects a communication symbol representing the *f* sound and says it aloud. During an Odd One Out activity, her teacher presents her with an array of four pictures (e.g., fish, fan, man, fat), allowing Cara to demonstrate her phonemic awareness by pointing to the picture that does not belong. During center time, Cara practices her phonemic awareness skills using a computer software program with speech output called Simon Sounds It Out™. When other children are on the floor manipulating letter tiles to form words, Cara participates using larger magnetic letters on a slant board. With these simple adaptations and AAC supports, Cara is developing critical phonemic awareness skills along with her peers.

Across the hall in the first-grade classroom is Tyler, a student with cerebral palsy and limited verbal ability who uses his electronic communication device during word analysis activities. His device is programmed with a variety of phoneme pages that generate letter sounds rather than letter names during these phonics activities. He is learning to read and spell by analogy using a page that is organized in an onset-rime format. He is able to select known rime patterns (e.g., -at, -an, -in) and generate word families by varying initial sounds. The AAC device pronounces the initial sound when selected, then the rime, and finally the blended word. Tyler is able to obtain more accurate speech feedback from the device during these activities than he can produce himself given his severely impaired articulation skills. When it is time to read or spell words that he is learning, Tyler navigates to pages specifically designed for those purposes.

AT/AAC and Self-Selected Silent Reading

The purpose of the *self-selected silent reading (SSSR)* component of literacy instruction is to encourage students, including those with complex communication needs (CCN), to see themselves as readers by providing them with interesting, accessible, and age- and developmentally appropriate texts to read on a daily basis (Erickson, Koppenhaver, & Yoder, 2002; Steelman, Pierce, & Koppenhaver, 1993).

These may include texts appropriate for browsing (e.g., catalogs, magazines), for emergent reading (e.g., wordless picture books, captioned photo journals, language experience stories illustrated with digital photos, multimedia texts with speech support), for beginning reading (e.g., predictable books, decodable texts), and for more skilled reading (e.g., fiction and nonfiction texts related to classroom themes or content areas). Thus, SSSR offers students daily opportunities to read books of their own choosing without evaluation. Teachers should assist students in choosing books that are both highly motivating and written at their independent reading level (Wigfield & Guthrie, 1997). If students regularly choose high-interest books that are too difficult, they may not develop fluency and/or an appreciation of books.

Physical Barriers to Self-Selected Silent Reading   Many of the AT/AAC supports discussed in the guided reading section are applicable here. As described earlier, teachers may want to modify traditional print books to make them physically accessible to students with motor impairments. Large-print books may be used to make text more accessible to students with low vision. Commercially available products such as LeapPad® by LeapFrog (www.leapfrog .com) and Fisher Price's Read with Me system (www.fisher-price.com) can be used to support independent reading. These systems enable a student to read words aloud by touching an electronic pen to words on the page. A range of book titles, from preschool through upper elementary, are available in this format. Another AT option discussed previously is to provide students with books and magazines in electronic formats; these can be obtained via organizations such as Bookshare (www.bookshare.org), the American Printing House for the Blind (http://www.aph.org/), and other online sources listed in Resources.

Communication Barriers to Participation in Self-Selected Silent Reading   The purpose of independent reading, as stated earlier, is to provide students with opportunities to read books of their own choosing for enjoyment. Communication is an important part of this process. Students with complex communication needs must have a way to tell others what books they would like to read. One low-tech solution is to use a communication board containing scanned images of book covers to facilitate this process. As an alternative, students could be presented with a picture menu of book topics or titles from which to choose. Another solution that supports a higher level of independence is to have a series of accessible interactive books available on the computer during self-selected reading time. Interactive books have user options that enable students to have a narrator read the book aloud, pronounce unfamiliar words, show related video clips, and explain new and/or difficult vocabulary in the story. These communication scaffolds can dramatically increase student engagement and comprehension during self-selected reading and can reduce the need for teacher or peer support.

In addition to book selection and access, students with complex communication needs must have a means of sharing thoughts and opinions about books they have read. Students might keep a reading log, adding communication symbols such as *thumbs up* or *thumbs down* to rate each story and share their ratings with peers. For students using electronic AAC devices, more complex displays could be designed using generic phrases such as "I really liked it," "It was boring," or "You should definitely read this!," as well as specific vocabulary (e.g., character names, places) that they can use to generate their own comments about books they have read.

Cognitive Barriers to Participation in Self-Selected Silent Reading

Some students with language impairments and/or poor decoding skills have interests in texts that are written at a higher reading level than they can access independently. High-interest, low vocabulary texts are useful for such students and are available in print form from such companies as Scholastic and High Noon. Start-To-Finish books (Don Johnston) also support students with low reading abilities and have an interest level of 8–16 years. Multiple formats (paperbacks, computer books, audiobooks) accommodate different learning styles and abilities.

A variety of AT/AAC supports can help students learn about topics before they read about them and organize or summarize what they've read. Movies or video and text from the Internet can support their development of background knowledge. Graphic organizers can help students keep track of characters or main events as they read, thereby increasing comprehension and decreasing verbal memory demands.

Students with significant cognitive impairments who do not have conventional literacy skills may still enjoy independent reading activities such as looking at pictures in books, browsing through catalogs, or reading language experience stories that combine photographs and simple text. Ultimately, the goal is to make sure that all students, regardless of their perceived intellectual capacity, have regular opportunities to interact with a variety of reading materials that they choose.

AT/AAC and Writing

Students in general education classrooms are expected to write for a range of academic and social purposes. They participate in various aspects of the writing process including topic selection, planning, writing, revising, and editing. They also learn to use resources for writing such as individual word banks (e.g., Word Walls), pictures, graphic organizers, and storyboards. Because students with severe disabilities often have motor, linguistic, and/or cognitive impairments that interfere with writing development, AT/AAC supports are essential to their participation in the writing process.

An important thing to remember when considering the writing needs of students with severe disabilities is that writing is an extraordinarily complex activity. Students must generate ideas about what to write, decide what language to use to express those ideas, translate that language into print, and monitor for accuracy and legibility. A number of barriers exist, some imposed externally (such as topic or length constraints) and some originating from within the writer (e.g., knowledge of topic, awareness of writing conventions, physical ability to construct text). AT/AAC technology can provide valuable support for students with disabilities as they navigate this complicated process.

Physical Barriers to Participation in Writing   From a physical standpoint, a writer's ability to hold a pencil, form letters, and edit a document influences his or her degree of success and independence. Low-tech supports for writing include pencil grips and chubby crayons or pencils that improve grasp, or even gel pens which move across the page more easily. Paper with raised lines can help a writer manage spatial elements of writing. For students who have

more severe problems with handwriting, word-processing programs provide a way to compose text with greater accuracy and less fatigue. Some teachers may be reluctant to introduce a keyboard for writing, especially for younger writers, because they believe children should develop their handwriting. However, if a student must devote his or her cognitive resources to the physical act of forming letters rather than the expression of ideas, he or she may tire easily and write much less than intended. Keyboard access may enable the student to construct text of greater length while experiencing less fatigue. Keyboards can have a traditional QWERTY layout, a high frequency or alphabetic layout, or vary in size and letter configuration. Nontraditional or alternative keyboards can be smaller in size (e.g., MacMini by TASH International) to accommodate users with good fine motor control but limited range of movement, or they can be larger than usual (e.g., Big Keys Plus by Greystone Digital) to support users with visual or fine motor concerns.

Intellikeys (Intellitools) is an example of a flexible alternative keyboard that comes with a variety of preconfigured overlays arranged in alphabetic, qwerty, and high frequency key configurations. It also enables teachers to design new overlays tailored to students' specific physical abilities and/or writing needs. For example, an overlay can be programmed so that students can select words, phrases, or sentences with a single touch and have them appear in a word-processing document. Hundreds of teacher-created overlays and lesson plans that can be used to support writing instruction are available to download from the Intellitools web site.

When keyboard support alone does not substantially improve a writer's ability to translate text effectively, word prediction software presents an efficient way to increase rate and accuracy. Word prediction software programs such as Co:Writer (Don Johnston), WordQ (WordQ), and WriteAway (Information Services) all operate under the same principle. As users type letters, the software program guesses, usually based on grammar, recency, and frequency, which words the user might be trying to construct. The program offers a selection of word options that change as each letter is typed (see Figure 9.5 for word prediction software constructed by CoWriter). In many of these programs, the writer can hear word choices by placing the cursor over each word. Once the writer selects a word, it is typed. These programs automatically capitalize the beginning of each sentence, put spaces between words, and then shift the sentence to a word processing window once a punctuation key is hit. Most word prediction software can be accessed via multiple input methods (e.g., onscreen keyboard with scanning, head mouse, trackball) to accommodate a range of physical needs.

While word prediction software may increase rate and spelling accuracy during writing, it also may influence a writer's production of written text in other, less desirable, ways. For example, a writer may opt to use words suggested by the program rather than the words he or she originally intended to write because it is easier and faster to do so. In addition, a writer who can recognize and select correctly spelled words may not develop the skills to spell the same words independently. In fact, recent research suggests that for some users, word prediction may have a negative impact on generative spelling development and therefore should be used in conjunction with systematic spelling instruction (Hart, 2006). As with any AT option, the pros and cons of using word prediction software must be carefully weighed for each student.

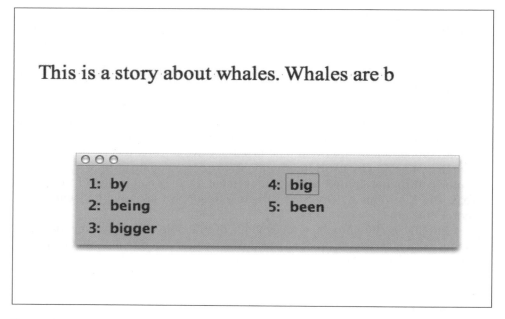

Figure 9.5.   Example of word prediction software.

Communication Barriers to Participation in Writing   Writing is a form of communication and a social interactive process (Nystrand, 1990). As writers, students must be able to effectively communicate ideas to their readers. They must also be able to communicate their reactions to written text produced by others. In order to participate fully in this social interactive process involving the writer, the reader, and the text, students with CCN may require the use of AAC supports.

Low-tech AAC supports such as simple communication boards can enable students to choose topics to write about, create patterned stories, or make comments about other students' writing (e.g., "That's funny," "I like that," "I don't understand"). Emergent writers with limited spelling ability may benefit from graphic support for translating their ideas into text. Software programs like Writing with Symbols (Widgit) and PixWriter (Slater Software) allow students to compose using a combination of picture symbols and text.

Students with significant disabilities often need scaffolds for producing written narratives (Soto, 2006). Software programs like Kidspiration (Inspiration) and Draft:Builder (Don Johnston) provide a variety of scaffolds for planning and organizing ideas. Teachers can easily create graphic organizers such as semantic webs, timelines, story maps, or cueing charts that students can use to construct more cohesive texts.

As discussed earlier, high-tech AAC devices allow students to produce both preprogrammed and generative utterances. This allows for quick access to pre-stored, generic messages during writing activities (e.g., "How do you like my story?" or "I don't know what to write about next"), as well as the possibility of constructing, storing, and printing out novel text. Most high-tech devices also offer the word-processing and word-prediction functions described earlier, so access to language is limited only by the user's literacy abilities.

Cognitive Barriers to Participation in Writing   Certainly, supporting the physical and communication demands associated with writing is important. However, writing is largely a cognitive act. The complex nature of composing even simple texts can be a challenge for students with severe disabilities. There are a number of ways AT can support the cognitive demands associated with writing during the planning, translating, and reviewing processes.

Planning involves idea generation, goal setting, and organizing. Teachers can provide structural support for planning by creating semantic webs and other graphic organizers (e.g., a graphic sequential timeline) students can use to construct more organized text. Computer software such as Inspiration, Kidspiration (Inspiration), and Draft:Builder (Don Johnston) can help students with planning by providing a way to brainstorm, to get ideas out by using pictures, and to arrange the ideas by linking them. Computer software can also support the planning process by enabling students to create a graphic representation of the story or text they would like to write. For example, Imagination Express (Riverdeep) is a thematic educational software program that allows users to first create scenes using backgrounds and realistic stamps and then compose text to describe those scenes.

Translating ideas into written text is especially difficult for students with language difficulties. Tools like sentence frames can be used to simplify the task. For example, students can write patterned stories using a cloze procedure (e.g., "I like fruit. I like _____. I like _____. I like _____"), filling in the blanks by selecting from symbol options on a communication display. As writing skills develop, stories can have more complicated structures (e.g., "I have a pet. He is a _____. His name is _____. He likes to eat _____), with the student still responsible for customizing the frames to his or her own liking. Even when these students know exactly what they want to write, spelling difficulties may slow their pace so much that the message gets lost. For some of these students, word prediction and/or voice recognition software may help with the translation process.

Reviewing is an important part of the writing process because it is during this time that students have the opportunity to review their work, or the work of their peers, to determine whether what was written matches the intent of the writer. Readers can help writers understand whether their compositions are interesting, understandable, or confusing to others. AT/AAC supports for the reviewing process include simple communication boards containing appropriate evaluative comments (I like it/I don't like it/I don't understand it), talking word processors that allow students to read aloud and/or edit what they have written, and high-tech AAC devices that enable students to read written text aloud and communicate spontaneously during the reviewing process.

AT/ACC and Writing: A Case Example

Davon is a third-grade student with autism. He rarely initiates conversation with others but does respond verbally when spoken to. When Davon tries to compose text without assistive technology, his best efforts consist of word lists or short phrases. In order to compose, Davon benefits from photographs to help him develop a story, and then word prediction software and talking word processors to translate thoughts into written text. For Davon, word prediction software is particularly useful because he has a rich sight vocabulary.

He has no difficulty recognizing the words he wishes to write and appreciates the routine associated with using word prediction. When Davon uses technology, he is able to compose several sentences at a time that are grammatically correct and, more important, tell a story.

SUMMARY

In this chapter, we have described some of the ways that AT/AAC supports can be used to make high-quality literacy instruction more accessible to students with significant disabilities. We have focused on the need to use technology as a tool to minimize barriers and increase participation in literacy learning contexts typically found in general education settings. Of course, successful inclusion of students with AT/AAC needs in comprehensive literacy instruction requires more than access to appropriate technology, placement in a general education classroom, or exposure to the general education curriculum. As discussed earlier, successful inclusion also requires a team whose members can work together to integrate an often complex array of technologies for communication, learning, and participation in the classroom (Erickson & Koppenhaver, 1995; Koppenhaver, Spadorcia, & Erickson, 1998).

Although most preservice training programs in special education and speech-language pathology now include at least some introductory coursework in AT/AAC, few provide opportunities for implementing AT/AAC solutions within student teaching or clinical experiences involving literacy instruction. Consequently, many new graduates enter the workforce without the knowledge and skills they need to maximize literacy outcomes for their students with disabilities and function effectively as AT/AAC team members. Likewise, more experienced professionals who have had little or no AT/AAC training as part of their own educational experience typically have a limited awareness of the AT/AAC tools required to make the general education literacy curriculum accessible to their students with disabilities. The need for improved preservice and in-service training, technical support, and ongoing professional development opportunities is compelling and will remain so in years to come as new assistive technologies and evidence-based AT/AAC intervention strategies are developed (Whitmire, 2001).

Professional organizations such as the Rehabilitation Engineering and Assistive Technology Society of North America (RESNA) and the International Society of Augmentative and Alternative Communication (ISAAC) provide members with a community of professionals with interests in AT and AAC. In addition, listserv groups such as the Quality Indicators in Assistive Technology (QIAT) offer ongoing support and information about AT innovations. Finally, annual conferences such as Closing the Gap and California State University Northridge (CSUN) Technology and Persons with Disabilities Conference enable teachers to keep abreast of AT/AAC-related research and technological advancements. However, they choose to educate themselves, professionals who develop and maintain AT/AAC expertise will have the potential to provide their students with unprecedented access to high-quality literacy instruction. That increased access should translate into better literacy outcomes, greater educational, vocational, and social opportunities, and a better quality of life for their students with AT/AAC needs. (Whitmire, 2001).

Chapter 10

Organizing Literacy Instruction

Elizabeth B. Keefe

This chapter will focus on how to conceptualize and organize appropriate literacy instruction for all students that is brain-based, differentiated, and founded on the principles of universal design. As noted by Copeland in Chapter 1, students with moderate or severe disabilities are capable of mastering literacy skills if they are given access to appropriate and challenging instruction. Researchers have found that literacy instruction is often based on a hierarchy of discrete skills that in fact become a barrier to access to literacy for students who cannot demonstrate that they can master the lowest levels of the discrete skills (Farrell & Elkins, 1995; Kliewer et al., 2004; Mirenda, 2003; Ryndak, 1999). The chapter will address two major challenges. The first challenge is to break away from the hierarchical approach to literacy instruction while still addressing individualized education goals and objectives. The second challenge is to avoid *retrofitting* existing curriculum and lesson plans (Udvari-Solner et al., 2002) and instead to find ways to plan for all students from the beginning of the planning process.

LITERACY UNIT AND LESSON PLANNING TOOLS

Many reading programs and standard literacy curricula are not designed to meet the needs of students with moderate or severe disabilities. Teachers, therefore, will have to use supplementary planning tools to ensure that curriculum and instruction meet the needs of all the students in their classroom regardless of ability level. The planning and implementation tools shared in this chapter will help teachers attain that goal.

Literacy Planning Wheel

Teachers can plan literacy instruction for all students right from the start. The use of the Literacy Planning Wheel helps teachers avoid the temptation to break literacy instruction into nonfunctional units by approaching unit planning from a broad perspective that takes into account literacy standards and individualized education program (IEP) goals (see Figure 10.1). One of the advantages of this planning wheel is that it can be used with any type of text at any grade level.

Any good planning tool should be flexible and have the ability to be modified depending on a classroom situation. This process can be greatly enhanced

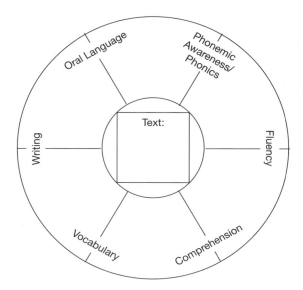

Figure 10.1. Example of a Literacy Planning Wheel.

by working collaboratively with colleagues as appropriate within a classroom, grade level, content area, and school. In general, to use the Literacy Planning Wheel the following steps are recommended:

1. *Choose* text that is appropriate for the curriculum standards and subject area(s) addressed in the unit. A book, a series of books by one author, textbooks, a particular genre of literature, poetry, plays, environmental print, or newspaper and other media are examples of text that could be used for language arts. The Literacy Planning Wheel can facilitate the integration of literacy instruction into other core subject areas and electives and can use text such as books or sets of books, a textbook, historical documents, newspapers and other media, instruction books, environmental print, or even lecture notes. The length of text chosen will vary according to grade level and length of time available for the unit.

2. *Brainstorm* ways in which the different areas of literacy instruction (oral language, phonemic awareness/phonics, fluency, vocabulary, comprehension, and writing) can be addressed using this text.

3. *Clarify and expand* the ideas generated by the brainstorming activity. Look at all of the brainstorming ideas. Which activities address the standards appropriate to your classroom? Which ideas can lead to a series of lessons that will provide brain-based instruction and allow students to meet the standards and/or individualized education program (IEP) objectives? Can these lessons be made accessible to all students in the classroom? Which aspects of the lessons can be used to assess whether the students have mastered the standards and/or IEP objectives?

4. *Select* a coherent group of lessons that can be realistically implemented in the time frame available. Any lesson-planning format will work with the Literacy Planning Wheel.

5. Complete an *evaluation and reflection* of the unit after it is completed. What areas of the unit went well? What would you change next time? Did the unit allow students the opportunity to meet standards and/or IEP goals as expected?

Literacy Planning Matrix

An alternative planning tool that also facilitates a more holistic approach to planning literacy instruction is the Literacy Planning Matrix (see Figure 10.2). This matrix allows teachers to consider each of the five major areas of literacy instruction and to look for opportunities to address these areas through oral language, reading, and writing. As with the Literacy Planning Wheel, this conceptual planning tool is flexible and can be modified to be responsive to individual teacher needs.

The following steps (similar to those for the Literacy Planning Wheel) are recommended to use the Literacy Planning Matrix:

1. *Choose* the text that is appropriate for the curriculum standards and subject area(s) addressed in this unit, using the same guidelines as stated for the Literacy Planning Wheel.

Date: _____

Developed by: _____

Text(s): _____

Grade(s): _____

Standards: _____

_____

	Oral language	Reading	Writing
Phonemic awareness			
Phonics			
Fluency			
Vocabulary			
Text comprehension			

Figure 10.2. Example of a Literacy Planning Matrix.

2. *Brainstorm* ways in which the different areas of literacy instruction (phonemic awareness, phonics, fluency, vocabulary and comprehension) can be addressed through oral language, reading, and writing using the text as the organizing framework.

3. *Clarify and expand* the ideas generated by the brainstorming activity. Look at the brainstorming ideas. Which activities address the standards appropriate to the classroom? Which ideas can lead to a series of lessons that will provide brain-based instruction and allow students to meet the standards and/or IEP objectives? Can these lessons be made accessible to all students in your classroom? Which aspects of these lessons can be used to assess whether the students have mastered the standards and/or IEP objectives?

4. *Select* a coherent group of lessons that can be realistically implemented in the time frame you have available. Any lesson-planning format will work with the Literacy Planning Matrix.

5. Complete an *evaluation and reflection* of the unit after it is completed. Which areas of the unit went well? What should be changed next time? Did the unit allow students the opportunity to meet standards and/or IEP goals as expected?

The use of holistic planning tools such as the Literacy Planning Wheel or the Literacy Planning Matrix provide students with access to a kaleidoscope of literacy opportunities rather than one rung of a ladder (Kliewer et al., 2004).

SPECIFIC INSTRUCTIONAL PLANNING STRATEGIES FOR STUDENTS WITH DISABILITIES

Brain-based teaching, differentiated instruction, multiple intelligences, and cooperative learning make it easier to include students with moderate or severe disabilities. The conceptual planning tools described above ensure that all students have access to all areas of literacy instruction and are not trapped at the bottom of the *literacy ladder*. However, strategies still need to be developed to ensure that students' individual educational needs are being addressed. It is not enough for students with moderate or severe disabilities to be merely present in general education classrooms, they must also be meaningful participants and full members of the classroom.

Program-at-a-Glance

The Individuals with Disabilities Education Improvement Act of 2004 requires that an interdisciplinary team develop goals and objectives for each student with disabilities. These goals and objectives are part of a student's IEP. It is essential that the special and general education teacher have readily accessible information about students with disabilities and their objectives. The IEP document itself is overwhelming for many educators to make into a living document. One of the roles of the special education teacher is to summarize the IEP for the general educator and other members of the educational team in a way that makes the information accessible and useful. One tool for accomplishing this is Program-at-a-Glance (e.g., Janney & Snell, 2000). The Program-at-a-Glance includes basic information about a student's strengths, objectives, and management needs on one

PROGRAM–AT–A–GLANCE

Karen's Objectives	Karen's Strengths

Academic:
- ✓ Match words to pictures
- ✓ Identify sight words
- ✓ Count 1–20
- ✓ Addition/subtraction

Social/communication
- ✓ Use assistive technology to communicate with peers and adults
- ✓ Initiate social interactions
- ✓ Respond to peers/adults
- ✓ Spend more time with peers

Self-help
- ✓ Help prepare meals
- ✓ Help clean up
- ✓ Choose food/drinks
- ✓ Help with grooming

Motor
- ✓ Move arms and legs
- ✓ Improve fine motor
- ✓ Use stander/treadmill

- ❖ Works hard
- ❖ Is patient
- ❖ Has great smile
- ❖ Understands a lot more than people think!
- ❖ Cooperates
- ❖ Is very responsive
- ❖ Has great potential to learn
- ❖ Is friendly

MANAGEMENT ISSUES
- ▪ Educational Assistant will toilet at approx. 12:30
- ▪ Educational Assistant will tube feed in AM
- ▪ Peer buddies can help in class/at lunch and transitioning between classes

Figure 10.3.   Example of Program-at-a-Glance.

page in straightforward language. Figure 10.3 demonstrates a Program-at-a-Glance the author developed for a 16-year-old student with intellectual and physical disabilities who is successfully participating in general education high school classes for five out of six periods a day.

Infused Skills Grid

Once the Program-at-a-Glance has been completed, educators need to work together to ensure that the general education classroom provides opportunities for the students to meet their IEP objectives. One tool used to achieve this is the Infused Skills Grid (see Figure 10.4), which is completed by the educational team (Castagnera et al., 1998). Ideally, the team will include the general education and special education teachers and any therapists working with the students. Sometimes parents may want to be part of the planning process. The Infused Skills

Infused Skills Grid

School name: _____   School year: _____

Student name: _____   Course: _____

Age: _____   Advocate/teacher: _____

Grade: _____   Parent/guardian: _____

Infused skills

Activities/subjects/environments

Check here
if the infused
skill was
identified by:

Family

Student

Peers

School

Figure 10.4.   Example of Infused Skills Grid.

Grid is a matrix that allows the educational team to see how a student's individual goals can be infused throughout the day in general education settings. It is important to note that the Infused Skills Grid looks at the needs of the individual student to see how skills can be addressed in general education rather than asking if the student can meet the demands of the general education classroom.

The Infused Skills Grid achieves several important goals. First, it communicates to the team opportunities for a student's individual goals, including literacy skills, to be met in general education. Second, it ensures that all team members are aware of the student's goals. Third, the grid reassures the special education

teacher, therapists, and parents that the student's individual objectives will be addressed in the general education setting. Finally, the grid identifies any skills that
cannot be addressed in general education. When this occurs, the team may decide that the goal is no longer needed or that the general education environment
can be modified so that the skills can be addressed. In rare cases, the student
may need to leave the general education classroom in order to work on the skill.

The Principle of Partial Participation

Students with moderate or severe disabilities are often denied access to quality
literacy instruction because they cannot participate in all aspects of a particular
program or lesson in the same way as their general education peers. For example, if the student cannot fully participate in a literacy program such as Open
Court, Success for All, or Four Block, then he or she is removed from general education for literacy instruction.

It is essential to consider the principle of partial participation (Baumgart et
al., 1982) when designing literacy instruction for students with moderate or severe disabilities in general education settings. The principle of partial participation is that most students with disabilities can participate meaningfully in some
aspect of an activity, lesson, or program. Instead of asking if the student can do
a particular activity, we can ask what individualized objectives the student can
achieve by participating in some part of the activity. Research has demonstrated
that when students are given access to partially participate in a general education curriculum, they often achieve at higher levels than expected (e.g., Mirenda,
2003; Ryndak et al., 1999).

Modification Questions

Once opportunities for meeting the needs of a student with intellectual disabilities in the general education classroom have been identified—considering the
principle of partial participation and using Program-at-a-Glance and Infused
Skills Grid—the next step is to determine what specific adaptations need to be
designed. A useful strategy to decide on appropriate modifications is to ask the
following curriculum adaptation questions as lessons are being planned (see Figure 10.5):

1. Can the student participate in this activity in the same way as his or her general education peers?

2. Can the student participate in the same lesson with adaptations in the environment, materials, support, and/or expectations?

3. Can the student partially participate in some aspect of the lesson?

4. Can the student participate in a similar or parallel activity within the same
   classroom?

5. If the answer to all of the above questions is no, does the student need to
   leave the general education classroom for an alternative activity? Could one
   or more general education peers also participate in this alternative activity?

In addition to deciding which adaptations are needed, the educational team must
also discuss who will provide the necessary adaptations and support for the stu-

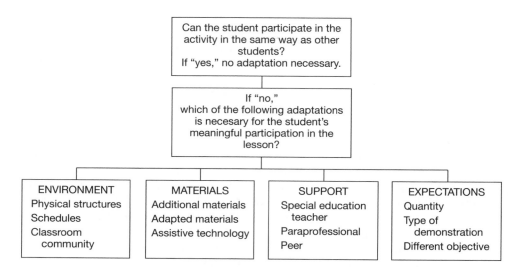

Figure 10.5. Example of curriculum adaptation planning questions.

dent. Finally, who will be responsible for evaluating and documenting the progress of the student? This kind of planning requires the establishment of strong collaborative relationships between general and special educators. (See the end of the book for a list of resources to help in the collaborative planning and implementation of accommodations and modifications for students with disabilities.)

SUMMARY

This chapter has described planning tools that can be used to implement best practices in literacy instruction and inclusive education for students with moderate or severe disabilities. Students with these disabilities need to be included in planning from the very beginning. Unit planning is related to appropriate text and guided by standards rather than limited to IEP goals. Tools to ensure that IEP objectives are addressed are included, and the importance of meaningful participation in literacy instruction is stressed.

for Life

Throughout this book we have discussed the serious consequences individuals with moderate or severe disabilities may experience when caregivers, teachers, or other practitioners have low expectations of the individuals' potential to become literate citizens. Too often these low expectations result in no or limited instruction and restricted access to the everyday literacy activities and materials that build understanding of language and literacy. The ultimate outcomes of these low expectations are adults who lack basic literacy skills and who are thus further excluded from their typical age peers in school, employment, and community settings.

Fortunately, there is a renewed interest among researchers and practitioners in examining literacy instruction for individuals with moderate or severe disabilities. Increasingly schools and families are recognizing the importance of literacy in the lives of individuals with significant disabilities and providing them access to this potentially empowering skill. Much of this work has been done with children with disabilities (e.g., Katims, 1994). Fewer programs, however, have addressed literacy instruction for adolescents or adults with significant disabilities (Farrell & Elkins, 1995; Gallaher, van Kraayenoord, Jobling, & Moni, 2002; Young, Moni, Jobling, & van Kraayenoord, 2004).

RESEARCH WITH OLDER LITERACY LEARNERS

The research focus on literacy in young children versus adolescents or adults is not remarkable. The majority of research on acquisition of reading skills by children without disabilities focuses on early childhood because this is a critical period for learning language and foundational literacy concepts. Language and literacy learning take place across the early childhood years, culminating in acquisition of beginning conventional reading and writing skills during the first few years of formal schooling (Ehri & Snowling, 2004). Basic reading and writing skills are generally acquired by third grade unless a child is having difficulty learning these skills or has not received appropriate instruction. The majority of efforts to improve reading skills of children in the nation's schools, for example, concentrate on children in K–3 (e.g., Reading First programs). Less is known about effective instruction for older students who struggle with reading (e.g., those with learning disabilities), so it is not surprising that there have been fewer investigations of literacy instruction for older individuals with moderate or severe disabilities.

Sadly, another reason that literacy learning of older individuals has received less notice is that for many years, the prevailing view in education was that older adolescents and adults with intensive support needs could not benefit from academic instruction. Experts believed that older students had moved beyond the age when they could acquire new academic skills. Educators recommended that educational programs for these learners should center primarily on functional and employment skills (Gallaher et al., 2002).

In fact, it is typical to find that educational programs for individuals with moderate or severe disabilities become increasingly focused on functional life skills (e.g., employment, meal preparation) as these students move into adolescence and young adulthood. Farrell and Elkins (1995), in describing educational programs for secondary students with Down syndrome, noted that curricula for older students becomes more focused on "nonacademic living skills in preparation for integration into the community (as if reading and writing were not to be considered essential life skills)" (p. 274). This trend has been confirmed through our own experience within secondary schools where we have frequently seen individualized education program (IEP) teams make decisions to stop academic instruction (and sometimes even direct language and communication therapy) once students reach high school age. Team members justified these decisions based on the belief that if students haven't mastered these skills (basic reading, writing, and numeracy) by adolescence, they won't ever acquire them.

The belief that older individuals with cognitive or severe disabilities cannot benefit from academic instruction is not, however, supported by research. Several researchers and practitioners have successfully demonstrated that with appropriate supports and individualized instruction, adults with significant disabilities can continue to acquire and expand literacy skills (e.g., Foley & Staples, 2003; Moni & Jobling, 2001; Pershey & Gilbert, 2002; Young et al., 2004). Some researchers have noted that adolescence and adulthood are actually optimal times for these individuals to further develop literacy learning (e.g., Farrell & Elkins, 1995). New understandings about the nature of language and literacy, the development of effective instructional practices, and the growth of technology all have contributed to more successful literacy education practices that can benefit older learners in multiple ways.

The positive findings of studies such as those mentioned above call for a shift in our view of the learning capabilities of adults with disabilities. Instead of thinking that academic instruction should cease at age 22 or younger, we need to consider that individuals with moderate or severe disabilities are capable of lifelong learning. Adults with and without disabilities can and do benefit in multiple ways from opportunities to learn new skills including literacy and language. Learning new literacy skills enhances self-esteem, creates social connections with others, opens up new leisure pursuits, increases participation in the community, and may lead to new employment opportunities or opportunities to participate in postsecondary education programs (Foley & Staples, 2003; Hamill, 2003; Pershey & Gilbert, 2002; Young et al., 2004). Farrell and Elkins (1995) summed up this new view of learning when they stated

We need, too, the Vygotskian vision that sees learning as a lifelong process in which individuals are always on the threshold of new interests and activities, trying new skills with the help and guidance of family, friends, expert helpers, teachers, or employers. Along with this view of the continuously developing person, we need a clear-headed understanding of how reading and writing are learned by everyone throughout life. (p. 279)

Literacy learning of older individuals is an expanding area of research and practice that offers exciting possibilities for individuals with significant disabilities and their families. The remainder of this chapter contains descriptions of instructional approaches and activities researchers and practitioners have found effective for adolescents and adults with moderate or severe disabilities, suggestions for age-appropriate materials and activities, and examples of adolescents and adults who exemplify lifelong literacy learning.

Literacy Instruction for Adolescents and Adults with Moderate or Severe Disabilities

Successful literacy instructional programs for adolescents and adults with intensive support needs share several common features. First, to be most effective, instruction must be based on the lives, experiences, and interests of the older students. Remember Brinkerhoff and Keefe's description of brain-based learning in Chapter 2? Just as with younger students, it is important to teach literacy skills to adults within meaningful contexts (i.e., in ways that relate to their prior and current experiences and involve them emotionally) rather than relying on decontextualized instruction. Authentic literacy activities such as reading about students' hobbies, writing cards to family members, learning sight words needed on the job, creating language experience stories based on shared visits to community sites, and other student-centered activities have all been used successfully to enhance literacy development of adults with significant disabilities. Moni and Jobling (2001), for example, reported on a successful literacy program for young adults with Down syndrome built around four themes: students' lives (families, friends, hobbies, interests), popular culture, students' communities (e.g., media, use of the Internet to explore the community), and social action aimed at increasing community participation. All the students in this program learned new skills and became more proficient readers and writers as a result of this contextualized literacy instruction.

Second, and not surprisingly, instruction that requires active student participation is more effective than passive learning activities. Learners with cognitive and severe disabilities need to engage in dynamic learning activities to acquire and retain skills (Iacono, 2004). Active learning helps to deepen their understanding of the purposes of literacy and helps them to see its application to their lives. Many of the instructional strategies found in other chapters of this book (e.g., shared writing) are effective with older learners in part because they require active student participation.

Third, instructional sessions should occur frequently and consistently and include repetition of key skills through varying contexts (Foley & Staples, 2003; Moni & Jobling, 2001). It is important to provide frequent opportunities for practicing new skills, both within instructional sessions and outside of these sessions in other areas of the individual's life. Doing so facilitates generalization of skills from the classroom setting to the student's everyday experiences. Concrete prompts such as pictures of story characters, graphic organizers used to create written texts, or actual physical objects such as a model of the human heart to accompany a text on health are also useful. These items can act as aids to memory, help students see relationships between events or concepts, and help convey meaning of new vocabulary words (Kluth, 2003).

Fourth, teachers can use technology to support students' literacy learning (Erickson, Koppenhaver, & Yoder, 1994). Computers and the multitude of literacy-related software programs available have opened up access to new literacy learning opportunities for many individuals with significant disabilities. Technology allows individuals to work at their own pace and provides the individualized supports they may require to actively participate in literacy learning. Learning to use computer programs to create texts and obtain information also allows those with cognitive and severe disabilities to participate in an activity that is highly valued in today's world. Literacy activities related to computer use are motivating to most individuals, and learning computer skills may increase opportunities in work situations.

Figure 11.1 shows a letter from a young woman with severe disabilities describing one of her recent teaching experiences in a university classroom. Michelle and her friend and facilitator Jeanne frequently visit my graduate classes on literacy to teach the graduate students in those classes about effective instruction for adults with intensive support needs. Michelle signs, uses an occasional word, and utilizes technology such as computers to communicate with others and to engage in various literacy activities. She created the text using a computer software program that allowed her to use both words and pictures to create a message. Only a few short years ago Michelle was not always perceived by those around her as capable of literate citizenship. Technology and practitioners who listened to her dreams and provided the individualized instruction

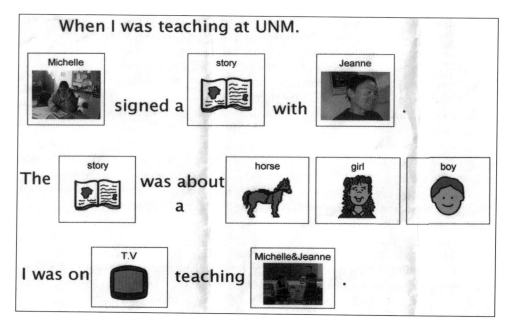

Figure 11.1.   A letter Michelle created using words and pictures.

and support she needed have facilitated her transformation from someone perceived as having nothing to talk about to someone who presents regularly in professional settings. Her story illustrates the power of high expectations and appropriate instruction and supports such as technology.

Not all technology support must be high tech, however. Low-tech support can be just as important and useful as complex electronic devices. Foley and Staples (2003), for example, described how they used choice boards, picture schedules, and pictorial task analyses to facilitate communication and literacy development of adults with autism in the adults' workplace.

A fifth component found in effective literacy instruction for adults with significant disabilities is basing instruction on student-selected goals (Moni & Jobling, 2001; Pershey & Gilbert, 2002). It is critical to ask what the older student wants to learn or accomplish and to tailor the instructional program to this purpose. Doing so enhances motivation and facilitates learning that leads to meaningful outcomes rather than acquisition of discrete skills that the individual never uses outside the instructional session. Student-directed instruction also fosters autonomy and self-determination. One of the primary goals for adolescents is learning to make their own choices and decisions. Seeking the input of adolescents and adults about what they want to learn acknowledges that they are not "children in adult bodies" (Foley & Staples, 2003, p. 326) and fosters their motivation to learn and, ultimately, their self-determination.

A final factor affecting the success of literacy instruction for adults with moderate or severe disabilities is the amount of time provided for instruction. Because most adults with intensive support needs learn at a slower pace than their typical peers, it is important to provide consistent instruction sustained over a sufficiently long time period for students to acquire and demonstrate skills. In fact, some of the most effective programs described in the literature were maintained across several years. For example, Foley and Staples (2003) and Moni and Jobling (2001) examined adult students' progress in a literacy program across 2 years. Pershey and Gilbert (2002) reported results of a successful literacy tutoring program for a woman with a cognitive disability across 7 years of instruction.

In describing their work with adults who had moderate or severe disabilities, Foley and Staples (2003) pointed out that if participants in their intervention had been assessed at the end of only a few months of instruction, they might have been viewed as incapable of acquiring literacy skills because the assessment would have revealed only very small changes in the participants' skills. These individuals needed a sustained time period in which to grasp, apply, and generalize new skills. However, at the end of 2 years of consistent instruction, all of these individuals, including those with significant learning challenges, showed measurable gains in literacy skills.

The length of time needed for adults to learn and be able to fluently apply new skills requires practitioners providing literacy instruction to rethink the ways in which these services are offered. Rather than providing short-term services or expecting participants to quickly acquire and begin to use literacy skills, agencies and others providing literacy instruction should plan to continue instructional programs for a period of several years, rather than for only a few weeks or months. This is especially important in planning for generalization of skills beyond the classroom setting. Students need extended time to learn and then practice new skills in a variety of settings and contexts if the skills are to be truly meaningful.

Age-Appropriate Literacy Materials

Literacy activities and materials for adults with intensive support needs must be appropriate both for the older students' developmental levels and their ages (Foley & Staples, 2003; Young et al., 2004). Finding engaging materials that meet both of these criteria can be difficult. There are an increasing number of appropriate published materials available for adults at the beginning stages of literacy, but practitioners will likely still need to create materials that are individualized for their students' interests and skill levels. Some suggestions for age-appropriate materials that meet a range of literacy levels include

- Wordless picture books that are appropriate for adults (e.g., *Tuesday* by David Wisner)
- Books on nonfiction topics that include numerous photographs and minimal text
- Magazines and catalogs devoted to students' particular interests (e.g., magazines focusing on sports, fashion, gardening)
- Language experience stories written by older learners and illustrated with drawings or photographs
- Newspapers
- Cookbooks and picture recipes
- Predictable books on topics that are age appropriate
- Texts of familiar songs
- Adapted versions of novels such as those created for English language learners that have simplified vocabulary and story lines
- Poetry
- Books on tape, CD with accompanying written text, or e-books with screen readers
- Published curricula and literacy materials designed for older learners (see Resources for a list of some appropriate materials and ordering information)

Literacy Activities

Many of the instructional activities described in previous chapters of this book are appropriate and effective for adolescents and adult learners if the topics and content of the activities are adjusted to be age appropriate. Following are some additional activities that have been shown to be useful in facilitating literacy learning of older learners.

Reading to Preschoolers   As mentioned earlier in this chapter, it is important to find literacy materials for older beginning and emergent readers that meet their current literacy skill levels and that are age appropriate. One way to provide early literacy instruction in an age-appropriate way is to set up opportunities for older beginning readers to read to young children. This allows the beginning reader to work with predictable texts or simple picture books, something that meets their current literacy skill level, and also puts them in a valued, age-appropriate social role as a teacher or mentor to young children.

As an example of this activity, a local high school teacher worked with the emergent readers in her class to master the book *Brown Bear, Brown Bear, What Do You See?* The simple repetitive text in the book was a good match for the students' current skill levels. Working with the book allowed them to master many important early literacy concepts, such as understanding the relationship between spoken language and print, how to move through a book from front to back, and how to use pictures as an aid to understanding the storyline. The content of the book, however, is not age appropriate for teenagers, and using such inappropriate materials is potentially stigmatizing. To transform the activity into one that was age appropriate, the teacher let students know at the beginning of the instructional unit that although the content of the book was geared toward *little kids*, the purpose of the activity was for them to be able to go to the preschool housed on their high school campus and read to the children there. Volunteering in the preschool placed these young adults in a helper role, something they rarely got to experience because they almost always were placed in the position of *being* helped rather than helping others. It provided a way for them to practice their new literacy skills, and it even offered an opportunity to explore a potential career option as a preschool aide.

Book Clubs   Another age-appropriate literacy activity for older students is to join a book club. Book clubs are a popular social activity among adults across the country. Besides providing a place to discuss literature, these groups offer opportunities for social interaction and community participation. Clubs meet in a variety of settings (e.g., bookstores, coffee shops, members' homes) and much of the fun involved is the conversation and interaction among members. During the past few years, individuals with disabilities have also joined or created book clubs as a way to acquire new literacy skills and expand their social interactions with others. Clubs meet regularly in community venues and discuss a literary selection while enjoying interactions with their friends. Figure 11.2 describes a successful local book club whose members are adults with moderate or severe disabilities. It is easy to see from this description how the Valencia Book Club offers its members opportunities to develop language and literacy skills as well as to become more active members of their local communities. Mary Clark, the staff person who created the club and supports its members, described a recent meeting in which members of another local book club mingled with the Valencia Book Club members at a bookstore, asking what book they were reading and how they are enjoying it. This illustrates how engaging in a literacy activity valued by typical peers can lead to increased social interaction and participation as well as to enhanced literacy skills.

Theater   Many adolescents and young adults enjoy participating in theater. Like joining a book club, joining a theater group offers more than just opportunities to enhance literacy skills. It also offers opportunities for fun and friendship. Theater productions facilitate community inclusion because they have a variety of roles and related jobs that allow individuals with a range of in-

The Valencia Book Club is part of the Los Luna Community Program's Employment, Volunteerism, and Community Membership. It is an innovative literacy and technology program. Initially, adults with developmental disabilities gathered in the community to share their journal writings over coffee about attending the state fair. Since then, the focus of the book club has been to meet once a month at different coffee shops in the local community to share a high-interest, age-appropriate book of the month.

In preparation for book club meetings, club members go to the library each week and research the book, topic, or author chosen for discussion at the next meeting. Members have learned to access the Internet with support and to print out information and illustrations about the topic of the month they will share with other members at the next meeting. Some club members type out their information using a word processing program with auditory support. Those with conventional reading skills are asked to practice reading aloud to support staff or peers in preparation for the next gathering.

During a recent club meeting, members focused on the book *March of the Penguins.* Several members volunteered to read factoids or to sign about penguins and their environment. For emergent readers, words were highlighted with picture cues to enhance their understanding and to develop early literacy concepts. One independent reader was chosen to read a chapter of the book to the other club members. The club then participated in a follow-up activity to reinforce comprehension of what they had read and heard and to further facilitate learning basic literacy skills. For this particular month, they watched the *March of the Penguins* on DVD and discussed the movie. They compared the movie to the book, exploring which version they preferred and why.

Figure 11.2.   Description of a successful book club.

terests and skill levels to participate. For example, some individuals fill the role of actor, others create scenery, others manage lighting, and some work as ushers or ticket sellers.

Theater offers many opportunities to acquire and enhance literacy skills. As noted in Chapter 8, acting out a story can aid in comprehending a plot or understanding the meaning of new vocabulary. If the theater experience includes writing the play itself, then opportunities for developing reading, writing, speaking, and listening skills are involved.

An outstanding example of using theater to develop literacy skills and increase community participation recently took place in a local high school. Several special and general education teachers and a speech pathologist teamed together to help their students, with and without disabilities, to develop a semester long project that culminated in the performance of a play students wrote based on *Where the Wild Things Are.* Although the book on which the play was based was intended for young children, the play was created to appeal to all ages.

Students created the text for the play, developed elaborate costumes and sets, and spent hours learning and rehearsing their lines. Typically developing students worked regularly with their partners with disabilities on a variety of literacy skills (e.g., understanding the storyline, creating and reading the text, memorizing lines). One of the most remarkable things about the production was that narrators *spoke* their lines using sign language, an AAC device, and spoken English and Spanish, reflecting the diversity of the students involved in the play. Teachers paired students who had significant cognitive and physical challenges with typically developing peers so that everyone experienced authentic participation. All participants benefited both by enhancing their literacy skills and by developing relationships with peers they would not have otherwise met.

SUMMARY

The recognition that literacy learning progresses from birth across the lifespan has significant implications for the types of services and supports provided to adolescents and adults with moderate or severe disabilities. This more comprehensive understanding of how literacy develops opens up exciting opportunities for learning that can lead to increased personal empowerment and increased participation in social, school, and employment settings for individuals with significant support needs. Instead of being seen as unable to acquire new knowledge and skills, older individuals with disabilities are increasingly being viewed as capable and offered opportunities to continue developing critical academic skills. New research findings regarding effective instructional practices combined with innovative technology that provides genuine access to learning activities are all contributing to an increased focus on lifelong literacy learning for individuals with moderate or severe disabilities.

References

Allington, R.L. (1983). The reading instruction provided readers of differing reading abilities. *Elementary School Journal, 83*(5), 548–559.

Allington, R.L. (2006). *What really matters for struggling readers*. Boston: Pearson, Allyn, & Bacon.

Allor, J.H. (2002). The relationships of phonemic awareness and rapid naming to reading development. *Learning Disability Quarterly, 25*, 47–57.

Al Otaiba, S., & Hosp, M.K. (2004). Providing effective literacy instruction to students with Down syndrome. *TEACHING Exceptional Children, 36*, 28–35.

The American heritage dictionary of the English language [Electronic version] (4th ed.; 2000). Boston: Houghton Mifflin; Bartleby.com

American Speech-Language-Hearing Association. (1982). Definition of language. Retrieved December 15, 2005, from http://www.asha.org/NR/rdonlyres/1F248614-EEF7-4D54-98AD-F3A0692EFC51/0/19130_1.pdf

American Speech-Language-Hearing Association. (2004). Roles and responsibilities of speech-language pathologists with respect to alternative communication: Technical report. *Asha Supplement, 24*, 1–17.

Armbruster, B.B., Lehr, F., & Osborn, J. (2001). *Put reading first: The research building blocks for teaching children to read: Kindergarten through grade 3*. Washington, DC: The Partnership for Reading.

Armstrong, T. (2000). *Multiple intelligences in the classroom*. Alexandria, VA: Association for Supervision and Curriculum Development.

Baer, G.T. (2003). *Self-paced phonics: A text for educators*. Upper Saddle River, NJ: Merrill Prentice Hall.

Baumgart, D., Brown, L., Pumpian, I., Nisbet, J., Ford, A., Sweet, M., et al. (1982). Principle of partial participation and individualized adaptations in educational programs for severely handicapped students. *Journal for the Association of Persons with Severe Handicaps, 7*(2), 17–27.

Bear, D., Invernizzi, M., Templeton, S., & Johnston, F. (1999). *Words their way: Word study for phonics, vocabulary, and spelling instruction* (2nd ed.). Upper Saddle River, NJ: Prentice Hall.

Beck, I.L., & McKeown, M.G. (2001). Text talk: Capturing the benefits of the read-aloud experiences for young children. *The Reading Teacher, 55*, 10–35.

Beck, I.L., McKoewn, M.G., & Kucan, L. (2002). *Bringing words to life*. New York: Guilford Press.

Bedrosian, J., Lasker, J., Speidel, K., & Politsch, A. (2003). Enhancing the written narrative skills of an AAC student with autism: Evidence-based research issues. *Topics in Language Disorders, 23*, 304–324.

Berninger, V., & Gans, B.M. (1986a). Assessing word processing capacity of the nonvocal, nonwriting. *Augmentative and Alternative Communication, 2*, 56–63.

Berninger, V., & Gans, B.M. (1986b). Language profiles in nonspeaking individuals of normal intelligence with severe cerebral palsy. *Augmentative and Alternative Communication, 2*, 45–50.

Betts, E.A. (1946). *Foundations of reading instruction, with emphasis on differentiated guidance*. New York: American Book Company.

Beukelman, D.R., & Mirenda, P. (2005). *Augmentative and alternative communication: Management of severe communication disorders in children and adults* (3rd ed.). Baltimore: Paul H. Brookes Publishing Co.

Beukelman, D.R., Mirenda, P., & Sturm, J. (1998). Educational inclusion of AAC users. In D.R. Beukelman & P. Mirenda (Eds.), *Augmentative and alternative communication: Management of severe communication disorders in children and adults* (3rd ed.; pp. 391–424). Baltimore: Paul H. Brookes Publishing Co.

Bloom, B.S. (1956). *Taxonomy of educational objectives, Handbook I: The cognitive domain.* New York: David McKay Company, Inc.

Bondy, A.S., & Frost, L.A. (1995). Educational approaches in preschool. In E. Schopler & G. Mesibov (Eds.), *Learning and cognition in autism* (pp. 311–333). New York: Plenum.

Boudreau, D. (2002). Literacy skills in children and adolescents with Down syndrome. *Reading and Writing: An Interdisciplinary Journal, 15,* 497–525.

Boyle, J.R., & Walker-Seibert, T. (1997). The effects of a phonological awareness strategy on the reading skills of children with mild disabilities. *Learning Disabilities: A Multidisciplinary Journal, 8,* 145–153.

Browder, D.M. (2001). Functional Reading. In B. Wilson & D.M. Browder, *Curriculum and assessment for students with moderate and severe disabilities* (pp. 179–214). New York: Guilford Press.

Browder, D.M., Flowers, C., Ahlgrim-Delzell, L., Karvonen, M., Spooner, F., & Algozzine, R. (2004). The alignment of alternate assessment content with academic and functional curricula. *The Journal of Special Education, 37,* 211–233.

Brown, L., Branston, M.B., Hamre-Nietupski, S., Pumpian, I., Certo, N., & Gruenewald, L. (1979). A strategy for developing chronological and age-appropriate and functional curricular content for severely handicapped adolescents and young adults. *Journal of Special Education, 13,* 81–90.

Brown, L., Wilcox, B., Sontag, E., Vincent, B., Dodd, N., & Gruenewald, L. (2004). Toward the realization of the least restrictive environment for severely handicapped students. *Research and Practice for Persons with Severe Disabilities, 29,* 2–8.

Cahill, L., & McGaugh, J.L. (1995). A novel demonstration of enhanced memory associated with emotional arousal. *Consciousness and Cognition*(4), 410–421.

Calhoon, J.A. (2001). Factors affecting reading of rimes in words and nonwords in beginning readers with cognitive disabilities and typically developing readers: Explorations in similarity and difference in word recognition cue use. *Journal of Autism and Developmental Disorders, 31*(5), 491–504.

Calhoon, J.A., & Leslie, L. (2002). Longitudinal influences of rime neighborhood size on rime recognition. *Journal of Literacy Research, 34*(2), 39–58.

Cardoso-Martins, C., Michalick, M.F., & Pollo, T.C. (2002). Is sensitivity to rhyme a developmental precursor to sensitivity to phoneme?: Evidence from individuals with Down syndrome. *Reading and Writing: An Interdisciplinary Journal, 15,* 439–454.

Carlisle, J.F., & Rice, M.S. (2004). Assessment of reading comprehension. In C.A. Stone, E. Silliman, B.J. Ehren, & K. Apel (Eds.), *Handbook of language and literacy: Development and disorders* (pp. 521–540). New York: Guilford Press.

Castagnera, E., Fisher, D., Rodifer, K., & Sax, C. (1998). *Deciding what to teach and how to teach it: Connecting students through curriculum and instruction.* Colorado Springs, CO: PEAK Parent Center, Inc.

Colasent, R., & Griffith, P.L. (1998). Autism and literacy: Looking into the classroom with rabbit stories. *The Reading Teacher, 51,* 414–420.

Cole, C.M., Waldron, N., & Majd, M. (2004). Academic progress of students across inclusive and traditional settings. *Mental Retardation, 42* (2), 136–144.

Conley, C.M., Derby, K.M., Roberts-Gwinn, M., Weber, K.P., & McLaughlin, T.F. (2004). An analysis of initial acquisition and maintenance of sight words following picture matching and copy, cover, and compare teaching methods. *Journal of Applied Behavior Analysis, 37,* 339–350.

Connors, F.A. (1992). Reading instruction for students with moderate mental retardation: Review and analysis of research. *American Journal on Mental Retardation, 96,* 577–597.

Connors, F.A., Atwell, J.A., Rosenquist, C.J., & Sligh, A.C. (2001). Abilities underlying decoding differences in children with intellectual disability. *Journal of Intellectual Disability Research, 45*, 292–299.

Cooter, R.B., & Flynt, E.S. (1996). *Teaching reading in the content areas: Developing content literacy for all students.* Columbus, OH: Merrill/Prentice Hall.

Corson, D. (1993). *Language, minority education and gender: Linking social justice and power.* Clevedon, England: Multilingual Matters.

Cunningham, P.M., Cunningham, J.W., & Allington, R.L. (2002). Research on the components of a comprehensive reading and writing instructional program. Retrieved January 7, 2005, from http://www.wfu.edu/academics/fourblocks/research.html

Cunningham, P.M., Moore, S.A., Cunningham, J.W., & Moore, D.W. (2004). *Reading and writing in elementary classrooms: Research-based k-4 instruction* (5th ed.). Boston: Allyn & Bacon.

Cupples, L., & Iacono, T. (2000). Phonological awareness and oral reading skill in children with Down syndrome. *Journal of Speech, Language, and Hearing Research, 43*, 595–608.

Cupples, L., & Iacono, T. (2002). The efficacy of 'whole word' versus 'analytic' reading instruction for children with Down syndrome. *Reading and Writing: An Interdisciplinary Journal, 15*, 549–574.

Davidson, J.W. (2005). *The American nation: Beginnings through 1877.* Upper Saddle River, NJ: Pearson Education Inc.

Denham, A.P., & Zabala, J.S. (1999). Assistive technology consideration guide for IEP teams. [Adapted from Georgia AT Project (GPAT), Wisconsin AT Initiative (WATI), Kentucky AT Guidelines, and the SETT Framework].

de Valenzuela, J.S., Copeland, S.R., Qi, C.H., & Park, M. (2006). Examining educational equity: Revisiting the disproportionate representation of minority students in special education. *Exceptional Children.*

Dowhower, S.L. (1999). Supporting a strategic stance in the classroom: A comprehension framework for helping teachers help students to be strategic. *Reading Teacher, 52*, 672–688.

Downing, J.E. (1999). *Teaching communication skills to students with severe disabilities.* Baltimore: Paul H. Brookes Publishing Co.

Downing, J.E. (2002). *Including students with severe and multiple disabilities in typical classrooms: Practical strategies for teachers* (2nd ed.). Baltimore: Paul H. Brookes Publishing Co.

Downing, J.E. (2005). *Teaching literacy to students with significant disabilities: Strategies for the K-12 inclusive classroom.* Thousand Oaks, CA: Corwin Press.

Dubin, F., & Kuhlman, N.A. (1992). The dimensions of cross-cultural literacy. In F. Dubin & N.A. Kuhlman (Eds.), *Cross-cultural literacy: Global perspectives on reading and writing* (pp. v–x). Englewood Cliffs, NJ: Regents/Prentice Hall.

Ebbinghaus, H. (1913). *A contribution to experimental psychology.* New York: Teachers College, Columbia University.

Ehren, B.J., Lenz, B.K., & Deshler, D.D. (2004). Enhancing literacy proficiency with adolescents and young adults. In C.A. Stone, E.R. Silliman, B.J. Ehren, & K. Apel (Eds.), *Handbook of language and literacy: Development and disorders* (pp. 681–701). New York: Guilford Press.

Ehri, L.C. (2005). Learning to read words: Theory, findings, and issues. *Scientific Studies of Reading, 9*, 167–188.

Ehri, L.C., Nunes, S.R., Willows, D.M., Schuster, B.V., Yaghoub-Zadeh, Z., & Shanahan, T. (2001). Phonemic awareness instruction helps children learn to read: Evidence from the National Reading Panel's meta-analysis. *Reading Research Quarterly, 36*, 250–287.

Ehri, L.C., & Robbins, C. (1992). Beginners need some decoding skill to read words by analogy. *The Reading Teacher, 27*(1), 13–27.

Ehri, L.C., & Snowling, M.J. (2004). Developmental variation in word recognition. In C.A. Stone, E.R. Silliman, B.J. Ehren, & K. Apel (Eds.), *Handbook of language and literacy: Development and Disorders* (pp. 433–460). New York: Guilford Press.

Elder, P., & Goossens, C. (1996). *Communication overlays for engineering training environments: Overlays for adolescents and adults who are moderately/severely developmentally delayed.* Solana Beach, CA: Mayer- Johnson Co.

Elkonin, D.B. (1973). Reading in the U.S.S.R. In J. Downing (Ed.), *Comparative reading*, (English translation; pp. 551–579). New York: Macmillan.

Erickson, K.A. (2003). Reading comprehension in AAC. *The ASHA Leader, 8*(12), 6–9.

Erickson, K.A., & Koppenhaver, D.A. (1995). Developing a literacy program for children with severe disabilities. *The Reading Teacher, 48*(8), 676–684.

Erickson, K.A., Koppenhaver, D.A., & Yoder, D.E. (1994). *Literacy and adults with developmental disabilities.* National Center on Adult Literacy Technical Report (TR94-15). Philadelphia: National Center of Adult Literacy

Erickson, K.A., Koppenhaver, D.A., & Yoder, D.E. (2002). *Waves of words: Augmented communicators read and write.* Toronto, Ontario, Canada: ISAAC Press.

Ewing, G. (2000). Update from the executive director. In *Metro Toronto Movement for Literacy Newsletter.* Retrieved January 12, 2005, from http://www.mtml.ca/newslet/july00/page1.htm

Farrell, M., & Elkins, J. (1995). Literacy for all? The case for Down syndrome. *Journal of Reading, 38*, 270–280.

Fifield, D. (2005). *March of the penguins.* Washington, DC: National Geographic Society.

Fisher, D., & Frey, N. (2003). *Improving adolescent literacy: Strategies at work.* Upper Saddle River, NJ: Merrill/Prentice Hall.

Fisher, M., & Meyer, L.H. (2002). Development and social competence after two years for students enrolled in inclusive and self-contained educational programs. *Research and Practice for Persons with Severe Disabilities, 27*(3), 165–174.

Foley, B.E. (1993). The development of literacy in individuals with severe congenital speech and motor impairments. *Topics in Language Disorders, 13*(2), 16–32.

Foley, B.E. (1994). The development of literacy in individuals with severe congenital speech and motor impairments. In K.G. Butler (Ed.), *Severe communication disorders: Intervention strategies* (pp. 183–199). Gaithersburg, MD: Aspen.

Foley, B.E., & Pollatsek, A. (1999). Phonological processing and reading abilities in adolescents and adults with severe congenital speech impairments. *Augmentative and Alternative Communication, 15*, 156–174.

Foley, B.E., & Staples, A.H. (2003). Developing augmentative and alternative communication (AAC) and literacy interventions in a supported employment setting. *Topics in Language Disorders, 4*, 325–343.

Foley, B.E., & Staples, A.H. (2006). Assistive technology supports for literacy instruction. *Perspectives on Augmentative and Alternative Communication, 15*(2), 15–21.

Fromkin, V., Rodman, R., & Hyams, N. (2003). *An introduction to language* (7th ed.). Boston: Thomson Heinle.

Gagne, R.M., & Driscol, M.P. (1988). *Essentials of learning for instruction* (2nd ed.). Englewood Cliffs, NJ: Prentice Hall.

Gallaher, K.M., van Kraayenoord, C.E., Jobling, A., & Moni, K.B. (2002). Reading with Abby: A case study of individual tutoring with a young adult with Down syndrome. *Down Syndrome Research and Practice, 8*, 59–66.

Gardener, H. (1983). *Frames of mind.* New York: Basic Books.

Gardill, M.C., & Jitendra, A.K. (1999). Advanced story map instruction: Effects on the reading comprehension of students with learning disabilities. *The Journal of Special Education, 33*, 2–17.

Gaskins, W., Ehri, L., Cress, C., O'Hara, C., & Donnelly, K. (1996/1997). Procedures for word learning: Making discoveries about words. *The Reading Teacher, 50*(4), 312–327.

Goswami, U. (2001). Early phonological development and the acquisition of literacy. In S. Neuman & D. Dickinson (Eds.), *Handbook of Research in Early Literacy for the 21st Century* (pp. 111–125). New York: The Guilford Press.

Guilmet, G.M. (1979). Maternal perceptions of urban Navajo and Caucasian children's classroom behavior. *Human Organization, 38*, 87–91.

Gunning, T.G. (2002a). *Assessing and correcting reading and writing difficulties* (2nd ed.). Boston: Allyn & Bacon.

Gunning, T.G. (2002b). Building writing strategies. In *Assessing and correcting reading and writing difficulties* (2nd ed.; pp. 458–495). Boston: Allyn & Bacon.

Hamill, L.B. (2003). Going to college: The experiences of a young woman with Down syndrome. *Mental Retardation, 41*, 340–353.

Hammill, D., & Larsen, S. (1996). *Test of written language-3.* Austin, TX: PRO-ED, Inc.

Harris, K.R., & Pressley, M. (1991). The nature of cognitive strategy instruction: Interactive strategy construction. *Exceptional Children, 57*, 392–404.

Hart, P. (2006). Spelling consideration for AAC intervention. *Perspectives on Augmentative and Alternative Communication, 15*(2), 12–14.

Hasbrouck, J.E., & Tindal, G.A. (1992). Curriculum-based oral reading fluency norms for students in grades 2 though 5. *Teaching Exceptional Children, 24*, 41–44.

Hasbrouck, J.E., & Tindal, G.A. (2006). Oral reading fluency norms: A valuable assessment tool for reading teachers. *The Reading Teacher, 59*(7), 636–644.

Hayes, J.R., & Flower, L.S. (1980). Identifying the organization of writing processes. In L.E. Gregg & E.R. Steinberg (Eds.), *Cognitive processes in writing* (pp. 3–30). Hillsdale, NJ: Lawrence Erlbaum Associates.

Hedrick, W.B., Katims, D.S., & Carr, N.J. (1999). Implementing a multimethod, multilevel literacy program for students with mental retardation. *Focus on Autism and Other Developmental Disabilities, 14*, 231–239.

Hiebert, E.H. (1991). Introduction. In E.H. Hiebert (Ed.), *Literacy for a diverse society: Perspectives, practices, and policies* (pp. 1–6). New York: Teachers College Press.

Hunt, P., Farron-Davis, F., Beckstead, S., Curtis, D., & Goetz, L. (1994). Evaluating the effects of placement of students with severe disabilities in general education versus special education classes. *Journal for the Association of Persons with Severe Handicaps, 19*(3), 200–214.

Hunter, M. (1994). *Enhancing teaching.* New York: Macmillan College Publishing Co.

Iacono, T.A. (2004). Accessible reading intervention: A work in progress. *Augmentative and Alternative Communication, 20*(3), 179–190.

Individuals with Disabilities Education Act (IDEA) of 1990, PL 101-476, 20 U.S.C. §§ 1400 *et seq.*

Individuals with Disabilities Education Act Amendments of 1997, PL 105-107, 20 U.S.C. §§ 1400 *et seq.*

Individuals with Disabilities Education Improvement Act of 2004, PL 108-446, 20 U.S.C. §§ 1400 *et seq.*

Iverson, J.M., & Thal, D.J. (1998). Communicative transitions: There's more to the hand than meets the eye. In A.M. Wetherby, S.F. Warren, & J. Reichle (Eds.), *Transitions in prelinguistic communication* (pp. 59–86). Baltimore: Paul H. Brookes Publishing Co.

Iverson, P., Kuhl, P.K., Akahane-Yamada, R., Diesch, E., Tohkura, Y., Kettermann, A., et al. (2003). A perceptual interference account of acquisition difficulties for non-native phonemes. *Cognition, 87*, B47–B57.

Jackson, L., Ryndak, D.L., & Billingsley, F. (2000). Useful practices in inclusive education: A preliminary view of what experts in moderate to severe disabilities are saying. *Journal for the Association of Persons with Severe Disabilities, 25*, (3), 129–141.

Janney, R.J., & Snell, M.E. (2000). *Modifying schoolwork.* Baltimore: Paul H. Brookes Publishing Co.

Joe, J.R., & Miller, D. (1987). *American Indian cultural perspectives on communication,* Monograph Series. Tucson: University of Arizona.

Johnson, C.J., Beitchman, H.J., Young, S., Escobar, M., Atkinson, L., Wilson, B., et al. (1999). Fourteen-year follow-up of children with and without speech/language impairments: speech/language stability and outcomes. *Journal of Speech, Language, and Hearing Research, 42*(3), 744–760.

Johnson, D. (2001). *Vocabulary in the elementary and middle school.* Boston: Allyn & Bacon.

Johnson, D.W., & Johnson, R.T. (1989). *Cooperation and competition: Theory and research.* Edina, MN: Interaction Book Company.

Johnson, D.W., Johnson, R.T., & Holubec, E. (1993). *Circles of learning.* Edina, MN: Interaction Book Company.

Johnson, J.M., Baumgart, D., Helmstetter, E., & Curry, C.A. (1996). *Augmenting basic communication in natural contexts.* Baltimore: Paul H. Brookes Publishing Co.

Joseph, L.M. (2002). Facilitating word recognition and spelling using word boxes and word sort phonic procedures. *School Psychology Review, 31*, 122–129.

Joseph, L.M., & McCachran, M. (2003). Comparison of a word study phonics technique between students with moderate to mild mental retardation and struggling readers without disabilities. *Education and Training in Developmental Disabilities, 38*, 192–199.

Joseph, L.M., & Seery, M.E. (2004). Where is the phonics? A review of the literature on the use of phonetic analysis with students with mental retardation. *Remedial and Special Education, 25,* 88–94.

Kabrich, M., & McCutchen, D. (1996). Phonemic support in comprehension: Comparisons between children with and without mild mental retardation. *American Journal on Mental Retardation, 100,* 510–527.

Kahn-Freedman, E. (2001). Finding a voice: Poetry and people with developmental disabilities. *Mental Retardation, 39,* 195–200.

Kaiser, A., & Grim, J.C. (2006). Teaching functional communication skills. In M.E. Snell & F. Brown (Eds.), *Instruction of students with severe disabilities* (6th ed.; pp. 447–488). Upper Saddle River, NJ: Pearson Prentice Hall.

Katims, D.S. (1994). Emergence of literacy in preschool children with disabilities. *Learning Disability Quarterly, 17,* 100–111.

Katims, D.S. (1996). The emergence of literacy in elementary students with mild mental retardation. *Focus on Autism and Other Developmental Disabilities, 1*(3), 147–158.

Katims, D.S. (2000). *The quest for literacy: Curriculum and instructional procedures for teaching reading and writing to students with mental retardation and developmental disabilities.* Reston, VA: Council for Exceptional Children.

Katz, J., Mirenda, P., & Auerbach, S. (2002). Instructional strategies and educational outcomes for students with developmental disabilities in inclusive "multiple intelligences" and typical inclusive classrooms. *Research and Practice for Persons with Severe Disabilities, 27,* 227–238.

Kay-Raining Bird, E., Cleave, P.L., & McConnell, L. (2000). Reading and phonological awareness in children with Down syndrome: A longitudinal study. *American Journal of Speech-Language Pathology, 9,* 319–330.

Keefe, E.B., & Van Etten, C. (1994). *Academic and social outcomes for students with moderate to profound disabilities in integrated settings.* Paper presented at The Association for Persons with Severe Handicaps, December, Atlanta, Georgia.

Kennedy, E.J., & Flynn, M.C. (2003). Training phonological awareness skills in children with Down syndrome. *Research in Developmental Disabilities, 24,* 44–57.

Kliewer, C., Fitzgerald, L.M., Meyer-Mork, J., Hartman, P., English-Sand, P., & Raschke, D. (2004). Citizenship for all in the literate community: An ethnography of young children with significant disabilities in inclusive early childhood settings. *Harvard Educational Review, 74,* 373–403.

Kluth, P. (2003). *You're going to love this kid!: Teaching students with autism in the inclusive classroom.* Baltimore: Paul H. Brookes Publishing Co.

Koppenhaver, D.A. (2000). Literacy in AAC: What should be written on the envelop we push? *Augmentative and Alternative Communication, 16,* 270–279.

Koppenhaver, D.A., Spadorcia, S.A., & Erickson, K.A. (1998). How do we provide inclusive literacy instruction for children with disabilities? In S.B. Neuman & K.A. Roskos (Eds.), *Children achieving: Best practices in early literacy* (pp. 77–96). Newark, DE: International Reading Association.

Kulhavey, R.W., Stock, W.A., Verdi, M.P., Rittschof, K.A., & Savanye, W. (1993). Why maps improve memory for text: The influence of structural information on working memory operations. *European Journal of Cognitive Psychology, 5*(4), 375–392.

Lane, H.B., Pullen, P.C., Eisele, M.R., & Jordan, L. (2002). Preventing reading failure: Phonological awareness assessment and instruction. *Preventing School Failure, 46,* 101–110.

Langer, J.A. (1991). Literacy and schooling: A sociocognitive perspective. In E.H. Hiebert (Ed.), *Literacy for a diverse society: Perspectives, practices, and policies* (pp. 9–27). New York: Teachers College Press.

Langer, J.A., & Flihan, S. (2000). Writing and reading relationships: Constructive tasks. In R. Indrisano & J.R. Squire (Eds.), *Perspectives on writing: Research, theory, and practice* (pp. 112–139). Newark, DE: International Reading Association.

Leslie, L., & Calhoon, J.A. (1995). Factors affecting children's reading of rimes: Reading ability, word frequency, and rime neighborhood size. *Journal of Educational Psychology, 87*(4), 576–586.

Liberman, I.Y., Shankweiler, D., Fischer, F.W., & Carter, B. (1974). Explicit syllable and phoneme segmentation in the young child. *Journal of Experimental Child Psychology, 18,* 201–212.

Light, J.C., & Binger, C. (1998). *Building communicative competence with individuals who use augmentative and alternative communication.* Baltimore: Paul H. Brookes Publishing Co.

Logan, K.R., Bakeman, R., & Keefe, E.B. (1997). Engaged behavior: Effects of instructional and teacher variables for students with severe disabilities in general education classrooms. *Exceptional Children, 63,* 481–497.

Martin, B. (1967). *Brown bear, brown bear, what do you see?* New York: Henry Holt & Company.

Mathes, P.G., & Fuchs, D. (1997). Cooperative story mapping. *Remedial & Special Education, 18,* 20–28.

McCoy, L.J., & Sundbye, N. (2001). *Helping the struggling reader: What to teach and how to teach it* (2nd ed.) Lawrence, KS: Curriculum Solutions, Inc.

McGill-Franzen, A., & Allington, R.L. (1991). The gridlock of low reading achievement: Perspectives on practice and policy. *Remedial and Special Education, 12,* 20–30.

McLaughlin, T.F., & Skinner, C.H. (1996). Improving academic performance through self management: Cover, copy, and compare. *Intervention in School and Clinic, 32,* 113–118.

Millar, D.C., Light, J.C., & McNaughton, D.B. (2004). The effect of direct instruction and writer's workshop on the early writing skills of children who use augmentative and alternative communication. *Augmentative and Alternative Communication, 20,* 164–178.

Miller, G. (1956). The magical number seven, plus or minus two: Some limits on our capacity for processing information. *The Psychological Review, 63,* 81–97.

Mirenda, P. (2001). Autism, augmentative communication, and AT: What do we really know? *Focus on Autism and Other Developmental Disabilities, 16*(3), 141–152.

Mirenda, P. (2003). "He's not really a reader. . .": Perspectives on supporting literacy development in individuals with autism. *Topics in Language Disorders, 23,* 271–282.

Mirenda, P., & Erickson, K.E. (2000). Autism, AAC and literacy. In A. Wetherby & B. Prizant (Eds.), *Communication and language issues in autism and PDD: A transactional developmental perspective* (pp. 333–367). Baltimore: Paul H. Brookes Publishing Co.

Moni, K.B., & Jobling, A. (2000). LATCH-ON: A program to develop literacy in young adults with Down syndrome. *Journal of Adolescent and Adult Literacy, 44*(1), 40–50.

Moni, K.B., & Jobling, A. (2001). Reading-related literacy learning of young adults with Down syndrome: Findings from a three year teaching and research program. *International Journal of Disability, Development, and Education, 48,* 377–394.

Moore, V.M., Metzler, C., & Pearson, S. (2006). Connecting across the community: Pen pals in inclusive classrooms. In E.B. Keefe, V.M. Moore, & F.R. Duff (Eds.), *Listening to the experts* (pp. 107–113). Baltimore: Paul H. Brookes Publishing Co.

Morgan, M., Moni, K.B., & Jobling, A. (2004). What's it all about? Investigating reading comprehension strategies in young adults with Down syndrome. *Down Syndrome Research and Practice 9,* 37–44.

Murphy, J.F., Hern, C.L., Williams, R.L., & McLaughlin, T.F. (1990). The effects of the copy, cover, compare approach in increasing spelling accuracy with learning disabled students. *Contemporary Educational Psychology, 15,* 378–386.

Nation, K., & Norbury, C.F. (2005). Why reading comprehension fails: Insights from developmental disabilities. *Topics in Language Disorders, 25,* 21–32.

National Joint Committee for the Communicative Needs of Persons with Severe Disabilities. (1992). Guidelines for meeting the communication needs of persons with severe disabilities. *Asha, 34* (March, Supp. 7), 1–8.

National Reading Panel (NRP) (2000). *Report of the National Reading Panel: Teaching children to read. Reports of the Subgroups.* (NIH Publication 00-4754). Washington, DC: National Institute of Child Health and Human Development.

No Child Left Behind Act of 2001, PL 107-110, 115 Stat. 1425, 20 U.S.C. §§ 6301 *et seq.*

Nystrand, M. (1990). Sharing words: The effects of readers on developing writers. *Written Communication, 7*(1), 3–24.

O'Connor, R.E., & Bell, K.M. (2004).Teaching students with reading disability to read words. In C.A. Stone, E.R. Silliman, B.J. Ehren, & K. Apel (Eds.), *Handbook of language and literacy: Development and disorders* (pp. 481–498). New York: Guilford Press.

O'Connor, I.M., & Klein, P.D. (2004). Exploration of strategies for facilitating the reading comprehension of high-functioning students with autism spectrum disorders. *Journal of Autism and Developmental Disorders, 34,* 115–126.

Ochs, E. (1986). Introduction. In B.B. Schieffelin & E. Ochs (Eds.), *Language socialization across cultures* (pp. 1–13). New York: Cambridge University Press.

Oelwein, P.L. (1995). *Teaching reading to children with Down syndrome: A guide for teachers and parents*. Bethesda, MD: Woodbine House.

Olson, R.K., Forsberg, H., & Wise, B. (1994). Genes, environment, and the development of orthographic skills. In V.W. Berninger (Ed.), *The varieties of orthographic knowledge I: Theoretical and developmental issues* (pp. 27–71). Dordrecht, The Netherlands: Kluwer Academic Publishers.

Perfetti, C.A., Beck, I., Bell, L., & Hughes, C. (1987). Phonemic knowledge and learning to read are reciprocal: A longitudinal study of first grade children. *Merrill-Palmer Quarterly, 33,* 283–319.

Pershey, M.G., & Gilbert, T.W. (2002). Christine: A case study of literacy acquisition by an adult with developmental disabilities. *Mental Retardation, 40,* 219–234.

Pierce, P.L., & Porter, P.B. (1996). Helping persons with disabilities to become literate using assistive technology: Practice and policy suggestions. *Focus on Autism & Other Developmental Disabilities, 11,* 142–148.

Polloway, E.A., Smith, T.E.C., & Miller, L. (2004). Written expression. In *Language instruction for students with disabilities* (3rd ed; pp. 432–480). Denver: Love Publishing.

Pressley, M., Symons, S., Snyder, B.L., & Cariglia-Bull, T. (1989). Strategy instruction research comes of age. *Learning Disability Quarterly, 86,* 360–406.

Putnam, J.W. (1998). *Cooperative learning and strategies for inclusion*. Baltimore: Paul H. Brookes Publishing Co.

Rasinski, T.V. (2003). *The fluent reader*. New York: Scholastic.

Ray, K.W. (2006). When kids make books. *Educational Leadership, 62*(2), 14–18.

Reichle, J., Beukelman, D.R., & Light, J.C. (Eds.) (2002). *Exemplary practices for beginning communicators: Implications for AAC*. Baltimore: Paul H. Brookes Publishing Co.

Reutzel, D.R., & Cooter, R.B. (2003a). *Strategies for reading assessment and instruction: Helping every child succeed* (2nd ed.). Upper Saddle River: NJ: Merrill.

Reutzel, D.R., & Cooter, R.B. (2004). *Teaching children to read: Putting the pieces together* (4th ed.). Upper Saddle River, NJ: Merrill/Prentice Hall.

Reutzel, D.R., Hollingsworth, P.M., & Eldredge, L. (1994). Oral reading instruction: The impact on student reading development. *Reading Research Quarterly, 29,* 40–62.

Rey, H.A. (1947). *Curious George takes a job*. Boston: Houghton Mifflin.

Rivera, M.O., Koorland, M.A., & Gueyo, V. (2002). Pupil-made pictorial prompts and fading for teaching sight words to a student with learning disabilities. *Education and Treatment of Children, 25,* 197–207.

Romski, M.A., & Sevcik, R.A. (1996). *Breaking the speech barrier: Language development through augmented means*. Baltimore: Paul H. Brookes Publishing Co.

Rowland, C., & Schweigert, P. (1993). Analyzing the communication environment to increase functional communication. *Journal of the Association for Persons with Severe Handicaps, 18*(3), 161–176.

Ryndak, D.L., & Alper, S. (2003). *Curriculum and instruction for students with disabilities in inclusive settings*. Boston: Allyn & Bacon.

Ryndak, D.L., Morrison, A.P., & Sommerstein, L. (1999). Literacy before and after inclusion in general education settings: A case study. *Journal for the Association of Persons with Severe Disabilities, 24*(1), 5–22.

Samuels, S.J. (1979). The method of repeated reading. *The Reading Teacher, 32,* 403–408.

Sapon-Shevin, M., Ayres, B.A., & Duncan, J. (2002). Cooperative learning and inclusion. In J.S. Thousand, R.A. Villa, & A.I. Nevin (Eds.), *Creativity and collaborative learning* (2nd ed.). Baltimore: Paul H. Brookes Publishing Co.

Schirmer, B.R., & Bailey, J. (2000). Writing assessment rubric: An instructional approach with struggling writers. *TEACHING Exceptional Children, 33,* 52–58.

Sendak, M. (1963). *Where the wild things are*. New York: Harper Collins.

Sharpe, M.N., York, J.L., & Knight, J. (1994). Effects of inclusion on the academic performance of classmates without disabilities. *Remedial and Special Education, 15*(5), 281–287.

Sheehy, K. (2002). The effective use of symbols in teaching word recognition to children with severe learning difficulties: A comparison of word alone, integrated picture cueing and the handle technique. *International Journal of Disability, Development, and Education, 49,* 47–59.

Siegel, E., & Wetherby, A. (2006). Nonsymbolic communication. In M.E. Snell & F. Brown (Eds.), *Instruction of students with severe disabilities* (6th ed.; pp. 405–446). Upper Saddle River, NJ: Pearson Prentice Hall.

Sims, C. (2006). Language planning in southwest American Indian communities: Contemporary challenges and issues. *Current issues in language planning.*

Singer, B.D., & Bashir, A.S. (2004). Developmental variations in writing composition skills. In C.A. Stone, E.R. Silliman, B.J. Ehren, & K. Apel (Eds.), *Handbook of language and literacy: Development and Disorders* (pp. 559–582). New York: Guilford Press.

Smith, M.M. (1989). Reading without speech: A study of children with cerebral palsy. *The Irish Journal of Psychology, 10,* 601–614.

Smith, M.M. (2005). *Literacy and augmentative and alternative communication.* Burlington, MA: Elsevier Academic Press.

Snell, M.E., & Brown, F. (2006). *Instruction of students with severe disabilities* (6th ed.). Upper Saddle River, NJ: Pearson Education Inc.

Snell, M.E., & Janney, R. (2000). *Collaborative teaming.* Baltimore: Paul H. Brookes Publishing Co.

Snowling, M.J., Hulme, C., & Mercer, R.C. (2002). A deficit in rime awareness in children with Down syndrome. *Reading and Writing: An Interdisciplinary Journal, 15,* 471–495.

Soto, G. (2006). Supporting the development of narratives skills in children who use AAC. *Perspectives on Augmentative and Alternative Communication, 15*(2), 7–11.

Stanford, P., & Siders, J.A. (2001). E-pal writing. *TEACHING Exceptional Children, 34,* 21–24.

Stanovich, K.E. (1986). Matthew effects in reading: Some consequences of individual differences in the acquisition of literacy. *Reading Research Quarterly, 21,* 360–407.

Stanovich, K.E. (1998). Twenty-five years of research on the reading process: The grand synthesis and what it means for our field. In T. Shanahan & F. Rodriguez-Brown (Eds.), *Forty-seventh yearbook of the National Reading Conference* (pp. 44–58). Chicago: NRC.

Staub, D., & Peck, C.A. (1994). What are the outcomes for nondisabled students? *Educational Leadership, 52,* 4, 36–40.

Steelman, J.D., Pierce, P.L., & Koppenhaver, D. (1993). The role of computers in promoting literacy in children with severe speech and physical impairments. *Topics in Language Disorders, 13*(2), 76–88.

Steelman, J.D., Pierce, P.L., & Koppenhaver, D.A. (1994). The role of computers in promoting literacy in children with severe speech and physical impairments. In K.G. Butler (Ed.), *Severe communication disorders: Intervention strategies* (pp. 200–212). Gaithersburg, MD: Aspen.

Sturm J., & Koppenhaver, D.A. (2000). Supporting writing development in adolescents with developmental disabilities. *Topics in Language Disorders, 20,* 73–92.

Sylwester, R. (1995). *A celebration of neurons: An educator's guide to the human brain.* Alexandria, VA: Association for Supervision and Curriculum Development.

Technology-Related Assistance for Individuals with Disabilities Act of 1988, PL 100-407, 29 U.S.C. §§ 2201 *et seq.*

Tomlinson, C.A. (2001). *How to differentiate instruction in mixed-ability classrooms.* Alexandria, VA: Association for Supervision and Curriculum Development.

Topping, K. (1987). Peer tutored paired reading: Outcome data from ten projects. *Educational Psychology, 7,* 604–614.

Topping, K. (1989). Peer tutoring and paired reading. Combining two powerful techniques. *The Reading Teacher, 42,* 488–494.

Torgesen, J.K. (2000). Individual differences in response to early interventions in reading: The lingering problem of treatment resisters. *Learning Disabilities Research & Practice, 15,* 55–64.

Torgesen, J.K., & Mathes, P.G. (2000). *A basic guide to understanding, assessing, and teaching phonological awareness.* Austin, TX: Pro-Ed.

Torgesen, J.K., Wagner, R.K., Rashotte, C.A., Rose, E., Lindamood, P., Conway, T., & Garvan, C. (1999). Preventing reading failure in young children with phonological processing disabilities: Group and individual responses to instruction. *Journal of Educational Psychology, 91*, 579–593.

Treiman, R. (1983). The structure of spoken syllables: Evidence from novel word games. *Cognition, 15*, 49–74.

Treiman, R. (1985). Onsets and rimes as units of spoken syllables: Evidence from children. *Journal of Experimental Child Psychology, 39*, 161–181.

Troia, G.A. (2004). Phonological processing and its influence on literacy learning. In C.A. Stone, E.R. Silliman, B.J. Ehren, & K. Apel (Eds.), *Handbook of language and literacy: Development and Disorders* (pp. 271–103). New York: Guilford Press.

Udvari-Solner, A., Villa, R.A., & Thousand, J.S. (2002). Access to general education curriculum for all: The universal design process. In J.S. Thousand, R.A. Villa, & A.I. Nevin (Eds.), *Creativity and collaborative learning* (2nd ed.). Baltimore: Paul H. Brookes Publishing Co.

U.S. Department of Education, National Center for Education Statistics. (1995). *Listening to Children Read Aloud, 15*. Washington, DC: Author.

Vaughn, S., & Klingner, J. (2004). Teaching reading comprehension to students with learning disabilities. In C.A. Stone, E.R. Silliman, B.J. Ehren, & K. Apel (Eds.), *Handbook of language and literacy: Development and disorders* (pp. 541–555). New York: Guilford Press.

Villa, R.A., & Thousand, J.S. (2000). *Restructuring for caring and effective education* (2nd ed.). Baltimore: Paul H. Brookes Publishing Co.

Villa, R.A., & Thousand, J.S. (2005). *Creating an inclusive school* (2nd ed.). Alexandria, VA: Association for Supervision and Curriculum Development.

Wagner, M., Newman, L., Cameto, R., Garza, N., & Levine, P. (2005). *After high school: A first look at the postschool experiences of youth with disabilities. A report from the National Longitudinal Transition Study-2 (NLTS2).* Menlo Park, CA: SRI International.

Wetherby, A.M., & Prizant, B.M. (1989). The expression of communicative intent: Assessment guidelines. *Seminars in Speech and Language, 10*, 77–91.

Wetherby, A.M., Reichle, J., & Pierce, P.L. (1998). The transition to symbolic communication. In A.M. Wetherby, S.F. Warren, & J. Reichle (Eds.), *Transitions in prelinguistic communication* (pp. 197–230). Baltimore: Paul H. Brookes Publishing Co.

Wetherby, A.M., Warren, S.F., & Reichle, J. (1998). Introduction to transitions in symbolic communication. In A.M. Wetherby, S.F. Warren, & J. Reichle (Eds.), *Transitions in prelinguistic communication* (pp. 1–11). Baltimore: Paul H. Brookes Publishing Co.

Whitmire, K. (2001).The evolution of school-based speech–language services: A half century of change and a new century of practice. *Communication Disorders Quarterly, 23*(2), 68–76.

Wigfield, A., & Guthrie, J.T. (1997). Relation of children's motivation for reading to the amount and breadth of their reading. *Journal of Educational Psychology, 89*, 420–432.

Wilcox, M.J., & Shannon, M.S. (1998). Facilitating the transition from prelinguistic to linguistic communication. In A.M. Wetherby, S.F. Warren, & J. Reichle (Eds.), *Transitions in prelinguistic communication* (pp. 385–416). Baltimore: Paul H. Brookes Publishing Co.

Winterton, W.A. (1976). The effect of extended wait-time on selected verbal response characteristics of some Pueblo Indian children. Unpublished doctoral dissertation, University of New Mexico, Albuquerque.

Wisener, D. (1997). *Tuesday.* New York: Clarion Books.

Wolfe, P. (2001). *Brain matters: Translating research into classroom practice.* Alexandria, VA: Association for Supervision and Curriculum Development.

Yoder, D.E. (2001). Having my say. *Augmentative and Alternative Communication, 17*, 2–10.

Yoder, D.E., Erickson, K.A., & Koppenhaver, D.A. (1997). *A literacy bill of rights.* Chapel Hill, NC: University of North Carolina at Chapel Hill, Center for Literacy and Disability Studies.

Yopp, H.K. (1988). The validity and reliability of phonemic: Awareness tests. *Reading Research Quarterly, 23*, 159–177.

Yopp, H.K. (1992). Developing phonemic awareness in young children. *Reading Teacher, 45*(9), 696–703.

Young, L., Moni, K.B., Jobling, A., & van Kraayenoord, C.E. (2004). Literacy skills of adults with intellectual disabilities in two community-based day programs. *International Journal of Disability, Development, and Education, 51,* 83–97.

Zabala, J.S. (1995). *The SETT framework: Critical areas to consider when making informed assistive technology decisions.* Houston, TX: Region IV Education Service Center. (ERIC Document Reproduction Service No. ED381962).

Resources

Literacy Resources

Books

Allington, R.L. (2001). *What really matters for struggling readers: Designing research-based programs.* New York: Longman.

Browder, D.M., & Spooner, F. (2006). *Teaching language arts, math, and science to students with significant cognitive disabilities.* Baltimore: Paul H. Brookes Publishing Co.

Castagnera, E., Fisher, D., Rodifer, K., Sax, C., & Frey, N. (1998). *Deciding what to teach and how to teach it: Connecting students through curriculum and instruction.* Colorado Springs, CO: Peak Parenting Center.

Culham, R. (2004). *Using picture books to teach writing with the traits.* New York: Teaching Resources.

Cunningham, P.M. (2000). *Systematic sequential phonics they use for beginning readers of all ages.* Greensboro, NC: Carson-Dellosa Publishing Co.

Cunningham, P.M., & Hall, D.P. (1994). *Making words: Multilevel, hands-on, developmentally appropriate spelling and phonics activities.* Carthage, IL: Good Apple.

Cunningham, P.M., & Hall, D.P. (2001). *Making words: Lessons for home or school.* Greensboro, NC: Carson-Dellosa Publishing.

Cunningham, P.M., Hall, D.P., & Sigmon, C.M. (1999). *The teacher's guide to the four blocks.* Greensboro, NC: Carson-Dellosa Publishing.

Dennison, P.E., & Dennison, G.E. (1986). *Brain gym: Simple activities for whole brain learning.* Ventura, CA: Edu-Kinesthetics, Inc.

Dennison, P.E., & Dennison, G.E. (1987). *Edu-K for kids: The basic manual on educational kinesiology for parents and teachers of kids of all ages.* Ventura, CA: Edu-Kinesthetics, Inc.

de Valenzuela, J.S., & Niccolai, S.L. (2004). Language development in culturally and linguistically diverse students with special education needs. In L. Baca & H. Cervantes (Eds.), *The bilingual special education interface* (4th ed., pp. 124–161). Upper Saddle River, NJ: Merrill.

Downing, J.E. (2002). *Including students with severe and multiple disabilities in typical classrooms: Practical strategies for teachers.* Baltimore: Paul H. Brookes Publishing Co.

Downing, J.E. (2005). *Teaching literacy to student with significant disabilities: Strategies for the K-12 inclusive classroom.* Thousand Oaks, CA: Corwin Press.

Fisher, D., Frey, N., & Sax, C. (1999). *Inclusive elementary schools: Recipes for success* (2nd ed.). Colorado Springs, CO: Peak Parenting Center.

Griego-Jones, T., & Fuller, M.L. (2003). *Teaching Hispanic children.* Boston: Allyn & Bacon.

International Reading Association. (2002). *Evidence-based reading instruction: Putting the national reading panel into practice.* Newark, DE: International Reading Association.

Janney, R., & Snell, M.E. (2000). *Teachers' guides to inclusive practices: Modifying schoolwork.* Baltimore: Paul H. Brookes. Publishing Co.

Jorgensen, C.M. (1998). *Restructuring high schools for all students: Taking inclusion to the next level.* Toronto, ON: Paul H. Brookes Publishing Co.

Kalyanpur, M., & Harry, B. (1999). *Culture in special education: Building reciprocal family-professional relationships.* Baltimore: Paul H. Brookes Publishing Co.

Kibby, M.W. (1995). *Practical steps for informing literacy instruction: A diagnostic decision-making model.* Newark, DE: International Reading Association.

McCarthey, S. (2002). *Students' identities and literacy learning.* Newark, DE: International Reading Association.

Miller, J.F. (1999). Profiles of language development in children with Down syndrome. In J.F. Miller, M. Leddy, & L.A. Leavitt (Eds.), *Improving the communication of people with Down syndrome* (pp. 11–39). Baltimore: Paul H. Brookes Publishing Co.

Neuman, S.B., & Dickinson, D.K. (2006). *Handbook of early literacy research.* New York: Guilford Press.

Oczkus, L.D. (2003). *Reciprocal teaching at work: Strategies for improving reading comprehension.* Newark, DE: International Reading Association.

Oelwein, P.L. (1995). *Teaching reading to children with Down syndrome: A guide for parents and teachers.* Bethesda, MD: Woodbine.

Rasinski, T.V. (2003). *The fluent reader: Oral reading strategies for building word recognition, fluency and comprehension.* New York: Scholastic.

Sigmon, C.M. (2001). *Modifying the four blocks for the upper grades: Matching strategies to students' needs.* Greensboro, NC: Carson-Dellosa Publishing.

Suina, J.H., & Smolkin, L.B. (1994). From natal culture to school culture to dominant society culture: Supporting transitions for Pueblo Indian students. In P.M. Greenfield & R.R. Cocking (Eds.), *Cross-cultural roots of minority child development* (pp. 15–130). Hillsdale, NJ: Lawrence Erlbaum Associates.

Thousand, J.S., Villa, R.A., & Nevin, A.I. (2002). *Creativity and collaborative learning: The practical guide to empowering students, teachers, and families* (2nd ed.). Baltimore: Paul H. Brookes Publishing Co.

Tomlinson, C.A., & Eidson, C.C. (2003). *Differentiation in practice: A resource guide for differentiating curriculum (5–9).* Alexandria, VA: Association for Supervision and Curriculum Development.

Tomlinson, C.A., & McTighe, J. (2006). *Integrating: Differentiated instruction and understanding by design.* Alexandria, VA: Association for Supervision and Curriculum Development.

Tyner, B. (2004). *Small-group reading instruction: A differentiated teaching model for beginning and struggling readers.* Newark, DE: International Reading Association.

Villa, R.A., Thousand, J.S., & Nevin, A.I. (2004). *A guide to co-teaching: Practical tips for, facilitating student learning.* Thousand Oaks, CA: Corwin Press.

Voss, K.S. (2005). *Teaching by design: Using your computer to create materials for students, with learning differences.* Bethesda, MD: Woodbine House.

Wirt, B., Bryan, C.D., & Wesley, K.D. (2005). *Discovering what works for struggling readers: Journeys of exploration with primary grade students.* Newark, DE: International Reading Association.

Articles & Reports

Duran, E. (1991). *Functional language instruction for linguistically different students with moderate to severe disabilities* [ERIC EC Digest #E501]. ERIC Clearinghouse on Disabilities and Gifted Education. Retrieved September 9, 2001, from http://ericec.org

González, N., Moll, L.C., Floyd-Tenery, M., Rivera, A., Rendón, P., Gonzales, R., & Amanti, C. (1993). *Teacher research on funds of knowledge: Learning from households* (Educational Practice Report 6). Santa Cruz, CA: National Center for Research on Cultural Diversity and Second Language Learning.

National Joint Committee for the Communicative Needs of Persons with Severe Disabilities. (1992). Guidelines for meeting the communication needs of persons with severe disabilities. *American Speech Language Hearing Association, 34,* 1–8.

Sileo, T.W., & Prater, M.A. (1998). Creating classroom environments that address the linguistic and cultural backgrounds of students with disabilities. *Remedial and Special Education, 19*(6), 323–327.

Published Phonological Awareness Assessments and Instructional Programs

Name of assessment/instrument	Purpose/measure	Target population	Publisher
Lindamood Auditory Conceptualization Test	Use as a diagnosis instrument to assess phonemic awareness	K–1	PRO-ED Inc. Phone: 1-800-897-3202 Fax: 1-800-397-7633 Proedrd2@aol.com www.proedinc.com
Comprehensive Test of Phonological Processing (CTOPP)	An individual's awareness and access to the phonological structure of oral language Examines for short-term memory Examines for long-term memory	K–College (5.0–24.11)	AGS Publishing Phone: 1-800-328-2560 Fax: 1-800-471-8457 www.agsnet.com
Test of Phonological Awareness (TOPA)	Measures young children's awareness of individual sounds in words	K–2	PRO-ED Inc. Phone: 1-800-897-3202 Fax: 1-800-397-7633 Proedrd2@aol.com www.proedinc.com
Phonological Awareness Literacy Screening (PALS)	Screening tool	K–3	Univ. of Virginia Phone: 804-786-3925 Fax: 804-786-1703 http:// pals.virginia.edu

Name of assessment/ instrument	Purpose/measure	Target population	Publisher
Word Journeys: Assessment-Guided Phonics, Spelling, and Vocabulary Instruction	Assessing children's spelling and word knowledge abilities	K–12	Guilford Press Phone: 1-800-365-7006 Fax: 212-966-6708 Info@guilford.com www.guilford.com

Instructional Programs

Edmark Reading Program

This program teaches high-frequency words using a stimulus-shaping approach. The original program has two levels (Level 1 teaches 150 words; Level 2 teaches 200 additional words) in addition to supplemental materials such as homework and spelling activities. Programs to teach community words are available in print and computer versions.

Edmark Corporation
P.O. Box 97021
Redmond, WA 98107
Phone: 1-800-362-2890
Fax: 425-556-8430
http://www.edmark.com

MEville to WEville:
Early Literacy and Communication Supplemental Curriculum

This is a research-based literacy curriculum for early literacy learners. Many of the materials are appropriate for older learners.

AbleNet, Inc.
2808 Fairview Ave. N
Roseville, MN 55113-1308
www.ablenetinc.com

Patterns for Success in Reading and Spelling

This program consists of structured, sequential, multisensory lessons based on the Orton-Gillingham approach. It is designed for teachers, tutors, aides, and others who work with students with special reading problems. The program follows a sequence ranging from beginning letter–sound correspondence useful in the primary grades to the Latin and Greek word parts necessary for reading middle school and high school subject area text and literature.

PRO-ED Inc.
8700 Shoal Creek Boulevard
Austin, Texas 78757-6897
Phone: 1-800-897-3202
Fax: 1-800-397-7633
general@proedinc.com
http://www.proedinc.com

Picture Me Reading!

This reading program is based on the Integrated Cue Procedure in which a picture is embedded within a word. The program teaches 220 Dolch sight words using this method.

Picture Me Reading
3899 Kenwood Drive
Spring Valley, CA 91977-1024
Phone 619-462-3938
Fax: 1-800-235-6822
picturemereading@cox.net
http://picturemereading.com/index.html

Reading Rods

Reading Rods are interlocking manipulative that can be used when teaching and learning to read. The Rods are color-coded to define the function of the letter(s) or words, and to differentiate among consonants, vowels, blends, nouns, verbs, and so forth. Reading Rods can be purchased from many commercial publishers.

Learning Resources, Inc.
380 N. Fairway Drive
Vernon Hills, Illinois 60061
Phone: 1-800-333-8281
www.learningresources.com

That's Life! Literature Series

Books on various themes specifically developed for secondary students with disabilities. All books use color photographs and are high-interest, low vocabulary materials.

AbleNet, Inc.
2808 Fairview Ave. N.
Roseville, MN 55113-1308
www.ablenetinc.com

The Animated Literacy

Animated Literacy is a multisensory approach to learning sounds, letters, and words. The program helps children learn reading and writing with the use of alphabet stories, songs, gestures, and coloring books.

The Animated Literacy
P.O. Box 2346
La Mesa, CA 91943
Phone: 619-465-8278
www.animated-literacy.com

The Sensible Pencil
This is a comprehensive program for developing handwriting skills. It includes 200 lessons that teach both uppercase and lowercase manuscript letters and numbers.

ATC Learning, LLC
P.O. Box 43795
Birmingham, AL 35243
Phone: 1-800-633-8623
Fax: 205-968-0591
www.atclearning.com

Wilson Reading System
This program is a systematic, multisensory instructional program designed for individuals who have difficulty with written language in the areas of reading and spelling. The program is based on Orton-Gillingham philosophy and principles as well as current phonological coding research. The primary goal of the program is to help students become fluent, accurate readers.

Wilson Language Training Corporation
47 Old Webster Road
Oxford, MA 01540
Phone: 508-368-2399
www.wilsonlanguage.com

Literacy-Related Web Sites

Dolch Word Activities
This web site contains numerous ideas for using Dolch Words to facilitate student literacy.

http://www.gate.net/~labooks/xLPDolch.html

Misunderstood Minds
This web site covers the basic development of handwriting and text composition. It includes links to ideas for developing writing skills for individuals with disabilities. Be sure to click on the *Try It Yourself* link—it simulates what it is like to have graphomotor difficulty.

http://www.pbs.org/wgbh/misunderstoodminds/writingbasics.html

The Next Chapter Book Club
This is a program sponsored through The Ohio State University Nisonger Center with the purpose of facilitating literacy skills, creating social connectedness, and fostering community inclusion. The web site includes information about how to join the program to create your own book club as well as resources that are helpful in starting a club.

http://www.nextchapterbookclub.org/index.asp

Word Wall Activities
This web site has numerous ideas for organizing and using Word Walls in creative ways.

http://www.theschoolbell.com/Links/word_walls/words.html

Wordless Picture Books
This web site contains a list of wordless books appropriate for students of varying ages. Links are provided to other sites giving ideas for activities related to wordless books.

http://www.holbrook.k12.az.us/picbook/wordless.html

Publishing and Software Companies

Attainment Company
This company offers numerous literacy materials, many of which are appropriate for adolescents and adults with moderate or severe disabilities.

P.O. Box 9300160
Verona, WI 53593-0160
www.AttainmentCompany.com

Don Johnston, Inc.
This company offers a range of literacy learning software and computer access devices for individuals with disabilities. Products are focused on emergent-through-conventional readers at all age levels.

26799 W. Commerce Drive
Volo, IL 60073
Phone: 1-800-999-4660
www.donjohnston.com

Sundance Publishing
This publishing company offers books for readers at varying reading levels. Many of their nonfiction books are written on topics that appeal to older beginning readers. They contain full-color photographs with simple text that allow even emergent readers to acquire content knowledge as well as to enhance early reading skills.

P. O. Box 740
Northborough, MA 01532
Phone: 1-800-343-8204
www.sundancepub.com

Software Programs

Key Area	Concepts/skills	Software	Accessibility options
WS – PA*	Initial, medial, final sounds, blends	Teach Me Phonemics (Soft Touch)	Mouse, single switch, two-switch scanning, touch window
	Phonological awareness	Earobics (Cognitive Concepts)	Touch window, switch accessible
WS – P**	Word families, rimes, word discrimination	Simon Spells It Out (Don Johnston)	Single switch
	Decoding skills, high-frequency word repetition, matching words	All My Words (Crick Software)	Switch accessible
	Phonics, word recognition, rimes, patterns	Intellitools Balanced Literacy (Intellitools)	Intellikeys
	Phonics, word families	WordMaker (Don Johnston)	Touch window, single switch, trackball, mouse, joystick
	Short, long vowels	www.starfall.com	Trackball, joystick, Intellikeys
	Letters of the alphabet, consonants, short vowels, long vowels	Stickybear Phonics I (Stickybear Software)	Mouse, touch window
WS – WR***	Word identification with picture matching	Talking Series (talking nouns, talking verbs) (Laureate)	Touch window, keyboard, single switch, mouse, trackball, joystick
	Vocabulary practice in story context, sight word recognition	Let's Go Read series (Edmark/Riverdeep)	Touch window, single switch
	Word recognition, vocabulary, word selection	UkanDu Little Books (Don Johnston)	Switch accessible
MP****	Cloze activities	ClozePro (Crick Software)	Switch accessible
	Story mapping, sequencing	Kidspiration/Inspiration (Inspiration Software, Inc.)	Intellikeys, trackball
	Creates electronic books for independent reading choices, options for leveling	My Own Bookshelf (Soft Touch)	Single switch, two-switch scanning, touch screen, Intellikeys
	Fiction and nonfiction reading comprehension and fluency, independent reading or with assistance	Pair-It Books on CD-ROM (Steck-Vaughn)	Mouse, trackball, Intellikeys
	Multiple reading formats including word support for all levels	Start to Finish Books (Don Johnston)	Mouse, single switch

*WS–PA = Word Study, Phonemic Awareness
**WS–P = Word Study, Phonics
***WS–WR = Word Study, Word Recognition
****MP = Multi-purpose, including Guided Reading, Self-Selected Independent Reading, and Writing

E-Book Sources

Electronic book sources	Software required	Notes	Cost
http://www.tumblebooks.com/	Internet browser, Macromedia Flash plug-in (free download)	Animated, talking picture books; individual, school, and district subscriptions	Yes
http://www.ipicturebooks.com	Adobe Reader (free download)	Electronic versions of popular children's trade books	Yes
http://www.mightybook.com/	Internet browser, Macromedia Flash plug-in (free download)	Original animated picture books; text highlighted as it is read	Yes
http://www.magickeys.com/ebooks/	Internet browser, Macromedia Flash plug-in (free download)	Original narrated stories, clickable text	Yes

Online Book Sources

Location	Software required	Notes	Cost
Internet Public Library http://ipl.si.umich.edu/div/kidspace/storyhour/	Internet browser	For independent readers; illustration with text	No
International Children's Digital Library http://www.icdlbooks.org/	Internet browser; some versions may require free Java Webstart Plug-in or Adobe Reader	For independent readers; scanned versions of print books come in various languages	No
Kiz Club http://www.kizclub.com/Sbody.html	Internet browser, Macromedia Flash plug-in	Animated, talking picture books; leveled readers; text highlighted as it is read	No
	Internet browser	Scanned version of classic children's books arranged by age/reading level	No
University of Virginia Library http://etext.lib.virginia.edu/ebooks/subjects/subjects-young.html	Internet browser, Microsoft Reader (PC only), or Palm Reader	Classic children's literature in web-based, Microsoft Reader, or Palm Reader formats	No

Index

Page numbers followed by "*f*" indicate figures; those followed by "*t*" indicate tables.